THIRSTY

isbn: 1-4196-9071-x
isbn-13: 9781419690716

Visit www.booksurge.com to order additional copies,
and www.thirstybook.com

.

THIRSTY

ADVENTURES AND LESSONS IN REMOTE
GEOCHEMICAL OIL EXPLORATION
1997–2005

THOMAS C. BROWN

ACKNOWLEDGEMENTS

Thanks to Andy Falconetti, Ray Rector, Rowland Rincon, Jason Innes, Kurt Rieder, Kelly Heapy and all my family, N. Bassabra, J. Hughs, Rachel Grabel, Mike Koehmstedt, Melany Johnson, Tanner Humphrey, and Pierre of Gamba.

DISCLAIMER

Front cover photo: Rub' al Khali desert, Yemen, ©Thomas C. Brown
Rear cover (author) photo: ©Jason Innes
Cover design by Kelly K. Heapy

CONTENTS

FORWARD: THE SMELL OF MONEY

UNE OF 2003 found me in Bolivia's astonishing and schizophrenic capital city with a fistful of dollars in the bank and a quietly ambitious mountain climb in mind. I was finally back. Not just in South America, no, but in the "southern cone," the land where Ernesto Guevara and Eva Peron lived and died, land of the gaucho and the guerilla, of coca and Coca-Cola, a land blessed with preposterous natural beauty and, as my cabbie explained, over a hundred kinds of potatoes. Though it was my third time in the capital, I was wide-eyed and uncommonly giddy. I introspected as we drove through the concrete canyons of the city's downtown. Was I home? It sure felt like it sometimes. Was it, in truth, a Bolivian soul trapped in my chest? Had I a Latino libido? Or was I simply another gringo exploiter, wealthy by relocation? Did I have, as had so many foreigners before me, a secret agenda? If so, it was also a secret to me, but why was I so drawn here? Was it to climb, or to carouse with twenty-something *mestiza* girls? I could thankfully do both, but during the week required to adjust to the altitude, only the latter was possible, and I had been diligent. I wondered if there was still *singani* on my breath from the night before. Was it a strange gleam in my eye, the kind a mountaineer might have, or a headache in my pants that had yanked me back to Bolivia? Would I need an alpine rescue or penicillin? Only time could tell. I was running errands around the dirty, loud, and fascinating town, preparing for another journey deep into the hinterlands of a nation that had years before forced my proudly rational mind to renegotiate the terms it had made with my senses. I needed a little lunch and some beer. I would soon be accommodated.

I stepped out of the cab after paying the ebullient driver and continued toward my destination on foot. The city was La Paz, or "the Peace," though some will know that La Paz is actually co-capital of Bolivia with another city way off to the southeast named Sucre. The metropolis of roughly a million citizens was erected inside a wide and ridiculously steep-walled canyon at over two miles above sea level; the expansive basin always seemed to me the extended, cupped hands of the giant, perennially snowcapped Mount Illimani, ever presiding above La Paz, the highest peak in Bolivia's mighty Cordillera Real, or "royal range," of mountains. Illimani is as well known within Bolivia as it is unknown without. The iconic massif rises to more than twenty-one thousand feet, and though it appears to be just at the edge of town, it is actually twenty-five miles away. It is the classic, archetypal mountain we drew as children, a huge chunk of pyramidal granite topped with a perfect meringue of permanent snow. The peak could change from beckoning to minatory in a single moment. Its fickle moods and colors were displayed throughout the day for all in the city to see, and now, in Bolivia's dry winter, its upper reaches were traversed here and there by groups of mostly foreign climbers. As the afternoon waned into dusk, the leviathan simply radiated ripe orange and purple light from the east like a seraph. "Illimani" is the name given the peak by the local Aymara people; as with many of the peaks in the Andes, no Spanish names ever stuck. I shot provocative, I'll-come-thither glances over my shoulder at the mountain as I walked up the bustling main artery of the city known as the Prado. Yet another innocent pile of matter I had needlessly romanticized. I took a left up a clamorous side street leading steeply uphill from downtown La Paz. My plan was to climb Illimani on my own, without support, a reasonable goal for an alpinist with my experience on the peak's popular and easy normal route.

Mountaineering was widely discussed that day around town by locals and visitors alike. The La Paz newspapers were reporting that Illimani had just taken three lives, a Bolivian guide and two Americans, both U.S. embassy workers. All of them lived in La Paz. They each saw the mountain almost every day as they lived their city lives. I thought of them grimly, wondering if and when their bodies would be recovered after what was reportedly a long fall from the normal route. I ducked off the street and walked up a flight of stairs into a familiar restaurant for lunch, plopped my copy of the newspaper *La Razon* down upon the wooden tabletop before me, ordered, and opened the mountaineering guidebook that for days had been stuck in my right hand. I inspected a nice photo of the Cordillera Real range taken from the air, comparing the paper's photo of Illimani to the ones in my guide. I wondered about the conditions up high. Why had they fallen?

Just to the north of Illimani hulks another mountain named Mururata. A man who worked at my motel explained to me in some detail earlier that week the Aymaran legend of Illimani and Mururata, and though I understood only about half of his heavily accented Spanish, I got the gist of it nevertheless. Though the Incan tongue Quechua is certainly the more commonly spoken pre-Colombian language in modern La Paz, Aymaran is also still spoken by well over a million Bolivians. The Aymara lived above La Paz on the barren altiplano around Lake Titicaca well before the Inca extended their empire. They were country before country was cool. The greater peaks of the Cordillera Real are anthropomorphized in Aymaran myth. Mururata, a name that means "without a head" in Aymaran, is much wider than it is tall, more a flat-topped, snow-covered mesa than a peak. The mountain did appear headless, and it, like Illimani, was visible from parts of La Paz. According to the legend, Mururata was Illimani's wife. The man explained to me that Mururata hoped to run off with Huayna Potosi, another handsome six-thousand-meter-tall peak nearby that I had climbed during my last visit, but that her intent was discovered. She subsequently suffered what most would agree was a disproportionate reaction on the part of her spouse. He chopped off her head. I kept wondering where it landed.

Late afternoons in June were often chilly in La Paz. Long winter shadows began to lean out into the streets. I took a swig from a brown bottle of Paceña beer at my favorite table in the popular second-floor restaurant known as El Lobo. I looked away from my book and watched the street below me through a wide, smudgy window beside my table and its wooden bench seat. Older-model Japanese cars and wounded buses coughed and heaved up the steep cobblestone of Sagarnaga Street. Tilted and cracked slabs of concrete sidewalk thronged with mostly brown-skinned people below, a few dressed in smart business suits, and many more sporting more traditional garb: big, colorful, multilayered dresses and trademark bowler hats for the native *cholla* gals, and simple pants and rough-hewn, button-up shirts for their male counterparts. Denim-clad packs of college kids searched for hot food, cold beer, and adult situations. Intrepid and ragged street kids ran and played amid the congested traffic. A few of the older locals spoke less Spanish than I did. They spoke Quechua principally, perhaps Aymaran, and were among Bolivia's majority of indigenous peoples, representing about 60 percent of the republic's nine million nationals. Coca leaf was being sold out of huge plastic sacks to workers and farmers below me on the street corner, placed into smaller, more convenient satchels by *cholla* women with notably filthy bare hands. I knew because I had just bought some. Coca was fairly cheap, even for locals, and was practically free for me. Business was brisk.

The former Spanish territory known roughly as Alto Peru became a nation in 1825, just two years after the Monroe Doctrine was delivered up north in the young United States of America. Bolivia was named after the brilliant Venezuelan military commander Simón Bolívar, an historically towering figure who had just finished liberating much of the continent from Spanish control. Neither was his greatest general forgotten by the newborn Andean nation—Antonio José de Sucre is the namesake of Bolivia's other capital city. Since those heady days, Bolivia has generally been either invaded or completely ignored by its neighbors and the rest of the world. It was robbed of many of its riches by the Spanish, and would have among the lowest standards of living of South America's litter of newly emancipated countries for quite some time while its considerable mineral revenue was hastened to a wealthy elite and on out of the country. It didn't help that Chile stole Bolivia's only egress to the ocean in the War of the Pacific in 1883. Oops, no more coastline. On top of this throw lots of bad luck, corrupt leadership, a few more costly wars, and, well... sovereignty had not exactly been a great ride in Bolivia, especially for the poor, which was almost everyone. Most Bolivians had to work hard simply to maintain their "poor" status, pleased to be one rung up the economic ladder from indigent. But something new was happening. This little Latin backwater suddenly had something to sell to the rest of the world beside its charm and good looks. Bolivia had fossil fuel, and much more than anyone thought they did. Huge natural gas reserves had been discovered quite recently in the extreme southern part of the country, and my company had helped to find them. Where the cash would go was a completely different matter, but even the average person in the streets of La Paz knew about the golden egg. They also knew that the goose was on the take.

I stopped reading and put my book down, considering what an interesting group of mouths my stainless steel fork must have been in between washes. I looked absently around the fairly busy diner. My eyes finally settled on a woman seated nearby. She met my gaze, and I joined her at her table. We struck up a conversation. She was bundled up and from Belgium. She was traveling alone and was mesmerized, much as I was, by La Paz. We drank a few beers and chatted, and, at her suggestion, I agreed to join her on a brief foray to Copacabana the following day, a charming small town on the shores of Lake Titicaca that I had yet to visit. We said farewell and parted company. I quit the restaurant and ambled contentedly back to my hotel.

The next morning was luminous and even warm. As our big, comfortable bus climbed to the edge of the altiplano up some steep La Paz thoroughfare, my new acquaintance asked me what I did for a living. I told her plainly that I was in oil and gas exploration. I might as well have said that I hunted and killed unicorns and painted my face with their blood. She was clearly indignant, even aghast—she could hardly fathom how a climber and lover of nature such as myself could be "in oil." She likely would have eschewed my company completely had she known the prior day at El Lobo what I did for a living. But there we were, on a bus, surging toward Copa. Her tension was manifest. The silence was deafening. I cleared my throat, both amused and annoyed, and asked quite innocuously what she did for a living, seeking only to shift our conversation back to some less contentious topic. Her answer came like a thunderclap. She distributed Volvo truck parts to South America.

⌒

I have become all too accustomed to the brand of antipathy that so many self-proclaimed "green" people feel for the oil industry at large. Not for any specific company or incident, but a general, abiding rancor that is thrown like a blanket over the entire enterprise, one that suddenly has very distinct edges and exists quite separately from all other sectors of the world economy. And from their lives. I lived in Boulder, Colorado, for twenty years, where some individuals might rail against an oil guy like me in a bar or restaurant until their jaws grew tired and then jump in their big Fords and Toyotas and drive for a full hour up to their homes in the mountains. Only to turn around and drive the same routes back to their jobs in the city the next morning. But somehow, that's not a part of the equation for these people.

The fact is that the American way of life is made possible by oil and by the enormous skill and pluck of those men and women who cast about the globe finding it. America currently consumes roughly 25 percent of the world's petroleum, but only 5 percent of the planet's people are Americans. Whether you are flying to Bolivia for your vacation, commuting to and from your beautiful mountain home, or simply buying affordable truck-transported goods at your local grocery, you are creating a demand. The paint on your house or apartment, the fertilizers for the food you eat, the nylon in your jacket, nearly everything made of plastic in your kitchen, bathroom, and car, all of these materials are currently derived from or manufactured with petroleum. For most in America and Europe, saying you don't like the oil industry is a lot like saying how much you detest vineyards as you drink record amounts of wine.

Foreign oil fields are indeed the vineyards from which the American lifestyle springs. We have the world's most affordable gas at the pump except for Venezuela and a handful of other nations, cheap consumer goods, affordable air travel, food from all around the globe—all of these depend on oil. Many oil fields are clean, efficient, and safe. Some oil fields create jobs for local workers, generate local economic booms, and even benefit nations as a whole, but these are found most often in places like Canada and the United States. Many oil fields in the "developing" world fall woefully short of this. A few governments in poor countries have used oil revenue to raise the standard of living for a broad group of people there, but most have not. In fact, the enormous revenues from Latin America's fossil fuels have traditionally done nothing to improve the quality of life in their country of origin. You cannot shake your fist at the oil patch without also including corrupt foreign governments, regimes that look the other way while oil interests run wild inside their nations, often at the expense of the people and the environment, and often with the blessings or at least the full knowledge of Washington. Uncle Sam has worked hard to preserve many an oligarchy in democracy's clothes in nations with oil. Bolivia was no exception. But my Belgian friend hadn't any venom for the current president in Bolivia. She didn't even know his name. We love to blame the fox, but what about the guy who holds the henhouse door open? That guy has often been U.S. and European governments and their toadies in the capitals of "developing" nations.

The U.S. reached peak oil production in the seventies, but its thirst was growing ever stronger, and OPEC was proving feisty. Places like Ecuador and Nigeria were suddenly on the maps and the minds of the U.S. oil giants. They would have their way in both those nations for a long time. Oil companies operate to turn a profit, and if some crooked despot gives them a sweetheart deal, what do they do? They take it. They say "we're an oil company," and remind their critics that it's not their job to worry about social justice or bad government. In Equatorial Guinea, we now know that some very big U.S. oil companies made direct payments to President Obiang and his family to help maintain just such a deal. Bolivia only saw 18 percent of its oil and gas revenue for a long time, and that went to an already wealthy elite. In parts of Venezuela, private oil companies were still paying royalties as little as *1 percent* as late as 2004. These types of deals tend to produce profound resentment among voters and catapult leaders like Venezuela's folksy, fiery Hugo Chávez into power. No one should be surprised at what you get when you ask marginalized people to vote. Democracy and fair elections in exploited countries will produce many more such anti- "business as usual" presidents.

The latest upgrade, of course, is outright invasion of oil-rich nations for control of their crude, as well for the unregulated orgy of corporate profiteering that follows. Dubya was being more honest than he intended to be when he said "mission accomplished" from the deck of the USS Abraham Lincoln, an aircraft carrier returning home from Iraq in 2003. The only mission was to secure the oil, grab the massive profits to be had from no-bid contracts, and establish a permanent military presence in the Persian Gulf. And kill Hussein on television. Completely complicit was a U.S. media that covered itself pretending to cover the war while "imbedded" in the ranks of the military, literally and otherwise. This brave new war was too dangerous for journalism, we were told. Funny, in

Vietnam, journalism proved too dangerous for the war. For the most part, people in the United States have become comfortable with the conquest of Iraq, but one must wonder: what kind of leaders will this very violent and tangible oil grab thrust into power in the region? This was no under-the-table shenanigans that the average person couldn't see. This was and is massive civilian bloodshed and the prolonged agony of millions of people. Someone may emerge and gain power in the region who makes Chávez seem rather cuddly.

When I started working in the industry, I knew nothing of all this. Nor did I understand how much America depends upon and is made out of oil. It took working in the oil patch for ten years for me to truly understand my country, its foreign policy, and its perilous addiction to fossil fuels. I have met some of the smartest and most upstanding people I will ever meet in the patch, but like soldiers, most of them tend to avoid the "why" and concentrate instead on the "when" and the "where" of matters oil. Initially, I did much the same. Do I think that oil companies always behave nefariously? No. But they have often been willing to break the rules when no one was watching in order to further their own interests at the expense of the powerless and unrepresented. Governments have helped make sure that no one was watching many times in the past, and they continue to do so today. Washington tried to keep us from watching too closely in Iraq. If you pay taxes in the United States, your money funded both the destruction *and* the alleged rebuilding of that formerly sovereign state. Your money went to oilfield parts and services companies with unprecedented no-bid contracts, as well to pay for as many warm bodies as that petroleum acquisition team heretofore known as the Department of Defense deemed necessary. Sure, plenty of G.I.'s, but soldiers of fortune where they failed. Big fortune. Those Blackwater guys have to eat too. They write their own checks against taxpayer money.

Governments aside, the oil industry itself clearly receives far less scrutiny than it ought to. When it does arouse indignation, it is usually not because of its upstream practices, but because gas costs more than people think it should at the U.S. pump. While some energy companies have good upstream records vis-à-vis human rights and the environment, the standards to which they are held vary greatly from nation to nation. Such standards are often laughable in remote areas of the third world. There is no one there to watch, no one, at least, with a camera, a safe vantage, and a media connection. Companies are free to paint whatever picture they want to of their foreign operations. What happens in the field has traditionally stayed in the field in these places. Thanks to the proliferation of the Internet and the attendant emergence of independent journalism, there is every day more and better information at our fingertips regarding U.S. oil companies, both large and small, including their environmental and political report cards. Now, it's easier to find out who the bad guys are. While it would be naïve to expect these bad actors to suddenly sprout a conscience, a more cynical and better-informed American public could certainly try to avoid buying products bearing the names of those negligent and irresponsible firms that need to make reparations to injured parties, clean up a mess they've made, or put a stop to unethical practices. We all ought to keep an eye on what's going on out there in the industry, especially abroad—after all, we use more petroleum as a nation than does any other.

Of course, most Americans would rather not think about where their gas comes from. Most are aware of the Valdez disaster in Prince William Sound, Alaska, in 1989. The U.S. press *has* to cover domestic oil industry disasters, but they often become "screw-ups," honest mistakes that are just bound to happen once in a while. While the Valdez incident may be common knowledge, as is that company's explanation of what took place, there is more to that story than meets the eye. Other much more insidious events have transpired in the recent past in South America. They are generally overlooked by the mainstream U.S. media, remaining unknown outside the industry. The Ecuadorian government during the seventies obediently turned a blind eye to the activities of a certain prominent U.S. energy company operating in the deep jungles of the Napo Basin. The famous firm knowingly created a large-scale toxic nightmare there through negligent exploration, drilling, and production practices. They left some six hundred open pits filled with crude and waste products on their leases, an amount of oil equivalent to two Valdez tankers. Their drilling practices were deplorable, but no one except the Cofán people, who live there, seemed to notice. It has been aptly termed a "Chernobyl in the rainforest." You may have gassed up your car at one of their stations recently. I would like to think that American indignation would rise to higher levels over this than it did when Janet Jackson's breast was loosed on us all. But no one knows about it, and many who have not seen it firsthand would simply dismiss such reports as environmentalist hyperbole.

More Chernobyls are assuredly avoidable. More international exploration for oil and gas is not. After one hundred and forty years of oil consumption, our very society and nation run on petroleum. But the biggest plays in the United States are played out. M. King Hubbert, a Shell geophysicist, predicted in 1956 that U.S. production of oil would peak around 1970 and decline rapidly thereafter. He was right. The United States currently produces about six million barrels per day. Its daily consumption hovers around twenty to twenty-five million barrels. More sobering is that the worldwide Hubbert's peak is imminent or even behind us. According to many of the industry's cognoscente, global conventional oil production has already reached a terminal state of decline. Whether in ten years or in thirty, we will at some point have no choice but to change our ways.

We ought to start right now. We should be working like mad to develop renewable energy sources, alternative fuels, better vehicles, and better habits. It would be errant to imagine, however, that switching over to these can be a quick or painless process. Natural gas will be important during this inevitable transition; there is a good deal more of it domestically and globally than there is oil. Corn-sourced ethanol is a clear ruse, as the corn itself is fertilized with fossil-fuel-sourced chemicals like ammonia and moreover requires oceans of fresh water, but other bio-fuels will be better. Hemp, anyone? The fact remains, however, that America's manufacturing, agricultural, and consumer economy is predicated on a steady supply of the fuels and petrochemicals derived from oil. You can't make a truly durable plastic, a strong epoxy, or a reliable, flexible electrical insulator without it. Franklin D. Roosevelt's secretary of the interior, Harold L. Ickes, summed it up best when he said this: "We have passed from the stone age, to bronze, to iron, to the industrial age, and now to an age of oil. Without oil, American civilization as we know it could not exist."

There are many ways to reduce our dependency upon foreign-sourced oil right now. Nuclear power? Oh my. Even less popular than conservation. How about limiting the use of personal automobiles in cities to three times a week? Just like watering restrictions. Slap a dollar-per-gallon tax on gas at the pump and spend the money on smarter public transportation, viable alternative fuels, and more efficient engines. Gas that costs as much as it does in Europe, right here in the United States. That would make people think twice about that Sunday drive. You could ban gas-guzzling cars, auto racing, recreational off-roading and boating, road trips, cruises, lawnmowers and lawns. You could limit unnecessary air travel, switch the entire agricultural industry to organic fertilizers, downsize the beef industry, resurrect the fifty-five-mile-an-hour speed limit, ban the frivolous and excessive use of paint and plastic, and...

And gird for the riots.

What follows in the pages ahead are accounts from my eight years of exploration fieldwork for a small Colorado field services company called Falcon Ventures. Oil firms both large and small contracted the surveys I performed with Falcon. These companies sought to acquire more data about some specific "play" that was theirs to explore and exploit, an area that for one reason or another showed promise and would likely play host to a drill crew or two at some point. Most exploration data is gathered using the seismic method, an expensive, sometimes destructive, and often very effective means of "seeing" underground using a source of energy such as dynamite and a set of geophones, specialized microphones which record the echoes of the "shots" as they bounce off of underground structures. The echoes of these miniature earthquakes are precisely measured by specialized equipment, and a theoretical map of underground rock formations is produced. This is the bread and butter of oil exploration, the means by which a company decides where it will eventually commit to drilling. But even if the presence of trapping structures has been established in an area via seismic, one cannot be sure that these structures are "charged" with trapped product. A soil-gas survey may reveal that. In essence, our method "smells" where seismic "looks." And oil definitely smells. Almost all oil has some natural gas mixed into it. Thirty years ago, natural gas was typically flared off at the well as a nuisance, sometimes in rather large quantities; astonishingly, some of it still is, but this practice is finally being banned in nations like Nigeria and

Russia, places where the worst offenses were ongoing. Silly us. Turns out that the stuff is quite valuable after all. Oil is still the prize, but natural gas has become precious as well, and there's a lot of it left, even in the lower forty-eight.

Falcon has searched for oil and gas on five continents, from the cotton fields of Texas to some of the most forbidding and remote terrain on the planet. We work primarily on foot, without support, carry our sampling devices and instruments on our backs, and are often nowhere near medical facilities. Sometimes we go alone. In essence, we work without a net. Our method is not widely known of outside the oil patch. Even some industry veterans have managed never to hear of it. My colleagues and I at Falcon deploy small, highly sensitive chemical packets or "modules" in the ground at a depth of roughly two feet using portable, battery-operated hammer drills or simple steel drive tools and hammers where the electricity required to recharge our drills is not available. These ten-inch-long, pencil-thin pouches, which some have called "sniffers," remain in the soil for roughly three weeks, after which time we return, retrieve them, and finally ship them to a laboratory for analysis and interpretation. This method of collecting geochemical data for the purpose of exploration is known as soil-gas testing.

When I tell some people that this is how my company prospects for oil, they look at me as though I've seriously suggested to them that Bugs Bunny was really a nutria. On its surface, exploration geochemistry can certainly seem a bit absurd if you don't know the first thing about it. But our job at Falcon is to do the legwork, not to explain the science or sell the surveys to our clients. We are good at getting the samples in and out efficiently, losing few or none of them, and doing so in some nasty places where less robust types might experience a certain erosion of determination. Much of what is contained in these chapters is written more from the perspective of an outdoorsman and backcountry diplomat than an oil guy. In fact, none of us at Falcon are geologists—we have all learned, however, a great deal about oil, geology, geophysics, and geopolitics over the years—enough to get us in trouble, anyway. The truth is, one really needn't know much about Permian stratigraphy to tromp around putting soil-gas collectors in the ground. What one does need is to be fit and agile, to be effective in extremes of heat or cold, and to be comfortable working around dangerous snakes, elephants, killer bees, sheer rock walls, and, worst of all, treacherous people.

Hence, a few lucky climbers and a handful of others who were variously firefighters, outdoor survivalists, and general tough guys were afforded an opportunity to make some relatively handsome cash by working for Falcon. New "field-worker" is but old "wolf boy" writ large. We snuck into the world of oil exploration through the back door. The physical demands of our work, the objective hazards, and the often harsh and alien settings are patently enough to preclude the interest of most formally trained geo-whatevers seeking to make a living in the oil industry. Sticking soil samples into the jungle mud of the Congo and chopping your way for a full kilometer between each point with a machete for ten hours a day is not something for which most colleges can prepare you. Just as a lawnmower cannot be rendered a helicopter through simple reorientation, most geologists would not easily be converted into successful Falcon field-workers.

To better understand the soil-gas method, one first needs to know a little something about geochemistry. Two Colorado School of Mines scholars named Vorhees and Klusmann were among the first to advance the theory that the presence of significant quantities of hydrocarbons underground is reflected or expressed by anomalous chemistry in the soils at or near the surface above those bodies. The coveted black goo, we must remember, has been down there since before we were walking upright, and has had plenty of time to percolate. Oil wants to come to the surface. Most of it simply can't, as it is trapped underground in any of a great variety of ways, but small "micro-seeps," farts essentially, often do come all the way up, moving from areas of higher pressure deep in the earth to areas of lower pressure near the surface. The latest thinking is that these gases go pretty much straight up, all the way to the surface, where our samples wait like carrots.

The first oil well in the United States and probably the world was drilled at a site with visible surface seepage in 1859 in Titusville, Pennsylvania. That field would produce for thirty years, yielding the kerosene that would bring the first efficient indoor lighting to businesses, hospitals, and homes throughout the United States, Europe, and elsewhere. Thirty-two years later in a little southeast Texas town called Spindletop, the first producing well in all of Texas was drilled. The Lucas-1 well came in at seventy thousand barrels a day, blew several joints of pipe out of the bore hole, and was the first gusher in U.S. oil history. Of note is the fact that Spindletop was so named because the historic oil deposit there was expelling enough gas to kill the lower branches on a particular tree in the area. This seems rather counterintuitive—shouldn't it have killed the roots too?—but that's how the story goes. Although these are just two examples, it is true that surface expressions of volatiles have adumbrated larger reservoirs below them since the very first bit pierced the ground. They continue to do so today. Trace hydrocarbons at the surface sometimes mean that a whole lot more waits down below. *Multum in parvo.*

Our soil-gas modules adsorb these trace volatiles where they are present. Following each sample's three-week exposure period in the soil, it is placed directly into a special glass container and retains a chemical signature until it reaches the lab. Laboratory analysis of the samples is conducted using a mass spectrometer, a highly sensitive device that processes the adsorbent packets of chemicals within each module one at a time, recording any hydrocarbons that have bound to the adsorbents. Groups of "grid" or "exploration" modules that have chemical signatures similar to those that were placed near existing wells and above known reservoirs, these called "model" modules, are considered in a general sense to have been placed above significant quantities of oil or gas.

The modules are both manufactured and analyzed by a large, diversified East Coast corporation better known for its other products. This East Coast firm had already begun large-scale production of a new, patented membrane material made of Teflon. Given that their new material was chemically inert, repelled water, and admitted gases, it was the perfect medium in which to contain the adsorbent chemicals used in the field samples of a tiny, Denver-based exploration geochemistry company. East Coast firm purchased little Denver company in 1997, acquiring both personnel and proprietary exploration methodology upon doing so. A splendid new use for their new material had been found. Little Denver company had been executing soil-gas surveys for several years using cumbersome field sampling devices that were little more than inverted glass test-tubes. East coast firm wisely brought their top people aboard, redesigned the module, and upon sensing potential in the technique, beefed up the marketing end of things. After a dismal year in 1998, things began looking up. More contracts and bigger clients were surfacing as oil prices began to rebound from very sobering lows around ten dollars-per-barrel. The only remaining piece of the puzzle was a field services team, a group of serious outdoorsmen who were hard working, could work anywhere, and were above all trustworthy. After all, they would be the only ones who knew which samples were placed where. Falcon would be that team, and Falcon's owner, the most experienced of LDC's field-workers, would be my boss.

At a job's outset, we at Falcon receive a cooler full of modules and a set of coordinates that represent the proposed locations for each module; these are loaded electronically into hand-held GPS units. That's really all we need other than plane tickets. The survey design for any given project is generated entirely by ECF's geologists and sometimes those of the client, and could be anything from a tight regular grid to a set of far-flung lines following "known" underground structures. But the only way to really know what is down there is to drill. And that is expensive. Geochemistry is, according to some in the biz, the snake oil of petroleum exploration. Not everyone believes it works. It is likely attractive to some of those heads of exploration who do employ the method largely because of its affordability. It is dead cheap. The bottom line is that we provide more data, data that is not always compelling or easily understood, but is almost always useful to those who decide where to drill. And we do it quickly, without any impact. Drilling is always a poker game. If a company can afford to spend a puny hundred grand on a soil-gas survey, it can increase its odds of hitting a pay zone by a few percentage points before it goes "all in." Though the soil-gas method has seen some muddling failures, it has seen many more successes.

As far as Falcon went, the best and brightest among us simply wanted to work in those places that would most test our skills and determination. We wanted to prove our mettle. We craved the remote, the difficult, and the dangerous.

We got it in spades.

1 DUMPCAN

God gave me my money.

— John D. Rockefeller, founder, Standard Oil

The amount of poverty and suffering required for the emergence of a Rockefeller, and the amount of depravity that the accumulation of a fortune of such magnitude entails, are left out of the picture, and it is not always possible to make the people in general see this.

— Ernesto "Che" Guevara

I HAD JUST begun reading a biography of Ernesto Guevara when the big Oklahoma job started. I wasn't yet sure exactly who or what Che was, but I had already learned that he had a name for a favorite shirt he wore while he was in the field. He called it *la semanal*, which in Spanish means "the weekly," as he often wore it for seven or more days at a time without a wash. Personal hygiene was not among his priorities, a fact he wore proudly and literally on his sleeve.

Mr. Wedow might have called his red tank top *la mensual*, or "the monthly." Mr. Wedow also appeared to have other priorities. He had just finished splainin' to me that his brother, who was standing in the living room window of his home a hundred yards behind him, had a .30-30 rifle aimed at my head. I fumbled with my wallet, produced a company card, and presented it to the rotund man, glancing over his shoulder at the porch and noticing that there was indeed a figure in a big window to the left of the front door. The faded yellow house was backed up against a stand of cottonwoods and was falling apart, and if I had to guess what type of crop Mr. Wedow conjured from his parcel of rich Oklahoma soil, I would have said decaying furniture and truck parts.

"Now what did you say you were puttin' in the ground again?" Mr. Wedow squinted his eyes. He had coarse black hair growing all the way up his arms and across his big white shoulders, and looked vaguely ill beneath his blue and white ball cap. He must have been around forty-five. I could see gin blossoms on his cheeks and nose from where I stood. His face was round, flat, and damp, and somehow looked to me as though it might smell bad. I imagined his wife, the poor thing, saying "honey, your face just stinks today." Then I imagined my head exploding like a melon in the tawny, late afternoon Oklahoma sunshine. I *was* on *his* land. Apparently without permission.

"We put in soil gas detectors. Just little tubes with some chemicals in them. Harmless chemicals," I quickly added. I produced the sample I'd plucked from the ground ten minutes before from the front pocket of my Carhartts. The sample itself looked like a white shoestring. It was contained within a thin-walled jar of clear glass with a white plastic cap, and the whole dang weren't no bigger than a size C battery. I held it up for Mr. Wedow to eye.

"These pick up oil vapors? From five damn thousand feet down? That sounds like hocus pocus to me." He tilted his head and squinted appraisingly. He spoke quietly. His voice reminded me a bit of Jimmy Carter's.

"We prefer the term voodoo." I gambled on a bit of levity. Three seconds passed, then five. Finally, Mr. Wedow laughed and then segued into a fit of deep wet coughing that he eventually suppressed with some effort. He spoke.

"Well, all right. You go on and do your thing. As long as it ain't no environmental horseshit, we don't care. We like oil. Just call ahead next time. You gave Mrs. Rawson quite a scare. She's the one what called me after she seen you in her milo. Then I seen your damn Chevy nearly in my driveway, and, well..."

"Sorry about that. I thought my partner already talked to y'all." I loved the word "y'all." Far superior to the gender specific "you guys." I really loved the fact that this encounter was nearly over with. I was beginning to relax again.

"All righty. You be careful. So long..." I resumed breathing normally as Mr. Wedow turned around, crunched across the gravel driveway toward his house, and raised his right hand high in the air as though to wave, whether to me or the gunman I wasn't sure. I walked to my rented Chevy Blazer, got in, and headed blithely south on a dusty county road back toward the highway.

Thirty minutes later I was back in Duncan. Most of the waitresses at Nero's bar and grill called it "dumpcan." Nero's was attached to our motel, and they both sat roughly in the commercial center of town on Highway 81. This was where the modestly famous and wildly successful Erle P. Halliburton and his eponymous oil field parts and services company began. The huge multinational grew out of his New Method Oil Well Cementing Company, a business that took off around 1919 in the once prolific Healdton oil field outside of Ardmore, Oklahoma, fifty miles to the southeast of Duncan. Oil companies needed concrete. Their new wells were "cased" in cement after the target depth was reached and the product encountered. Duncan had grown larger due in part to the firm's presence. While it was not in the late nineties what anyone might call a boomtown, Duncan was doing just fine, and was still a center for oil field services providers.

It had not one but two Pizza Huts. It had a community college and a golf course. It was above all a stagnant morass of ennui, this as soothing to its elder denizens as it was confounding to its young pretty things. I drove through town toward the motel with the windows down and the Bad Brains on the stereo. It was warm outside, but autumn was in the angle of the sunshine and the smell of the air. I casually surveyed both sides of the main drag as I drove back to the hotel. A brown ponytail brushed a suntanned shoulder, a wayward Labrador was nearly hit by a Dodge Ram, a scoop of ice cream fell from its cone to plop on the warm, filthy sidewalk in front of Braum's, a "texahoman" restaurant chain I had never set foot in. I pulled into the parking lot at the motel.

The phone rang behind the bar at Nero's. It was 5:38 on a Thursday afternoon in late October. Nita picked up the cordless phone while presenting a mug of straw-colored beer to a chubby bald man in a weary green sports coat.

"Wait just a sec," she said into the phone before setting it down on the counter. The man slouched into the lacquered wooden bar and its fake brass trim, handing some cash to the sultry barkeep. His eye lingered on Nita's bottom with a secret, predatory delight as she turned and put the cash in the till. She returned to the bar, smiled politely, and handed the man fifty cents. She picked up the phone and slipped her free hand into the back pocket of her tight black jeans as the man walked away. "What's up, girl?" she said with a giggle. "So, did you do him?"

Nero's looked like any other neighborhood sports bar, with a little more glass and real wood than some, a couple of ceiling fans, and dark green carpet. The only things special about Nero's were the particularly fetching girls who worked there and the fact that you could get a side order of speed with your chicken fried steak. Nita had a breath of cheap flowery perfume lingering about her fondly. She reached across the top of her head with her free hand to stroke aside a shock of long, jet-black hair from between the phone and her ear. I pushed through the main entrance. She glanced over toward me and smiled warmly, waving a little "I am so goddamn lovely that all you boys just want to do *things* to me" wave. I smiled back, ordered a beer by holding up a finger, and sat down at my usual table.

And then the boys wanted to give things to you. And then share their things with you. And later, all the things would be separated once again and piled into the backs of F-150's and U-Hauls and driven away to separate places in the night. Nita's ex-husband was a huge, dipsomaniacal, Cope-chewing man-child with the poise of a four-year-old; he never failed to bring enough dumb-ass for everyone when he came to the bar to lean on her. Too many Swanson's Angry Man dinners. They had two kids together before it all unraveled. I liked to squeeze his head between my fingers during his frequent visits to the restaurant while I quaffed my chilly Coors at the table farthest from the bar.

My esteemed colleague Jack would be joining me soon. I spoke with him on the Motorola radio before I returned to the motel. I looked up from my recently purchased copy of *The Oklahoman*. Smiling faces greeted Nita as the night crew arrived to replace her. Star, Kim, and Cheryl would take the baton. They all waved little hellos to me as they raced about preparing for work. My favorite was Cheryl. Cheryl had a bad attitude and an underwear model's figure. She made no effort to hide the latter, and moved in a way that celebrated her boobs, a nice pair that one might suspect had been surgically enhanced, but were actually quite real—she had assured me of this at some point when we'd found occasion to discuss her anatomy. She was, rather sadly, a bit screwed up on "ups," this while raising a thirteen-year-old kid by herself, one Cody, to whom I'd been introduced in the bar one afternoon. He was a nice enough lad, fair-skinned like his mom, but he did seem to be on the verge of dying of acne, an affliction that had nearly consumed my head and stolen my social life as well in my early teens. Cheryl was a member of a small army of single moms in Duncan who generally received no child support and only the wrong kind of attention from the men around them. I smoked with her and listened to her sad story in her '88 Chrysler LeBaron beside the motel one cold night with the windows cracked and the heat on. The inside of her rusting burgundy ride smelled like dirty laundry, Cheetos, and Apple Pucker.

The term "ups" meant methamphetamine in Duncan—not a lot of cocaine there, nor the money to afford it—and meth meant that gals like Nita and Cheryl might not eat for three or four days at a time, high as kestrels, warbling like larks, and remaining collaterally sleek and slender for all the boys around town. Nita was doubtless high that afternoon. She approached my table with a mug of Coors. Nita had more than a little Native American blood pushing through her veins. She sat the beer down before me, pulled up a chair, and plopped her coveted butt down across from me at the smallish round table.

"Hi cowboy." The right side of her mouth curled up as she let the words drip from her lips. She had a beautiful face, almost Egyptian, was beige-skinned, and seemed to me to have been carved out of a huge block of flan by some virtuoso sculptor. I think it was her *texture*.

"Hello, Nita. Done for the day are we?" I asked in my best Sean Connery era James Bond. I leaned forward, moving my face closer to hers and placing my elbows on the slightly sticky brown tabletop. She bubbled.

I thought about being naked against her. She knew it. I pulled my beer closer.

"Finally. I didn't get shit for tips." She winced, and then her face brightened. "Did you find any oil today?" she cooed, devouring my eyes with hers.

"Yup. Got a bunch in my room. Wanna come see it?" I looked at her glossy scarlet lips. Her mouth was like a horizontal vagina, glistening with anticipation. I wondered which side her love button would have been on. Lefty or righty? Nita seemed to genuinely like us, particularly Jack, though her most common refrain was "y'all are so *weird*." Jack and I were unusual, at least as folks in Duncan went. When we weren't working, we were making potato guns out of PVC and shooting them at cattle, blacking out the "T" on "Touch" brand condoms with a magic marker over at Wal-Mart, or drinking, which was our most decidedly normal Oklahoman activity. We were both fascinated by Che Guevara and we both loved pro hockey, two things that commanded equally little interest in southeast Oklahoma. Though I had only known Jack, who also went by "Chunk," for the two weeks during which we had worked together in Duncan, we had become fast friends immediately. He was the biggest goofball I had ever met.

Just as Nita's nose nearly touched mine, Jack entered the bar. Nita quickly forgot about me. She turned her head with a zephyr of perfume and a swish of long straight hair, fixing her eyes on my partner. The only problem with all of this was that both Jack and I had girlfriends. Ones we really liked. Ergo, we had become wildly more attractive in our fidelity to some distant mystery girls, and now the game was on. Who could make one of the Colorado boys give it up first? Jack approached, nodded, smiled a hello to both of us, and sat down at our table. I ceased to exist. Nita locked on to Jack for ten minutes as he and I exchanged amused glances and he started in on his first beer.

"Don't get any on you!" This time Kim delivered the standard Nero's farewell, a most mysterious maxim, as Nita stepped out the front door. She left after having a hushed back and forth with Jack at our little table, a process that concluded with some naughty little nothing being whispered at point blank range into Jack's ear. His subsequent expression was one of stunned delight.

"What did she say?" He and I sat facing one another across cold mugs of Coors. His large grin was surrounded by two days' worth of stubble. He was a big, strong guy with movie star good looks, sandy blond hair thinning slightly on top, and a ruddy round face. His big blue eyes had the kindness of a good family doctor, and while intelligent, his preponderant quality was a prepossessing, ineffable boyishness. He was a *puer eternis* in the best sense.

"She said," he paused and looked at the ceiling, then back at me, "she said that you are in love with yourself and that you like to smell your own butt." We both laughed.

"Come on," I probed.

"OK...she said that I could just stick it in her anytime I wanted, but that she especially wants me to do her on a motorcycle."

"What? On a motorcycle? How the hell does that work?" I blurted, nearly spraying beer out my nose. We laughed some more.

"I think she meant draped over a parked one."

"Oh. I see. This is getting out of hand. Have you ever been pursued this fanatically by this many ladies?"

"No," Jack said simply, a look of disbelief on his face.

"Kinda makes the ego swell," I offered.

"Among other things," he said in his best Brooklyn accent. We giggled. I ordered two more cold ones from an ecstatic Cheryl. She just won fifty bucks on a scratch lottery ticket. She ain't never won nothin' before, she explained. Maybe her luck was changing.

2

Jack and I stayed up drinking beer until around eleven-thirty, went to sleep, and met for breakfast in Nero's at seven. His was over easy, and mine omelet. We would once again split up and head to different parts of the prospect for the day, as Jack was finishing up permitting while I installed samples on the permitted parts. I told him about my regrettable encounter with Mr. Wedow. It was no fault of his. We had simply overlooked the little slice of land the Wedow clan owned, and Mrs. Rawson, who was in her seventies, likely forgot about the call she received from Jack roughly a week before I actually got around to sampling her land.

Permitting meant trying to talk with all the landowners in the one-hundred-square-mile survey area, a rather Sisyphean task; many of these were, of course, ranchers and farmers. Ranchers got up early. Ranchers didn't like city folk. They were hard to find and sometimes hard to talk to. Jack was on his way to meet with an Elias Shelby, whose thousand-acre ranch was his only to a depth of about one meter or so—surface ownership only. Elias owned what was called a split estate. Anything below the surface was leased to energy companies by the state, and that lease was currently held by our client, one Vantage Petroleum. Eli was doubtless well aware of this, and also aware that he was powerless to stop any exploration efforts by the leaseholder, but we didn't want any more rifles being pulled out of their cases. It was still trespassing in the absence of prior verbal contact. If Vantage decided to drill on Eli's land, he would have to be compensated only for surface damage and the physical use of an acre or two of land as long as the well produced, a few thousand dollars at best, but Eli would make no money off the oil.

Jack and I both had a measure of admiration for ranchers and farmers. We discussed them over breakfast. Many of them had been around since the earth was cooling, and they seemed to us immune to the sort of materialism that permeated more modern lives. Their lot was determined by that most famous of schizophrenic bitches, Mother Nature herself, and they accordingly took nothing for granted. Generally speaking, they weren't the most erudite group of folks ever, and while trying to explain mineral ownership and the legality of leases to one or two among them was something like doing card tricks for a Basset Hound, most of them were by no means dull. I knew Jack didn't mind getting stuck with the permitting, but he would be much happier when it was over, when the legwork began for him too.

The coffee was always bad in Duncan. It wasn't supposed to be good. We paid the waitress, this time the inscrutable Sheila, and returned to our rooms to gear up for the field. I changed back into a pair of cheap hiking boots that I was quickly destroying, still wet from the day before. I was walking between six and ten miles every day through hummocky fields and muddy pastures. This was only my third job for Falcon and Jack's fourth, and the fact that I was being paid rather handsomely to do little more than wander about in fields all day still seemed incredible to me. As did the soil-gas method. I shared Mr. Wedow's skepticism concerning its effectiveness.

I left the hotel at 7:45 a.m. Jack had already headed out to the field when I hopped in my Blazer with a to-go coffee and a vague headache. I stopped in at the Kum & Go, where they were fresh out of the AA batteries required by my GPS. The porcine clerk explained that they'd be getting more on Monday. She looked at me as though I was visiting her in prison. I carried on to the next convenience store, popped in, and was quickly on my way north out of town. I took a left on Highway 7 toward Lawton as I had a dozen or more times before, still immune to any sense of monotony. I was, in fact, only beginning to find myself in the field, only beginning to apply the same ethic to fieldwork that for me had always applied to climbing: be tenacious, and welcome adversity. Great idea, but the only adversity in the fields and thickets northwest of Duncan were the occasional mean dog, nasty bull, or grumpy landowner. Not exactly sexy stuff.

I had actually tasted a bit of nastiness in southeast Texas on my first job for Falcon. I became acquainted with a new snake, a viper nearly weedy in its commonness and sometimes impressively aggressive and bold in its behavior, the cottonmouth. The fat pit viper known also as the water moccasin was not an uncommon sight as I soaked myself in the deep muck of the mangrove swamps. I learned how not to use a machete. The truly oppressive heat had tested my endurance. The woods could be surprisingly thick in the swampy backcountry around Deweyville, Texas—that job was nearly what we called a "tough guy" job or a "suffer-fest," but was too short in duration to qualify. And too close to civilization. Jack had the same appetite for hard jobs, and had been a part of the already legendary southern Bolivia job with our boss Logan and three other Falcon boys a dozen months before. He talked about it a lot. I was jealous. We were both hungry. We both wanted more.

I slowed my Blazer down and turned north off of Highway 7. The pavement ended with a great whump, and my Chevy quickly had a plume of brown Oklahoma dust behind it. I, like Jack, had a bit of a lead foot, and I realized that I was already doing sixty as the car started listing across big washboards. I eased up on the pedal, but too late. My piping hot and lidless to-go coffee spilled all over my crotch from its position between my legs. That really woke me up. I slowed the car to a stop, found some napkins from a lunch of a couple of days ago in the back seat, and padded at my genitals. I opened the car's door and hopped out to air out my lap. The sun was about to clear a great yellow omelet of low and distant clouds in the east. Although I had been to the Red River Valley once before on the Texas side for an execution or a pissing contest or something like that, I was unaware how pretty Oklahoma could be until we started the Duncan job. I breathed in deeply, watching a couple of pintails in a pond ringed by deep hoof prints and cow shit below me in a heavily grazed pasture. Some piebald Herefords lingered in the distance. The air smelled like autumn. A panoply of colors shimmered in the breeze; ashes, elms, and cottonwoods now preferred golds and ochers to the greens they wore just a couple weeks earlier.

A skein of Canadian geese honked their way southeast far above me, as weedy an animal as there was in the United States. I got back in the Blazer and continued north. I was only a couple of miles from where my first big, looping hike of the day was about to begin. The geese reminded me of one of my favorite jokes, one that functioned best when delivered outdoors and with the rough drawl of a wise old hunter. It went: "When geese fly in a 'v', why is one side of the 'v' always longer than the other?" I was a teen when this jest was first foisted on me, and I remembered the moment I spent filled with the anticipation of learning some deliciously clever new bit of outdoor lore. The answer, to my chagrin, was that one side was longer because there were more geese in it.

⌒

Jack and I were back at Nero's, sitting at the bar and talking with Nita, owner of the coveted Friday night bartending shift. Nero's usually got going pretty good on Fridays. It was just after eight o'clock, and everyone seemed to be in a good mood, including Chunk—he had finally finished permitting, and would begin installing modules with me in the morning. It seemed to be a day for jokes, and the three of us were all taking turns telling them. Jack loved my goose joke, good Michigan native that he was, and Nita thought it was stupid. Nita was high, and kept biting her lower lip and staring at Jack like a dog gazing at a ham. Krissy was working the floor behind us, the final member of our Duncan "fab four," which also included Nita, Cheryl, and Kim. Krissy was a relative celebrity in Duncan, having appeared locally in a Mattress World commercial.

It was my turn. "How many Falcon field-workers does it take to screw in a light bulb?" I grinned.

"I dunno," responded Nita. Jack listened intently, Jack and Coke in hand.

"Two. One to hold the light bulb, and the other to drink until the room starts spinning!" Peals of laughter filled the air. "On that note, I should like another beer, please."

"That's your fifth one, Mr. Fieldworker," Nita scolded. "You're gonna be drunk by ten. You have to dance, you know."

Jack chimed in. "Nita, Tom is sick, and his doctor said to drink plenty of liquids. You have to help him get better," he said earnestly.

I chuckled. The music was about to start in the big room adjacent the main bar where bands sometimes played. Tonight it would be a DJ, as everyone arriving was interested in a bit of line dancing, a phenomenon that was for me enormously entertaining to watch. Absolute conformity choreographed. I thought about how deeply appropriate that was, at the same time careful to shoo any meanness from my heart. Not all Duncanites were proudly identical, I reminded myself. And not all country music sucked. I loved what I thought was good country music, Allison Kraus or Steve Earle, but Alan Jackson? Still, we might get to see Krissy dance. She got off at ten. Even in a line she was delightful to watch.

Nita put a beer in front of me and busied herself filling other orders. Chunk and I resumed a conversation we'd abandoned forty-five minutes earlier, when the jokes started flying. We were imagining aloud what the funniest thing he could have said to Mr. Shelby that morning might have been. Apparently, Shelby was none too pleased about us going on his land, and had been rather brusque with Chunk. We would be "stealthing," or not marking, all of those samples that fell on his land for fear of him tampering with them or simply yanking them out of the ground.

"How about 'I'm collecting donations for the fight against SADS,'" I said.

"What is SADS?" asked Jack.

"Sudden adult death syndrome." Chunk convulsed with laughter. When he stopped laughing, he returned to a deep contemplation. Nita bent over to pick up a bill she dropped behind the bar. We both took the opportunity to look at her butt.

"Mmmm," Jack intoned, looking at me happily. "OK, how about, 'I'm selling edible chocolate nativity scenes, and they come in white chocolate, too, in case you're not into a brown baby Jesus.'" My mouthful of beer came out my nose. Nita turned and stared at me, as did a few others seated at the bar.

"What is your problem?" she shouted with an incredulous half-smile.

"Sorry, sorry. I'll clean it up." My beard and moustache were dripping with beer and snot, and my sinuses stung.

"See what I said! He's sick. He needs help," Jack bellowed. I humbly accepted some paper towels from Nita. It was going to be one of those nights.

3

The morning began with drizzle. After a rather late eight o'clock breakfast, Jack and I drove together to the field in the same car, my Blazer, and felt our hangovers rather keenly. We were up until nearly one the night before. Krissy's boyfriend tried to pick a fight with Jack in the dance hall, but was called off by members of the fab four, who explained that Jack was most assuredly not sleeping with his woman. He was scary, a wild-eyed southern boy you wouldn't want to tangle with, even if you were a lot bigger than he, as was Jack. Chunk knew how to fight too, having wrestled in high school, but the redneck likely would have reappeared with a knife or a pistol if Jack took his ass down in front of everyone. Jack wanted nothing less than a fight, anyway. He was the sort of guy who, upon finding a big spider on his bed, was more likely to catch it and put it outside than kill it. We had that in common.

The drizzle was our friend. It looked like it might break up when Jack and I started our walks, but it only set in more, a great gray blanket pulled over the land. The clouds hovered very low, more walking than flying, and visibility was reduced to not much more than a stone's throw. Patches of fog loitered in low areas, and a sheen of fresh, cool water covered the trees and reinterpreted their crimsons and canaries. Suddenly, Oklahoma had changed, become mysterious, even bewitching. The cool weather was perfect for fast hiking. The sounds were different. My breath, my footsteps—all different. It was much easier to move quietly through the wooded parts of the area. All the usually crispy leaves covering the ground were soaked with moisture. I even surprised a little group of wild turkeys on the far side of a sharp hill I traversed. They exploded into the air away from me only after I got within about thirty feet of them. I likely could have killed one with nothing more than a well-thrown cheerleader's baton had I been prepared and so inclined. When we met back at the car, it was two in the afternoon. We chewed some jerky and cashews as we sat inside the Blazer, feeling once again spry, our hangovers shed out in the field somewhere like snakeskins. We were both rather wet, but were enchanted with the weather.

"Want to go up north and finish those ten along that little road?" I asked.

"Yeah, let's do that." Jack handed me a chocolate bar with almonds, then unwrapped his own and bit off a third of it. He talked with a full mouth. "That ought to be a day. How many did you get on your walk just now, fourteen?"

"Fifteen. No wait, you're right—fourteen. What did you get?"

"I got fifteen, so that's twenty-nine, plus ten more is thirty-nine. That's a good day."

"Yeah, it is. If we get forty a day, we'll finish up in about, what, eight days? That means two days off before we can retrieve. The first samples we put in won't have full exposure until the sixth of November," I stated, pleased. One happy fact about our work was that each sample wanted the same exact exposure time, in days, as had all the other samples in the survey. On retrieval, it was only possible to pull out one day's worth of samples at a time. If you went for a "two-in-one," pulling two days of install in only one day, one group of samples would have a day less exposure than the other. That was to be avoided.

"We could go to Dallas," Jack said with a smile.

"That could be fun." We finished up lunch and drove north, working together from one car and making small out-and-back hikes to the last ten sample sites of the day. We finished these points in just over ninety minutes, and were soon back in Duncan and in dry clothes. We were seated at a large, round, lawn-furniture-style table near the indoor pool, the kind with a hole in the center for an umbrella. I entered my points into Falcon's laptop while Jack looked at our main map. We should indeed finish install in eight days, he agreed. The front office girl entered the pool room through the glass doors that led to the lobby. We had both forgotten her name. She spoke.

"Y'all are the Falcon guys, right?"

"Yeah. What's up?" asked Jack.

"You're supposed to call your boss. He just left a message since y'all weren't in your rooms."

"OK, thanks." Jack looked at me with raised eyebrows. He went into my room to use the phone. His room was upstairs and in another wing of the motel, while mine faced the pool on the first floor, near our work table. I could hear him talking with Logan, Falcon's owner, from where I sat. I couldn't make out much but an incredulous "no way" at some point in the conversation. Then another. Jack reemerged from my room. He walked back to the table and did not sit down, but stood facing me instead.

"Well?"

"Guess what."

"What?"

"Falcon just got another contract with Vantage."

"In Oklahoma too? Does Logan want us to do it?" This was good news indeed. More work. I took my eyes off the computer screen and looked up at him, smiling. He was awfully pleased about something. I eyed him quizzically, tilting my head.

"Yes, Logan wants us to do it. And no, it's not in Oklahoma." He spoke slowly. He was about to explode. He was like a kid who had just discovered his first bicycle on Christmas morning.

"Well, where is it?" I smiled wider.

"It's not really around here. It's in," he paused for effect, "it's in southern Bolivia." My jaw dropped. I stood up and grabbed Chunk. We jumped up and down and howled like coyotes until we nearly fell in the pool.

"You better not be joking," I barked, totally overwhelmed and giggling like a lunatic. I knew that he was not.

That night in the bar, we shared the news with Nita and Kim. They were impressed, happy for us, and suddenly aware that we were actually going to leave Duncan in just a few weeks and that they were not. It had also become clear that we were not going to start something romantic or even casually sexual with any of them. The game was over. We declined to drink in the bar the following Saturday night and sat instead by the pool, sipping a big California Zin out of plastic cups by ourselves, considering aloud what the Bolivia job might be like. We were going to the same part of the Chaco that had played host to the last Falcon job in Bolivia, a survey that had already risen to fable status. Jack was filling me in on the details. I drifted into a daydream as he spoke, aware that I was about to take a big step up as a field-worker. I was a triple A player going to the bigs. The show! I tried to imagine what was ahead, remembering how much even the Oklahoma job differed from what I had expected. I felt fortunate that Chunk would be joining me.

"So, this is officially a 'tough guy' job, right?" I interrupted him without meaning to, having returned from my reverie. "Sorry."

"That's OK, I'm blabbing." He took a sip from the black-looking Zin. "This isn't *a* 'tough guy' job. This is *the* 'tough guy' job."

The following weeks passed quickly as our anticipation grew. We finally dropped off two coolers full of samples at the Oklahoma City Airport's FedEx counter and boarded a small propeller plane headed for Denver. Duncan was quickly receding into memory. On the plane, I turned to Jack.

"You know what?" I asked.

"What?"

"We should have gone to the carnival in Duncan last weekend," I opined.

"Why?"

"We may not get the chance to play tic-tac-toe with a live chicken in Bolivia."

"True." Jack chuckled.

I looked out the plane's little window at the center-pivot-irrigated crop fields below, great tan and taupe circles stretching to the horizon. For one hundred and twenty years people had looked for oil in Oklahoma, simply drilling where the surface geology seemed promising in the old days, and now "looking" and "smelling" underground using fancy 3-D seismic and geochemical technology to find the last drops. For it was good to the last drop. But the price of a barrel of oil was only about fifteen dollars, and was about to go even lower. How long would it stay so low? The state's crude was used to fight the last world war. It had transformed the region's economy. And now it was almost gone, replaced by water from below, long since burned up, its carbon floating about in the atmosphere all around us. If our survey turned up anything new, it would most assuredly be miniscule compared to the once vast oil reserves of the Sooner state.

2 INTO THE CHACO

I looked at these guys, at this world, at these men who were overpaid and drank too much and were glib and cynical and bit the hand that fed them and showed up late and had no respect for authority, and I thought to myself: these are my heroes.

— Matthew Weiner

THERE WERE MORNINGS when the village of Nancarauintza declined time's invitation to a new day, and after one look outside, collectively pulled the door closed, returned to bed, and buried itself in blankets. December 19th was just such a day. The ground was soaked in the wake of a strong rain that had drenched the area the evening before, and even at eight in the morning, no one moved through town and not a single storefront was propped open. It was unusually cool for December and for late spring. Some would say that Pachamama, the earth mother, had answered their prayers. The water so desperately needed by the village's skinny cattle was standing about in pools and brown puddles; the sedges and low plants upon which they depended would, for a time, be restored to relative vigor. Some of the plots of corn might still take hold after a bone-dry spring had threatened to waste them. Those who lived farther from town would not have to make the journey to Nanca's well to fetch water for a whole week, maybe longer if they had good containers for catching rain. But the heat would return soon.

Nanca had not a single paved street other than the one that went from the highway to the big gas plant called Porvenir off to the east, and that was only paved for a couple hundred meters. Walking anywhere whatsoever was frustratingly difficult that morning. The soil in the area was full of silica, and after a heavy rain became almost preternaturally slippery. Pregnant clouds hung low above the tall, leafy trees at the little pueblo's edge, threatening further showers, and while it was around fifteen degrees Celsius outside, it felt much colder. Nanca's residents were more accustomed to temperatures in the thirties.

Juan was watching Highway 9 from the front steps of his family's house. Nanca was just east of the only road that connected the boomtown of Santa Cruz, three hundred and eighty kilometers to the north, to the village of Villamontes and the Argentine border to the south. Despite being right alongside the main artery of the Chaco, Nanca was in the middle of nowhere, a fact that the nineteen-year-old Juan deeply rued. He had been to Santa Cruz just once with his father three years ago, and wanted nothing more than to return there and stop living on the edge of the world. Juan noticed that no cars or trucks had passed by on the highway for some time. It was paved for only about thirty kilometers to the north, beyond which was mud, completely impassable in almost any vehicle after a storm like the one they'd just had. Even a horse would have to wrest its feet out with every step. He imagined the buses and big trucks that were mired there, and considered that he was similarly stuck in the sticks. Many of his friends hadn't even been to Villamontes, much less the great, horny Santa Cruz de la Sierra, and knew not what they were missing.

He stuffed some coca in his left cheek, noting that he hadn't much left, and threw some *bico* in his mouth atop the tender leaves. His mother and sister were lying in bed asleep just inside the worn wooden door behind him, less than eager to leave the warmth and relative dryness of their bed. He resolved to save a little coca for his father, who was still sleeping, or more accurately, was still passed out, beside them. He would want it for his hangover. A couple of bottles of *singani* had shown up at the neighbor's the night before, during the heaviest part of the storm. The rain and the booze both lasted until sometime in the wee hours, and the former was shared by six or seven *vecinos*, Juan among them. He was the youngest in the group, though, and didn't get to drink much of it.

Juan heard the whine of an engine approaching on the Porvenir road in the distance. His family's house was a stone's throw from the wide, sloppy road and all of its traffic. He knew it must be one of the gas plant Toyotas. That was the only vehicle that had a chance to make it down the road that morning. He stood and walked slowly and carefully toward the road, slipping and almost falling a couple times. It was indeed a formerly white Toyota HiLux pickup truck with a barely visible gas company logo on the door. Only the two half-circles of glass on the windshield that the beating wipers defined were not brown with snotty mud. The truck slowed to a stop. Its tires looked absurd, so thick with mud that they seemed twice their normal size. The hood and roof of the little Toyota were strewn with fist-sized clumps of soaked brown soil. The opaque driver's side window came down to reveal the plant's doctor.

"Hello Juan."

"Good morning, doctor. Someone hurt?" Juan's Spanish was delivered with a distinctly country accent, while the doctor spoke with the smoother tones of a university-educated urbanite.

"No—worse. I'm out of cigarettes. No one at the plant has any, it seems. Or they are hiding them from me." Juan laughed. "Any stores open?"

"No. You'll have to go to Tiguipa."

"Want to come?" The doctor smiled.

"Sure!" Juan walked around the front of the Toyota and let himself in. The doctor had the heat on.

"Do you know what? You might be the luckiest guy in town, up and around as you are this morning."

"Why?" Juan puzzled.

"Because you are going to be the first to hear the news."

"What news?"

"The gringos are coming back. In two weeks. They will need eight *macheteros*, like before. They want the same ones they used last year. But Rafa has gone away. And they don't want Otero. Too drunk."

Juan smiled. "You mean..."

"You could take his place. I will tell the foreman when I go back to the plant, if you want me to. I think you are strong enough." The doctor smiled and patted Juan on the shoulder. "Thirty dollars a week. Six or seven weeks."

"Thank you. Thank you!" Juan exulted.

2

I was seated in a window seat on a well-used 737 heading toward Santa Cruz's Viru Viru International Airport. Zane Curtis, a fellow Coloradan I had just met in Miami, occupied the aisle seat to my left. Jack Barnes and Logan Robles sat across the aisle from us, and the four of us had six seats to ourselves. Zane and I were again discussing southern Bolivia, having both been gently awakened moments before by the dull blue lambency of first light outside the plane's windows. Actually, Zane was talking and I was listening. This would be Zane's second trip to the Chaco to perform a Falcon soil-gas survey. We cruised above a great, soft ocean of gray clouds. Bolivians dreamt under blue blankets in the seats before and behind us.

"It sounds pretty hairy down there," I mumbled, rubbing some of the sleep out of my face.

"Psychics will lead dogs to your body," Zane stated blandly. I chuckled. Zane was bigger than I was, though not quite as large as Jack, and his black hair was braided into a long ponytail that reached the middle of his back. He wore round, wire-framed glasses and a Fu Manchu-style goatee, sideburns, and had a rather pale face with high cheekbones and smallish brown eyes. His look clearly required some maintenance. When I saw him in the Miami airport for the first time, I knew instantly that he was a Falcon boy, but he contrasted sharply with the rest of us, who were less well-groomed. He was married without children. He spoke fondly of his wife. He drank less than the rest of us did, and displayed less raw enthusiasm about our imminent jaunt as well. He was the type of guy, I was about to find out, whose highs were never too high and his lows never too low.

I spoke at length with each of my colleagues during the eight-hour flight. My discussion with Logan nearly took the form of a briefing about the imminent survey, whereas Jack and I talked a lot about the Duncan job, deciding that we each wanted to own a ranch on the high plains of Oklahoma. I was going to call mine the Flying Jew. He would call his Brandyshine. As usual, he and I laughed more than was normal. Zane and I talked primarily about the last Chaco job. He seemed like a tough lad, and smart as well. I was certain that he could "walk the walk" after discussing Falcon work with him, and knew that he would not be once again winging to Bolivia had that not been made abundantly clear during the last survey there. I didn't mind in the least the fact that he was just a bit aloof with me, and seemed quite clearly to regard me as a greenhorn. I was.

My three partners collaborated to paint a rather murky and unnerving picture of the Chaco for me. Though they had all worked there the year before on what had been Falcon's first Bolivian job, they agreed that the place to which we were hurrying was more than just a little alien. And dangerous. I had growing concerns about the language barrier. I purchased a tutorial Spanish book right after returning home from Duncan in early December, but had barely opened it during my three weeks off, preferring instead to fill myself with wine and screw up my relationship with my girlfriend. All that good behavior in Duncan for nothing—April and I broke up shortly after I returned to Colorado. She could not abide my peregrinations. She also hated it when I called her "the cruelest month." It was a black Christmas.

We began our descent into the city of Santa Cruz. I pressed my face against the window as the plane slipped silently into the bank of clouds below us. I made out lights along twisting roads and in small villages outside of the city. There was none of the straight-line design of the average U.S. town here. Jack and Logan were stirring. We were all of us feeling a bit rough. We'd turned a fair amount of suds into piss and left it in the plane's little bathrooms before shutting our mouths and eyes some scant hours before. Our plane descended lower still. I had already gathered during the flight that Logan thought Zane's cultivated appearance to be unseemly for a field-worker, and that he was giggling a bit behind Zane's back. Though Logan clearly respected him, he and Zane were cut from different cloth. I doubted that Logan even owned a comb. Neither did I. Logan was awake. Not five minutes later, he and Zane resumed their latest debate. Though we were about to touch down, the two picked up where they had left off hours earlier, returning to a heated discussion about whether one ought to climb ice with one rope or with the more modern dual-rope system. They were both good ice climbers, and Zane had actually worked as a private guide on a couple of big mountains in Ecuador. Ice climbing was, in my opinion, difficult and dangerous. For me, it was the perfect thing to think about if you needed to quash an untimely erection during, say, the course of a strictly nonsexual massage. It was the diametric opposite of sex. I much preferred climbing good sturdy rock.

Logan was insisting that two ropes were better. A great deal of energy was trapped within the rather small frame of our leader. He stood around five-foot-eight, and I would have put his weight at a slight buck-and-a-half. He seemed much larger, however, and was notorious for having the resiliency of a cartoon character. I had yet to work with Logan, but had enjoyed his company in Boulder, Colorado, where we had teamed up for a few rock climbs in Eldorado Canyon. He was a talented ascensionist, and had climbed some pretty hard routes both in Yosemite and in Colorado's Front Range. He and I both spent several years in our twenties living in vans, drinking cheap beer for dinner, eschewing haircuts and shavers, and thinking of nothing but climbing. And women.

Logan was still a bit of a slob. His mop of wild, curly black hair framed his tan Roman nose, square jaw, and strong chin nicely. He shaved only occasionally. He was clad normally in an old T-shirt and a pair of jeans, and had made no exception for the flight. Though he was wholly careless with regard to his personal appearance, he was handsome enough to get away with it. His brown eyes were usually full of raw enthusiasm, even if he was just doing the dishes, and this enthusiasm, while often contagious, could be a bit exhausting to be around at times. Add a little Argentine *yerba mate* tea or coca leaf, two popular, powerful stimulants I was about to explore extensively, and Logan could turn positively obstreperous.

All who knew him would agree that he was capable of being a bit more obtrusive in public than he meant to be, particularly when booze had a role; he was often completely oblivious to the general ire he sometimes inspired in bars and restaurants and airplanes with his maniacal fits of laughter and often brash polemics. This much had been evidenced that very evening. At times during the flight, unspoken objurgations were written plainly on the faces of certain nearby passengers, a fact that I had noticed, but he, as usual, had not. In general, he was never quite offensive, but was often ribald. He once explained to me that what other people thought of you was "none of your business." But Logan had undeniable charisma. He was a natural leader of men. He even looked Latino, and knew how to use that fact to his advantage while he was in Latin America. He led by example in the field. He was manic without the depressive, required little sleep, and could abide a fair bit of whiskey as well. He was a finisher who made people want to work hard for him and he was, beyond question, the heart of Falcon.

With a bark of the plane's tires, we were on Bolivian soil. We were all off of the plane in short order and standing in line at the immigration booth. In a few moments we had stuffed ourselves and our kits into a couple of taxis and were headed for the hotel Yotau. We all craved some horizontal sleep. We would check in to our hotel at around 8:30 a.m., and were free to sleep until lunchtime.

⌒

I lay in bed and stared at the ceiling, hearing the occasional sounds a big hotel makes over the hum of the air conditioner. This was not just any hotel. This was Santa Cruz's voluptuous home away from home for the DEA, oil bigwigs, and for me and my colleagues for one night—this was the Yotau. A heavy door slammed somewhere above me in the sizeable building. A few minutes later, a room-service cart squeaked by in the hallway outside my bedroom. The wide window to my right revealed a mass of dark clouds settling on the city. It was about to rain.

The digital clock on the nightstand next to my bed said that it was almost noon. I sat up and tossed aside my sheet and blanket. The Yotau's powerful AC had turned my bedroom cold. I looked vacantly at my legs, white from two months spent inside of work pants in Oklahoma. I swung them out of bed, stood up, and walked naked from the bedroom into the main room of my spacious suite. I padded across the tastefully furnished living room, much larger than the one in my Colorado rental, to a pair of sliding glass doors that opened to a balcony. I looked outside. A gusty wind bullied the date palm trees planted near the hotel and lifted skirts down on the sidewalk beside busy San Martin avenue. I placed a hand upon the inside of each of the warm metal door handles, palms facing out and down and knuckles nearly touching. They were heavy sliding doors of thick glass, and the sort of motion one makes when swimming underwater would open them. I threw the doors wide.

Humid heat poured across my skin. The din of honking cars and straining engines filled my ears and the room behind me. Someone spoke loudly in staccato Spanish directly beneath my balcony and a dog barked behind a high stone barrier across the street. The smell of flowers, car exhaust and wet garbage among a dozen others assailed me. The flowers were bougainvillea, and were painfully, brilliantly red. They poured over the tops of brick and cinder block walls defining property across the street and grew also, among others, in my balcony's planter. I moved outside. A young, long-legged woman walking with a friend noticed my naked torso from across the avenue, and though the balcony's low wall effectively blocked any view of my southern regions, she tapped her friend's shoulder and pointed at me. They giggled. I smiled at them and waved. More giggling. They were beautiful.

Rain from the lowland storm started in big plops. In the span of a couple of minutes, the wind ushered in curtains of water that would wash the streets Santa Cruz, drive her people indoors or beneath awnings and market tarps, and wet the long brown legs of skirt-wearing girls caught on the street without cash for a taxi. I smiled, turned, and walked back inside. I left the glass doors wide open and returned to my bedroom to dress.

It rained enough for an entire Colorado spring during the course of our lunch. The hotel restaurant was wrought of polished umber hardwood and glass and served a very good ceviche of *surubi*, a sweet white fish found in certain special stretches of Bolivia's rivers. I enjoyed the dish at a table with my back to a large window, studying the restaurant's patrons and chatting idly with Jack and Zane. Logan was out running an errand. We might have been in the restaurant of one of the finest hotels in South Beach, Miami—the Yotau was no less opulent or self-conscious—it lacked only a beach and a view. Chunk and Zane were convinced that first-generation cocaine money had built the Yotau.

Four groups were seated at tables in the restaurant. Two of them consisted of white tourists in various stages of hyperphagia. These groups contrasted sharply with a cadre of DEA boys seated around a large table for lunch, likely headed to the Chapare region to eradicate coca, which according to Zane was something like going to Nebraska to fight corn. They wore shorts, collared shirts, and running shoes, but uniformly buzz-cut heads and an overt machismo had betrayed their mission in Bolivia to Zane. He explained that they were about to undertake something called "Operation Dignity," an effort to eliminate a raw plant growing out of god's green earth, cultivated in Bolivia since before the U.S. Constitution was even dreamt of.

"They think they're Navy Seals." Jack chuckled. "We met some guys here last year who were DEA. I'd bet a hundred bucks that those guys are. We do not want to talk to them. They're really hard to not laugh at. Muy macho." He was amused.

They did act a little smug, even superior, and laughed too loudly. That much I had already noticed. We seemed to be their natural rivals. Perhaps because we were young, strong, and not on the same team as they were, despite also hailing from the United States. We were unkempt. They were clean cut. They were thugs. We were explorers. Or maybe it was the fact that we could legally enjoy the very thing that they had traveled south to eradicate and were not supposed to use, even in Bolivia. Logan pushed through the restaurant's swinging glass doors carrying a watermelon-sized bag of green leaf. He walked over and plopped down in a seat at our table.

"Got it!" he smiled.

⌣

"Most city folks in Bolivia wouldn't walk around town chewing coca, bro. City people don't chew. Only a backwards-ass hillbilly mofo would do that," Logan quipped.

"It would never even occur to the rare Bolivian who can afford to stay here to chew coca while he was here. Even though it's completely legal," said Zane.

"It used to be in Coca-Cola, ya know," Logan added. "Coca is to the rural working class in Bolivia what food is to most people."

We laughed. I would soon find out how true that was. I tongued the wad of green leaf in my cheek. Coca became psychoactive only after it was sprinkled with sodium bicarbonate. Baking soda. Mine was working very well. My right cheek and the front part of my tongue were numb, and I had this buzz, this not-so-subtle high that was nothing but pleasant. Logan and Jack each had a big *bolo* in their cheeks as well. The rain of the morning was gone. We were seated in tasteful reclining lawn chairs beside the Yo's lovely and extravagant outdoor pool under a strong sun and in our bathing suits. A couple of the DEA boys drank Paceña beer at a table on the other side of the pool. They were well aware of our coca-chewing ways. The ten-story Yotau formed an enclave around the pool area, and the hotel's exterior walls above us were like hanging gardens. Flowers and plants leapt from the planters of each room's balcony and hung down the beautifully masoned gray stone walls in violets, reds, and emeralds. The warm, redolent air was the smiling breath of grace. I was in the most opulent place I had ever been. And I was chewing coca.

"So, all these people here," there were maybe twenty people scattered around the pool, "think that Logan and Jack and I are total freaks?" I asked.

"Oh, yeah. Very much so," Zane said flatly. "But you're gringos. Gringos do the funniest things."

"Isn't that a TV show down here?" Jack deadpanned. "Gringos do the funniest things? Have you guys seen that?" We all looked at Chunk. Zane punched him in the arm.

3

It was time to leave. It was 8 a.m. in Santa Cruz and in New York, and I was watching one of those American morning "news" shows as I got dressed at the Yo, the kind that featured a cute female host doing her best impression of a journalist. Their lead story was about road rage. Everyone on the set down to the weatherman wore a smile as bright as an arc-welder and suffered from pitiable paroxysms of self-infatuation. It was less a news program than a circle jerk.

I stuffed my toothbrush, toothpaste, and still-wet swimsuit into my duffel. I admired my recently purchased Tramontina machete before wrapping it in my towel and putting it likewise in my large bag. I turned off the TV, wondering if Bolivians got road rage. Did they have irritable bowel syndrome? I wondered if they had attention deficit disorder and wanted whiter teeth. Did they take pills to avert depression? Did low-calorie donuts go through consumer taste tests in Bolivia? Did they show their lawns who's the boss? I closed the door to my room and shouldered my bag, walked downstairs, and found Jack seated in the hotel's polished stone and glass lobby. Logan was signing us out at the desk. Glancing through the twin, swinging glass doors of the main entrance, I noticed Zane speaking with Freddy, Vantage Petroleum's hapless looker-on who would accompany us to the job site. The pair stood beside a gray, late-eighties Land Cruiser that appeared to be in decent shape. Two other Toyotas, both pickups, were parked at the curb behind it. Soon we would all be driving to some gas plant called Porvenir, two hundred and fifty miles south of Santa Cruz and deep within the Gran Chaco.

"The chariots await, I see." I sat next to Chunk on a fancy black leather sofa.

"Yup. You should ride with me. I'm gonna drive that red one down." Jack's face was filled with raw anticipation and a trace of something else, something more serious. We were about to make the change back into field-workers. He wore a red and white T-shirt that said "Give Blood" across the front, and had already donned his work boots. "You look like you need some Chaco."

"Yeah," I said with a smile, "looks like that's what I'm getting."

Soon we were rolling in our new rides. Chunk was at the wheel, and I rode shotgun beside him. As I idly bullshitted with him, I gazed variously at the people on the streets, the buildings, and the cars around us. Every other car was a taxi, and most of these did not have clients within. I soon realized that the Yotau was in a very nice part of town, and that we had not really seen Santa Cruz at all. The main streets of Santa Cruz were arranged in big circles around the center, and on a map the city looked like an oblong dartboard. As we motored along the third ring, I remarked how disturbingly poor most of the town was. Throngs of homeless people squatted in parks. Shoeless kids ran through the streets. Rotund women

43

wearing white dresses were seated with their children on the sidewalks, their long black hair in braids, their backs against dirty beige walls, their small stands of gum and cigarettes and soda displayed hopefully to a world that was being slowly and surely invaded by the American-style superstore, the likes of which we had already seen around the Yotau.

Doorways in the buildings along the streets admitted people to sundry stores, photocopy vendors, dusty hardware outlets, and little chicken places, most of which had no glass in the windows. Discarded paper and plastic wrappers collected in every corner and crack. Half-completed multistory buildings stood around uncertainly throughout the city, their concrete skeletons unattended by workers, their rusted rebar poking the hazy turquoise sky. Young boys wearing tattered clothes cajoled drivers stopped at major intersections into windshield washes with the persuasiveness of trial lawyers. These cost the equivalent of three cents in U.S. money. No one seemed to be starving, but many were clearly hungry and hurting.

Our avenue grew grungy and increasingly walled by pedestrians near one or another of the city's large, open-air markets. The street simply burst with activity before us as we were forced to slow to a halt. Carts of fruit, bicyclists, pigs and goats, little kids—Freddy and Logan led us around the melee of commerce in a bumbling series of rights and lefts toward the teeming city's edge. This was the second-largest town in Bolivia after La Paz, but it was more of a capitalist hothouse than was the Andean capital, a center of trade both large and small. Here you could buy everything from oil wells to mandarin oranges to large quantities of cocaine. Lowland farmers and prostitutes alike sold their commodities in her streets. Machete-toting jungle dwellers from the Beni province in the north and pale-skinned Mennonites from south of town shared the sidewalks around the pungent markets and their rows of blue tarps. Grim-faced and bored policemen guarded a big bank, automatic rifles slung around their shoulders. There were more than a few beautiful young women scattered in the crowd, some wearing high heels and others looks of quiet desperation. We drove with the windows down, both part of the scene and insulated from it, in Bolivia but not really there yet. Finally, we were out of town. We motored south on the deceptively well-maintained start of the great Highway 9, the Chaco road, the main vein of southern Bolivia. We passed an enormous billboard that advertised Paceña beer and featured a sixty-foot-long, green-eyed and brown-skinned beauty resting on her curvaceous side. It said "Paceña is beer" in Spanish that even I understood. I wondered what marketing genius had trotted out that slogan. Beneath the billboard, a placid-faced woman seated on an overturned white plastic food bucket breast-fed an infant as she waited for a bus.

Ahead of us, Logan drove the Land Cruiser and Freddy the white pickup. After brief deliberation, Jack and I plugged the first *bolos* of the day in our cheeks. It was, after all, a road trip. Santa Cruz and the emotions it elicited receded behind us. The highway deteriorated steadily over the next couple of hours until we were trundling along deeply rutted and concrete-hard red dirt. After several dozen miles of uniform flatness directly south of Santa Cruz, the land changed slowly, began undulating, and eventually foothills appeared to our right in the west; they would remain there for the duration of our journey. These were the nadir of the mighty Andes, the foothills of the great range. I noticed a few impressive, vertical sandstone walls that formed the chests and shoulders of some of the big hills bumping past. Most exposed rock was a dusty red or beige, just like the sandstone found in western Colorado. We crossed the sharp-toothed mouths of several rugged canyons that terminated just west of the road to our right; it looked like strong acid and not rain had formed them. The flora was robust. This was the beginning of the dry Chaco forest, one of the most biologically diverse dry forests in the world. All but the steepest of hillsides and rocks were crowded with thorny plant life.

Thick and spiny brush, queen palm, and tall saguaro-style cacti mingled beside and beneath the higher-reaching *quebracho* and *palo santo* trees, broad-leafed trees that seemed out of place in such an arid area. The forest grew greener and thicker with every bend in the road, however, and finally leaned almost completely over the euphamistic "highway" in places. The humidity was growing. Here and there a pink *lapacho* tree stood alone beneath its auspicious crown of cotton-candy-colored blossoms, but for the most part, the woods were dirty green leaf and pewter shadow. Soon the dry, semi-deciduous tropical forest would do its best impression of a jungle, complete with two canopies and extensive vines in some places. I glimpsed several vertical-walled ditches cutting deeply through the land away from the highway and into the forest here and there, and at least one had water in it—Jack said that these were called *quebradas* in a contemptuous tone. I knew without having to ask that these would be formidable obstacles. It was some of the most daunting terrain I had ever seen.

We passed myriad tiny villages. The dwellings in many of them were something like the forts I built as a youth in the pine forest around Conifer, Colorado. While some were what you might call sturdy, despite extensive ventilation, others were nothing more than blue plastic tarps stretched tightly around crude wooden frames. We turned a bend and entered a flat area of benchland where the road suddenly improved and went straight for a while. We could see the other trucks about a quarter mile ahead of us—we were lagging behind. There was a lot to look at. On our right, thick forest climbed steeply away from the road, but to our left was a great open area that had been hacked and burned free of native growth and was being farmed, ostensibly by the people living in a group of shacks at the edge of the wide field. Some smiling kids ran alongside the truck to our left at the edge a broad, freshly-worked swath of brown earth. A man followed an ox and wrestled mightily with a primitive plow beyond them.

Before Jack could react, a pack of dogs exploded from the forest on our right and ran full speed into our path. We were lucky to hit only one of them. The wounded dog burst into yelps as it emerged from beneath the truck, which Jack brought to a very abrupt halt. The dog had run under the truck, which was doing about forty at the time, and was hit by some part of the undercarriage. We felt the impact inside the vehicle. The crying white and tan animal turned around and careened back into the forest behind us as a cloud of dust rose around the Toyota. He was running on three legs, visibly broken and likely hopeless. The guy with the plow checked his ox, stopped, and watched. The other dogs continued chasing, nipping and playing in the wide field. They were all painfully thin. The kids stopped to watch the injured dog disappear and then looked at us.

Jack looked at me heartbroken. "Fuck! What should we do?"

"If we had a chance to find it, I'd say we should go kill it." I looked at the kids. I looked at the man with the plow. "But we couldn't find him now. I just hope he dies fast," I muttered weakly.

"Should I go talk to them?" Jack was full of remorse. Logan and Freddy were no longer in sight ahead of us.

"I don't think dogs are really owned here. Just tolerated. Look how skinny they are. I doubt if they—well, fuck, I don't know. It wasn't your fault. They probably saw that."

Jack put the truck back in first and started slowly away. An eighteen-wheeler grew quickly and unexpectedly in the distance on the almost-two-lane dirt road ahead of us. It was one of perhaps a dozen vehicles we had met going north. It thundered by us with barely enough room, nearly removing our truck's side-view mirror and kicking up huge clouds of dust.

"That was too fucking close." Jack gripped the wheel tightly. "He's going faster than we have the whole way. I bet he's killed a few dogs. And chickens."

"And five-year-olds. Did you see what the side of it said?"

"No, what?"

"Schlumberger. We must be going the right way." Schlumberger was one of the biggest oil field service providers in the the world. Oil well parts and support for finding, drilling, and completing your new well. Even if it was in the actual middle of nowhere. We caught up to Logan, Zane, and Freddy in ten minutes. They had stopped to wait for us at a little roadside chicken stand in a dingy village of cinder block and plywood huts called Cabezas. Lunch awaited on greasy pieces of newspaper. I gnawed at my breast and imagined a dog slowly dying beneath the tangled leaves and thorns of an indifferent forest.

⌒

Che Guevara met his untimely end near a town called Vallegrande, just sixty miles northwest of where we ate chicken. The Argentine sansculotte's abortive efforts to foment a Cuban-style revolution in the hills just west of the Chaco proper were conducted in the same terrain in which we would work. Unlike the Cuban *campesinos*, those of southern

Bolivia met Che and his motley band with indifference. They did not go out of their way to feed him or help him hide. They did not misrepresent his position to the army that searched for him. Above all, they did not share his zealous desire for revolution. His fervency was met by people in southern Bolivia not with raised, clenched fists, but with nonplussed stares. Many there asked simply, "revolt against *what?*" His hungry and hunted movements through the tangled brush of southern Bolivia's foothills ended in a shootout in October of 1967. His body was put on public display in Vallegrande. His hands were cut off and sent to Cuba as proof of his demise.

Even in 1998, the presence of a government in the deep remoteness of the Chaco was scarcely noticeable. There weren't cops. The army had a post in Villamontes and Camiri too, where the Bolivian national oil company YPFB had extensive facilities, but for some one hundred and fifty miles of red dirt "highway" between the two there was no evidence of a government, a major power line, or an official street sign. Gas was sold not from pumps but jerry cans. It was like the old west, but with a few cars—many people still rode horses—and it was, roughly speaking, anarchy. But very few fought, stole, or killed. Folks got along. If you had a breech birth, a compound fracture, or just got bit by a nasty snake, it was among the last places you would want to be, but if you were a gringo who was tired of getting hassled by the man, this was the place for you.

Two such *norteamericanos* were Robert Leroy Parker and Harry Longabaugh, better known as Butch Cassidy and the Sundance Kid. The much-celebrated pair of bandits were also killed, allegedly, by soldiers of the Bolivian army after robbing the Concordia mine's payroll wagon in the polychrome desert west of the dusty frontier town of Tupiza in December of 1909, one hundred and eighty miles due west of where our job was about to begin. This popular story was promulgated by a writer named Arthur Chapman in a 1930 magazine article; Chapman placed their last stand in a tiny village named San Vincente, and his version has become widely accepted. But Chapman's sources were unknown, and Parker's sister claimed to have seen him some sixteen years later in the United States. A former Bolivian president and Western U.S. history buff, the late René Barrientos investigated the San Vincente site, exhumed remains, and concluded that the story was false. Of note is the fact that Barrientos was in command of the troops that killed Che Guevara.

We left Camiri behind us at about 4 p.m. It would finally take us twelve hours to go two hundred and sixty miles, and we would continue driving until well past nightfall before reaching Porvenir. Jack and I were flying on coca. In places the road was barely passable. Any urgently needed improvements were made on the spot by those unfortunate souls who were stuck there using machetes, shovels, and logs plucked from the forest. Whole busloads of people might be pressed into service, and any given bus carried its own platoon of potential laborers—a good thing, that, for it was just these buses that most frequently became mired. There was no department of transportation in the Chaco.

We had the right vehicles for the trip, but we had to stop and jump out a few times to move logs out of the way, push them back into place, or to assist one another with a second pair of eyes over some crevasse or obstacle that could not be seen by the driver. *Campesinos* here and there stared at us blankly until we waved and smiled, which always elicited a response in kind. Some noticed our *bolos* and pointed at their cheeks laughing, surprised to see gringos chewing. The day began to wane. After thirty crepuscular miles south of the village of Boyuibe, the world went black. Faint blurry slivers of orange light escaped from cracks in the brown walls of huts near the highway and cooking fires in the trees. The air was full of smoke. I was experiencing subtle visual effects from the coca. I couldn't focus my eyes as quickly or as well as normal. My vision was blue or white tinged at times. More than this, I felt like all of me, my entire consciousness, was trapped right behind my eyes. Though throbbing with a euphoric, narcotic vim, I felt like I was in the attic and the rest of my body was a great, dark, and empty house with no furniture or carpet. I was hollow and echoey. I was higher on coca than I had ever been on anything when we stopped at the padlocked gate of Porvenir and waited as headlights came down from the plant office to let us in. It was 10 p.m. when we followed a security vehicle through the gate and up a rutted dirt road to the main facility. We parked and stumbled inside the largest of several dark buildings looking for someone who could show us to our beds.

4

I did not sleep well. Morning crept into our room like a vapor. Logan awoke first; we had all slept in the same large cement bungalow in four separate steel-framed cots. The air was already uncomfortably warm and quite humid in the gray-walled room, and the single window admitted the pale light of dawn not through glass, but through hex-shaped openings in concrete cinder blocks. I stood up and slipped my pants on. When I sat back down and reached for my boots, Logan tapped me on the arm. He had slept in the cot beside mine, and was seated there rubbing his stubbly face. He pointed at my boots and made a gesture with his right hand as though he held a large cup of water and was pouring it on the floor.

"Centipedes," he said quietly. "Turn over your boots and shake 'em before you put 'em on."

The mess hall was a short walk uphill from our new home. Breakfast was served, announced by familiar scents as the four of us shuffled up to eat. Regal orange trees stood around the premises contentedly while the natural forest crowded against the chain-link fence surrounding the grounds like a phalanx of outcasts. The whole employee compound was manicured and tidy. It was a little slice of the first world. We met several plant employees over breakfast, all of whom were most friendly and eager to know if we liked Bolivia. A couple of them razzed us amicably about our manliness as we stood in line at the buffet, or more accurately, our ability to work in the thick stuff. They pointed out the glass window of the dining hall and kept saying *muy duro*, "very tough," all the while with big smiles on their brown faces. Logan told me quickly that they called the forest around Porvenir the "green monster." He and I laughed, reminded of Boston's Fenway Park. Logan was a Yankees fan. I liked the Sox. He was bantering with them, flipping them a little shit too, when suddenly he pointed at me and said something to them in Spanish. They exploded with laughter. I asked him what he had said, smiling at the amused pair of mechanics.

"I was just telling them how tough you guys are. I told them that you, bro, hold your socks up with thumbtacks." I laughed as one of them slapped me on the back. I walked with my blue tray and plate of breakfast to the long, Formica-topped table where Logan and Zane sat. They were both digging into big, steaming piles of yellow eggs and meat and toast across from the plant foreman, chatting with him effortlessly in Spanish. The bloke who plopped down opposite me at the table, a plant engineer, kept asking "how are you?" in poorly pronounced English and beaming when I responded with "fine, how are you?" Jack sat between Zane and me, and had a perplexed look on his sleepy, stubbly mug; he was trying his best to follow Logan's discussion with the plant boss. The breakfast was copious. I had two American-style pancakes, some scrambled eggs, and three strips of very thick bacon. I soon noticed that one of my strips had coarse black hair growing out of it. I neglected to eat that one. The orange juice was exceptional. The coffee was delicious, a double shot of espresso-style inky black brew in the bottom of a cup served with a little metal container of warm whole milk on the side. Others drank *yerba mate* tea. I noted an ice cream machine against the wall behind me. The food was good—my bacon was the only exception. Jack looked at it when I had a chance to point it out to him without drawing attention. He winced.

The plant's crewmembers were among the most educated of all Bolivians, at least in matters technical, and were for the most part very pleased to be working at Porvenir, which was a large compressor station for the abundant natural gas produced by the area's many wells. This was where the sales gas was put into a pipeline and sent to end-user markets like Brazil. The permanent staff was between fifteen and twenty men, among them a doctor and a couple of cooks. Every man's sky blue helmet was hung on a wooden peg near the white metal door of the dining hall as he ate. Most had names written on them in black marker. It was a cheerful room with a white plastic floor and four long, pale yellow tables, each of which sat about ten, five on each side, in matching plastic chairs. You could smoke there. Food was ready three times a day, and there was never too little. The plumbing worked well. There was always water. Modest lawns and fruit trees replaced the thorny native flora outside the glass windows of the mess hall. The snakes had been shooed away. It was, however relatively, a utopia. It missed only women and alcohol.

The plant's doctor spoke decent English. He was a big, husky man with a large nose, heavy-rimmed black bifocal glasses, and thinning gray hair; he had whiter skin than most at the plant, and must have been in his late fifties. He noticed from the next table that I spoke no Spanish and motioned me over to sit with him. He welcomed me, and I chatted with him briefly as he drank coffee and smoked an L & M cigarette. He ashed sloppily, staring at the wall as he talked to me in his neglected English, often missing the clear glass ashtray, often clearing his throat. He had an air of authority and struck me as intelligent, but seemed also to be a bit annoyed with life in general in a manner simultaneously droll and slightly sad. I asked him if there was malaria in the area and he shrugged his shoulders and said "who knows?" He was different than the rest and a bit of a mugwump, I suspected. I was beginning to understand that whiter skin often corresponded to a higher station in life in Bolivia. I shook his big soft hand as the four of us stood to leave. We quit the dining hall together and walked back to our quarters with full bellies. My gaze lingered on the chaotic foliage pressed against the plant's fence as we walked. I wondered if, after a few weeks therein, I would also call it the "green monster."

⌒

My face exploded in pain in three distinct places, my eyes pinched tightly closed, and I stumbled backward, machete dropped and hands swatting at some outrageously hostile flying insects which, either for some unknown trespass or for the sheer delight of attacking me, were treating me with extreme prejudice. I tripped on something behind me and landed on my sweat-soaked ass. I was dripping with brine as I got quickly to my feet and set them. I held my arms up before me as would a pugilist and opened my eyes, anticipating a second assault. None came.

Manuel and Juan cackled behind me. I felt like a lozenge in the hot, dry mouth of the forest, dissolving slowly as it savored me. I turned around to face my assistants, dropped my arms, and uttered a weak "fuck" to myself. My heart was racing.

"Que es?" I asked Manuel as I panted. He walked to my side, giggling like a little girl. He stopped before me and smiled. His wide grin revealed a great wad of coca leaf in his right cheek.

"Avispas. Matacaballos," he said quietly. He moved his left hand around randomly in the air with the tips of his index and middle fingers on the tip of his thumb. He made a buzzing noise between his tongue and green upper lip. His deep brown face was flat, and his nose went straight down from his forehead without going out very far. He did not sweat much despite what was to me oppressive heat. He had no facial hair. He was missing two front teeth between his canines. No fault of fighting, just too much Coca-Cola and not enough fluoride. Manuel was thirty years old.

"Ah!" I sighed, feeling the three bumps on my face. They stung a fair bit and were already growing. "Peligroso?"

"No, no mucho. Pero dolorosa," he muttered.

I knew *peligroso*—it was one of the first words I had learned on our first day. *Peligroso* meant dangerous. I had decided after four days that Chaco meant dangerous too. I turned and saw Juan standing behind us in the shadows, paused in the tight corridor, almost a tunnel, that I had hacked through the cat-claw thorns, vines, and dense bushes that rose to block our passage. Dusty, parched trees vaulted to a height of sixty feet around us, among them the unusual *toboroche*, a shorter tree with the shape of a bowling pin and thumb-sized, iron-hard thorns. The canopy blocked most of the pale blue sky above us, offering some shelter from the searing direct sunlight. It was ninety-five degrees Fahrenheit. I had taken the point for several hundred meters, and was about to let one of the others resume the cutting again. I finally stopped panting. My face throbbed where it was stung, while the inside of my left cheek was numb. I was mighty high on coca. Again.

Manuel wore sandals, a style of which the outlaw Josey Wales might have worn to a picnic or a casual midsummer shoot-out. In what was either some morbid act of machismo or a simple manifestation of Chaco prowess, he wore the last type of footwear I would have wanted there. If I had to choose between alpine ski boots and sandals, I would have taken the former. He walked slowly forward, stopping a few feet from a black object that hung about six feet off the ground, pointing at it with his machete. "La colmena." Upon noticing my incomprehension, he chose a different word, one that I was more likely to understand. "La casa."

I walked forward to look more closely, stopping beside my short, squat, and most expert colleague. A wasp's nest. They allowed us to come fairly close without attacking, but five or so of them circled the nest watching us, ready to fight. They were black, and larger than any I had ever seen. Nature's little pain grenade, hung at face level. We backed away.

I pointed at Manuel's sandals and smiled again, shaking my head. I then pointed at him and said "muy duro." I couldn't understand how he did it. The ground all around us was covered with a wickedly sharp-edged plant called *carajuata*. Like yucca, it had sword-shaped leaves radiating out from a central, low body, but each leaf had nasty rows of talon-shaped thorns that grabbed anything they touched. Tarantulas lived all over the place. Machetes slipped from sweaty hands and launched into the air. We had to climb up and down the vertical-sided, hard dirt walls of the *quebradas* that grew like a cancer throughout the area. Many of the myriad seismic lines we walked were becoming or destined to become *quebradas*—without living trees to hold the ground together during heavy rain, the soil washed away quickly along these twenty-foot-wide and miles-long scars left by cutting crews some years before. Seismic exploration had not been without consequence in the Chaco.

Then there were the snakes. We had already seen two from the *peligroso* category, as well as several others, both large and small, in shades of black, green, and yellow. Of the two bad-asses, one was certainly a *cascabel*, easily identified by its noisy tail. This was the tropical rattlesnake. The second was some unknown-to-us-gringos viper that the Bolivian guys called a *llopi*, pronounced "yo-pee." Both of these were medium-sized snakes, a meter long or so, and both were decidedly venomous. The word *cascabel* meant "bell" in Spanish, but the significance of *llopi* was a mystery to me; I only caught a glimpse of the second snake as Juan was on point when we scared it up. He had chased and killed at least one snake already, thinking it good sport, but had declined doing so with that one.

Manuel took the point as I grabbed my GPS and machete off the forest floor. I wondered silently if and when we would encounter some evil combination of these objective hazards. Juan had not moved, in the throes of his fourth or fifth super-*bolo*.

"Vamos." I used my new word.

"Sí, Tom," Manuel burped. "Vamos."

I pressed the heel of my hand against a wasp bump growing on my forehead. It was 3 p.m., and we had placed seven samples since starting at around nine in the morning. A half-kilometer between samples. Three and a half clicks in six hours. But each step had to be earned here. I pushed my hand into my cheek, squishing salty green juice from my plug of leaf onto my teeth and tongue. I had not eaten since around eight that morning, but was not hungry. I walked behind Manuel on the balls of my feet, machete ready, and vision set on "panafocus"—I tried to focus my eyes not on any one thing, but on everything. It was a new skill I was trying and apparently failing to learn while deep in the "green monster." The ever-dramatic head mechanic Ricardo continued to call the forest surrounding Porvenir this whenever I spoke with him, which was usually over dinner. We had all quickly realized, however, that he was a bullshitter, a city boy from Santa Cruz, and that we had spent more time in the nasty stuff in four days than he had in his whole life. It was a pretty good name for the protean forest of the Chaco, however.

—

"So what is it called again?" I asked, incredulous.

"The Vinchuca beetle. And the disease is called Chagas." Zane's eyes were glued to the crude trail before us as he steered our Land Cruiser slowly forward. His feet were busy working the brake and clutch as the truck's wheels rolled into and out of ruts and hidden holes; the suspension and drivetrain protested with clucks and groans. It looked as though the two-track would become impassable in a hundred feet or so. Our four *macheteros* bounced and jostled on the bench seat behind us.

"And it bites you when you are sleeping, and you die thirty years later?" I asked.

"Right. Not exactly thirty years. Around that. How close are we?" Zane almost sounded bored.

I looked at the screen of my GPS as I held it out of the Toyota's open window. "Four hundred meters. And there is no cure for it?"

"Correct. There's a center to study it in Cochabamba, but I don't imagine they get much funding. The bugs like to live in thatch roofs. They say a third to half of the people in the rural Chaco have it."

"Goddamn. You are fucking kidding me."

"I shit you not."

My mind reeled. The U.S. medical industry was rushing with celerity to the aid of hordes of North American women who through no fault of their own were in possession of dangerously small breasts. A killer disease resided unchallenged in the homes and bosoms of thousands of Bolivians. A figure holding a shovel appeared ahead of us. He wore a floppy, filthy, and remotely cowboy-style hat, and his open button-up shirt was soaked with sweat. As we neared him, something else appeared beside him in the road at his feet—a dead, caramel-colored horse. We stopped the truck ten feet shy of the man and his fallen mount, hopped out, and approached.

"Hola, che!" said Zane. *Che* meant "friend" in southern Bolivia, just as it did in Argentina, Mr. Guevara's homeland. Zane and I shook his hand, and the two continued to chat. The man was digging a hole at the road's edge adjacent to the horse, and had a fair amount of work ahead of him before the pit could accommodate the dead animal. The horse's body had not yet begun to bloat, nor did it smell, but flies were busily darning the air about its ears and eyes. It looked old. I wondered what effect the host's death had on the dozens of ticks tacked to its neck and mangy flanks. Zane turned and looked at me. "It looks like the road actually gets better ahead. Dude man says that we can probably drive it all the way to the main road."

"Too bad there's a horse in the way. I guess we're walking from here," I muttered. "It's only three hundred meters to the next point, but, according to the map," I produced my field book and the tattered photocopy folded in quarters inside of it, "this road hits the main one in about half a click. It sure would be nice to come out there instead of going all the way back the way we came in."

"Yeah. Better to drive over the horse."

"What?"

"Drive over the horse." Zane seemed a bit amused as he informed the man of his plan. The gentleman proved amenable. We got back in the truck.

Zane fired up the Land Cruiser and shifted it from 4-high to 4-low. He glanced at me with a wry smile and engaged the clutch. We crept forward. If we stayed to the far right, with the right side of the vehicle nearly scraping against a couple of tree trunks at the narrow road's edge, the left wheels would cross the horse's upper legs, and the right wheels not at all. Zane inched the truck forward until the left front tire touched the horse's right rear leg. Manuel sat behind Zane and had his head thrust out of the window. Felipe grinned beside him, the elder of Zane's two *macheteros*. The man with the shovel watched indifferently.

Zane gave it the gas. The left side of the truck rose up quickly and then dropped again as the horse's rear leg bone broke with a great pop. Shovel man's expression did not change. The guys in the back seat giggled wildly. In five more feet, the same tire pressed against the horse's front leg where it met the horse's body. Again the vehicle's left side raised and dropped with a louder, more sickening sequence of cracks as the front legs were broken. We crept forward until we were clear of the thing. Zane thanked the man with the shovel. We carried on to the next point, our boys talking in loud outbursts and laughing robustly.

"Good thing it was dead," Zane said flatly.

"Couldn't we have just moved it? We have six guys."

"But we didn't have to. That's the beauty of it." Zane smiled.

I sat across a chessboard from the doctor in the recreation room at Porvenir. I played white, and had opened with the queen's gambit, my most practiced and therefore strongest option against a very adept adversary, a former ranked master in Bolivia, a devious and skilled artist. Zane played Ping-Pong with Jack behind us. Logan chatted with one of the plant engineers across the room, drinking *mate*, smoking L & M's, and enjoying, as we all were, some free time. The doctor accepted my gambit, and several moves later I was placing some serious pressure on his kingside, a breakthrough game, it seemed—he had bested me a dozen times in the days since our arrival. I craved my first victory.

He had been an exceedingly gracious winner. He flattered my game after each of his wins, never gloated, offered only cursory advice, and was generally only pleased to be playing, playing someone who at least demanded his full attention and might even prove challenging from time to time. This was my game. More than winning, I wanted to know how he might react to being mated. I had a delicious discovered attack with a bishop. In ten more moves, I had my first win against the doc. He lit another in a long series of smokes. He looked at the board, at me, and then hailed the engineer with whom Logan was speaking. He said simply to him in Spanish that I had won. The engineer spoke to me through Logan, who stood similarly aside our chess table.

"He says that no one has ever beaten the doctor here at the plant," Logan translated. He was impressed, and slapped me on the back. The doctor smiled broadly, sucked on his smoke, and accepted his defeat with the humility of a sumo wrestler, seemingly pleased that the small group assembled in the rec room knew that another good player was present. I asked Logan to tell everyone that I was something like one-and-twelve against the man, but they would not have it—no one stationed at the plant had ever bested the most sagacious doctor, guest or otherwise. He seemed to enjoy my solitary win as much as I did. We replaced the pieces in their shoe box and folded the board closed.

"I just learned of this Chagas disease," I said darkly to the doctor.

"Oh, yes. Very bad. But what can we do?"

"Nothing, apparently..."

"How is Juan doing? He works with you, yes?" the doctor asked.

"He's not bad. Manuel is better with a machete. He chews a lot of coca," I said.

"Juan and his family are Guaraní. His mother does not speak Spanish. The Guaraní have lived on the land here since before Bolivia was a nation. Same with the Tapiete and others. Before they knew about gas here." The doctor spoke slowly. "Now trucks and pipelines cross their land, and where does the money go? Away from here."

"Guaraní? What do they speak?" I queried.

"Guaraní. But the tribe learned some Spanish, of course. They are not fortunate people. This was all their land, and now it is the land of the foreign oil man and big ranchers. Worse for them than gas are those big ranches. They are big pieces of land bought and sold by big people in faraway cities. They clear land that is not theirs to feed their cows. It is supposed to be Guaraní land. But, their workers all have guns. Now, some of the Guaranís have no land to farm." The doctor's voice was deep and gravelly, his face truculent.

"Where is the government in all of this?" I asked.

The doctor laughed. "In La Paz! Living in mansions! Counting the money. They do not care." He sighed, removing his smokes from his left breast pocket with his big left hand. "You know that my country has the highest percentage of natives in the Americas? It is like if your country had a hundred and sixty million Navajo and Sioux alive today. Imagine that!"

"Imagine the racism," I thought aloud.

"Might be worse than here. But now you know a little more about the Chaco. And Juan. I go to bed, Thomas. Your chess game has tired me." He smiled warmly and stood. I stood and shook his hand.

I stepped outside the rec room door behind the doctor and sat on the concrete steps in the darkness. An orange tongue of fire twisted and wagged atop one of the plant's tall gas flares, a fiery brooch pinned to the breast of the night, an eternal flame, an eerie homage to the twin prizes of the modern age, oil and gas. The boon and bane of our modern world. Depending on who you asked. I considered the lengths to which we went to find them. Were we that different from the Spanish conquistadors? Was oil any different than gold? I thought of Juan and the other *macheteros*, all of whom slept in a large dormitory a couple buildings west of ours; it occurred to me that they were all sleeping in perhaps the most posh accommodations of their lives. I wondered where Juan's family slept that night.

5

"There are other indigenous groups here besides the Guaraní. The Weenhayek live here too, but they are fewer. The Tapiete. They aren't being shot or anything like that, but they are being marginalized. Big gas pipelines and all the heavy truck activity around them, and big seismic programs, they frighten away the game these guys hunt. They have to travel farther to hunt now. Worse are the mines in Potosi and Oruro. The dam at a huge waste pond at one of the Compania Minera del Sur's mines burst a couple of years ago, releasing tons and tons of toxic mineral residue into the Pilcomayo River. The mine is owned by Sanchez de Lozada. They call him 'Goni.' I'm sure you've seen his name around, right? He was president before Banzer. The U.S. likes him."

"Killing lots of fish. Which these guys need," I responded.

"Right. The Pilcomayo is really badly polluted because of the mines. Anyway, it's a classic case of the natives having the civilized concept of land ownership thrust upon them, the idea that I can pay money to a distant government, in this case in La Paz, and then the land is mine to do whatever I want to with. They've lived here for centuries. They don't get that. The ranches probably are worse than oil. They don't just clear a couple of acres here and there to make well pads, drill, and then leave. They clear thousands of acres that supported game and fruit, or could be used to farm corn, and they put cattle on it. No one around here is going to eat those cows. Although sometimes they steal one or two. And the ranches don't provide many jobs to locals. Neither does oil and gas."

"But the government supposedly set aside protected land here for them?"

"Exactly—supposedly. The Yabog gas pipeline goes through six recognized indigenous community territories."

"And what about the Chaco war? I found a couple really old spent rifle cartridges out in the bush here. And last year when our company was working here, Burt, one of our guys, found an unexploded shell."

"Did you really? Well, the Chaco war was fought over oil in the early 1930's. Paraguay scrambled to annex as much of the Gran Chaco as it could as soon as it was decided that there might be a lot of oil here. Bolivia lost badly, and lost a lot of land. But as we now know, they ended up retaining the best parts. What Paraguay took has proven to be less rich. The O'Connor Block is pretty good. Where you guys are working. But the Itaú field looks to be huge. In gas, not oil."

We were in Villamontes, a small town about ninety minutes by car from Porvenir, sipping cold Paceñas and chatting with some guy named Earl at a dingy little hamburger joint on the rather uninspiring main plaza at the center of the backwater. We were on retrieval now, and after finishing up the day's work early, we all craved a bit of beer, something that the gas plant couldn't offer. Earl was from St. Louis, and was in the middle of a stint with the Peace Corps in Villa. He looked to be around our age, and had neatly-trimmed black hair and a short beard. He wore a Cardinals T-shirt and smiled a lot. He was tall, slender, and deeply tanned, with a big beak of a nose and a slightly underfed appearance.

"You sure know a lot about oil for a Peace Corps guy."

"Yeah," Earl stated significantly.

Jack sat beside me listening quietly to the discussion and likewise enjoying a cold one. He finally chimed in. "So we are the bad guys?" he remarked coolly.

"Well, I'm not going to say I'm your biggest fan. But it sounds like your method is low impact. The real problem is with the Bolivian government and oil firms who only care about their bottom line. I want to help these people get some effective representation here, but it's kind of like rooting for the Washington Generals," he stated.

"Who?" Jack asked.

"The team that always plays the Harlem Globetrotters," I said.

"Oh." Jack laughed tepidly. "Hey, I'm gonna go find Zane and Logan in the market. I'll be back in a few." He chugged his beer and stood to leave.

"OK. I think I'll just hang here."

"I have to go too." Earl stood and extended his hand to Jack. "Nice to meet you guys."

"Yeah." Jack shook his hand, as did I.

"Good luck, Earl," I said sincerely.

"You guys too. Be careful out there." Earl left a bit of cash for his two beers on the table and walked away. Jack lingered until Earl was out of site and sat down again.

"I don't like that guy," he mumbled.

"He sure knows a lot about the Chaco."

"Yeah, but he acts like we caused all the problems here."

"Well, we're not exactly helping fix them," I said absently. We ordered two more beers. Zane and Logan returned from the market, the latter carrying two big bags of coca leaf. They sat down with us at our table.

"Wuz up?"

"Beer-thirty." Jack pulled deeply on his bottle. "And a lecture from some dude about how bad we are," he muttered.

"What?" asked Zane. Logan flagged down our little waitress. She was cute, but not quite a woman yet. She wore a long, black braid of hair down her back and a white dress with a colorful embroidered band from side to side above her nascent breasts. She brought two big brown bottles of cold

Paceña Centenario and a sweet smile over to our white plastic table. The color of the glass bottles nearly matched that of her skin.

"Look, Zane! Her hair's almost as pretty as yours," Logan quipped mordantly.

"Fuck you," Zane grunted. Logan guffawed, glancing at Jack and me and back at Zane. "So who was this guy?"

"Earl. He gave us the scoop on the Guaraní and Ween-hay-something people. Oil is scaring their game away, and the upstream mines are polluting the Pilcomayo," I explained.

"Uh-huh," said Logan. "So we should leave."

"Right," said Jack with a laugh. "This place is huge. The right-of-way for a pipeline is what, forty feet wide? I don't see how that scares all the game away."

"It is their land though," Zane stated. "When all the timber is cut, the ore mined, and the oil pumped, there will be some very uneducated and unemployed people here, and their forest will be trashed."

"So this guy thinks that the Yabog line means that all the pigs and deer have buggered off to Paraguay?" asked Logan.

"I guess so," I said.

"I can believe that the river is dirty, but these native peoples don't live in a vacuum. They live in the world with the rest of us, and we have needs too," Logan said. "Juan's Guaraní, and he seems to like working in oil."

"Earl would say that the temporary jobs that these guys get with us and the seismic companies are quick fixes, and they don't really improve their lives. Or something like that," I stated.

"These guys loved all the seismic work! It's decent pay for unskilled labor! The last program here lasted over a year! If I were Juan, I would damn well want to work for a seismic company. Or for us. Even if it is just six weeks. Fuck, you get free coca with us!" We all laughed.

"Try to stay relevant," quipped Zane.

Logan was picking up speed as his *bolo* kicked in. "Listen, the people in this country who don't live in the woods and don't know how to need light and heat in their houses and their hospitals and their schools, and if these guys here have to bend a little, well, so be it. I mean, how many of them are there? A couple thousand? Ten thousand? There's what, like four million people in La Paz, Cochabamba, Santa Cruz, and Sucre? It's a great big changing world, and if you can't change with it, well...I mean, what are we supposed to tell them? That we're sorry we disturbed them? That we'll just leave and never come back until the end of time? So they can be as happy as if they were living by themselves on another planet?"

"No. We should pay them," Zane interjected.

"Who is 'we' though?" Jack asked.

"Us gringos. The multinationals we work for. The Bolivian government gets its take, and then we pay them, the people living here. Those tribes whose rights are trod upon in the rush to the oil and gas. We make sure that they get some money, even if it is modest, for the resources we remove. It would be peanuts for a company like Vantage to chuck a hundred grand their way. Think what that money could buy here," Zane stated seriously.

"Well, that might be nice..." Logan grinned condescendingly, abandoning his rant before it began. He paused, nursing his beer. He stared at the waitress. "Your hair is definitely prettier than hers. You'd look cute in that dress too." We all laughed some more as Zane pretended to stew. It was good to be in Villa—we all agreed that it was the Paris of the southern Chaco. Paris, Texas, that was.

⌒

In the stillness of the mosquito dawn we walked once again, dressed in skin that remembered every trespass of the forest's myriad pins and daggers like a document, soaked with sweat, our bodies hardened, our actions instinctive and unconscious, ragged denizens of the thorny and clogged bottom of an ocean of air, scuttling here or there with our crude tools, searching, always searching—the sweltering morning passed like a dream. Was it noon? So said my GPS. The sun seemed straight up, but it was so close to the tops of the cacti. It was touching them. I was walking. But my mouth was too dry for my tongue. I saw a shriveled man squatting in a clearing, cutting his own hair with a broken beer bottle. Or did I? Something was wrong. I saw myself from above, empty, unalive, my eyes black and I...I went back to myself and we stumbled and fell. I sat back up. The earth was moving. But I didn't have to hold on.

I needed water. I was...losing it? I stood up and stumbled backward a step. Juan. Juan and Manuel. Sitting on the ground. Looking hot. Too hot.

Too hot to sit down. They found shade. One shade. I had to go. Go to the car. I lifted up my shirt. I saw five ticks in me. My skin was red. I wasn't sweating. No sweat.

Water. Water. I had to go. To the car. "Yo voy to camioneta. I come back…vengo con coche. Con agua." They looked up and nodded, then down at something between their legs. I had to go. I could walk. I could.

⌐

"You have heat stroke." Zane was pouring water on us from two liter bottles. Jack didn't look too good. He sat beside me on the ground, head between his knees. I had never seen him so raddled. "You probably chewed too much coca too. Silly rabbits."

"More water. To drink, I mean."

Zane produced some Cabaña lemon soda from Ploma's cab. "Drink this. It's more better."

"OK." I was weak. Jack had had a bout of delirium as well. Our boys were all right. We were going to be fine. We had been working in the far north of the program, retrieving samples on the hottest day of the job. Here, the forest gave way to low, scrubby brush and saguaro-style cactus, prickly pear, and the ultra-thorny *pica pica* plant, an absolute bouquet of hypodermic needles. It was an island of desert in an otherwise forested area, and pernicious as well. The sun was like a blowtorch. There was no canopy, no cover whatsoever from the horrible fiery orb, but we still had to chop our way to the next point through walls of tangled concertina. My hands and arms were crisscrossed with shallow cuts and abrasions. It was around one hundred gringo degrees outside.

"I don't know how I, how we, made it back to the truck. We ran out of water fast, this morning, going out still," I muttered. I was beginning to feel relatively coherent again.

"I don't know," Jack was barely audible, "how we made it back to Carandaiti. I started freakin' out. I was fuckin' out there. We ran out of water at ten. Eight clicks from the truck." I looked at my GPS. It was three in the afternoon.

"Me too." I pulled another tick out of my lower back. That was number nine that day. Many more had been on me, but only nine had established themselves for lunch. In a few moments, we were rolling down another bad little dirt road back toward Porvenir, now well-known and well-liked by the locals living in the dozens of little mud brick and wood homes we passed every day. Sharing our coca had won us friends. They always waved as we passed, smiling faces framed by windows in ragged brown walls, lazy smoke from cooking fires barely rising from crumbling chimneys, skeletal dogs loitering about hopefully, chickens eating ants, and the occasional young boy or girl running barefoot alongside our trucks laughing. These people worked hard for meager returns. They worked without the machines that the North American farmer had taken for granted for seventy-five years.

The women wore tired but sometimes colorful dresses, and the men simple cotton T-shirts and sturdy denim pants. The baseball cap was quite popular among the men, though some wore leather cowboy-style hats. All the men had short hair and all the women long. Jack and I encountered one young boy with a Colorado Rockies T-shirt—how that shirt found its way deep into the Gran Chaco we could not fathom. To a person they were uncommonly kind and obliging. These people were not strictly members of any indigenous group. They called themselves simply *el Pueblo,* "the People," and were pretty happy to be there, miles from nowhere, scratching away at the dirt. For many of them, the gas plant and its fine doctor, who would always help a *campesino* in need, represented the only option they had ever had in a medical emergency. They liked the plant. They seemed also to think that we were faring pretty well in the bush for a bunch of white boys from way up north.

We bumped through the gates of Porvenir, all three trucks in a convoy. We would do so only a few more times. Just three days of retrieval remained.

6

Even as we walked through the madcap brush, even as our machetes sang and shivered through limbs and vines and thorny green flesh, history was paying the Chaco another visit. No war with a neighbor this time.

No insurrection led by an Argentine revolutionary or chicanery by gringo bandits, no—this was a discovery. A sea change would soon alter the course of the nation and, quite possibly, the continent. Bolivia had natural gas.

Not just a little. More than a lot. An international consortium comprised of various European and American interests was about to announce that it had established the presence of vast gas reserves at their Itaú field, near the Argentine border, not at all far from where we worked; these were estimated to be around 7.3 *trillion* cubic feet, a figure that would later be revised upward. Stop the presses. Shout it from the rooftops. Bolivia was suddenly on the world energy map. Reserves of this magnitude in Bolivia meant several things. While Brazil and Argentina would remain steady customers and likely want more than what they were already buying, Bolivia would want to develop other markets. The obvious choice was the energy-thirsty United States, but how would they get the gas there? Bolivia was landlocked, and had been since about 1884, when Chile stole her *litoral* district and only access to the sea, an injury still deeply felt by many Bolivians. There remained in Bolivia an abiding and profound resentment of Chile. But to sell her vast reserves, Bolivia would need a new pipeline to the Pacific through either Chile or Peru. The shorter and cheaper route would be through the former, and the longer, more expensive one through the latter.

It was an issue of national pride. Many would feel that no money from Bolivian gas should end up in Chilean hands. The question would prove most rancorous, and the gas would shape events in Bolivia for years to come. And where exactly would the money from all this gas go? Foreign energy firms had one of the sweeter deals on the continent in Bolivia—the nation itself received only about 18 percent of the revenue from its fossil fuels. Would the government change the Law of Hydrocarbons and ensure Bolivia a bigger take? Would they go so far as to renationalize the industry, which had been privatized just a few years prior? Would the quality of life improve for the average Bolivian?

It seemed possible, even likely, that a populist like Evo Morales would gain power in La Paz and become president through a fair and democratic election very soon, a mandate from Bolivia's indigenous. A leader like Evo could be a real threat to re-nationalize the oil and gas industry in a symbolic and possibly substantive move toward a populism which would include Bolivia's aboriginals. But what if the rich part of Bolivia didn't want to share? Would the oil and gas elite and their friends in the relatively larger middle classes of Santa Cruz and Tarija be a threat to begin a powerfully discordant and even separatist movement? Could Bolivia face a civil war, complete with foreign sponsors?

It was the final day of retrieval. Juan was laughing at Manuel as he climbed up the steep wall of a deep *quebrada*, his feet paddling at the sugary dirt as he grabbed successively higher roots—he gained the top and grabbed my hand. The coarse dirt stuck to Manuel's face and arms and chest where he sweated. He brushed himself off, explaining that he hated climbing as he giggled. We all turned and faced the forest. Juan led us in.

Our spirits were high. My Spanish vocabulary had grown to perhaps one hundred words. Communication between me and Juan and Manuel had improved considerably. The weather was relatively mild. The forest was not too thick. Only the flies perturbed us. I swung my machete back and forth through the air beside my head like a paddle and knocked them out of the air. They were after us, but we didn't care much. *Singani* and beer awaited, and the boys from Nanca were about to get paid. Some of them, certainly Juan and Manuel, who loved to drink, would likely not sleep until the following night.

With a great shout, we pulled out our final sample. I returned it to its home in yet another tidy screw-topped glass bottle just as I had hundreds of times before. A simple joy settled upon us as we walked back to the truck on a little goat trail, bending low as we traversed beneath thick branches, each of us sucking a big *bolo*. The "green monster" threw ticks, wasps, snakes, heat, and *quebradas* at us daily, tore our skin, dulled our machetes and our minds, and, at least when we had the option, drove us to drink. Only the aegis of *Pachamama*, the Incan earth goddess, had saved us from ruin, or perhaps it was simple dumb luck, but the sure thing was that we were all due a bit of surfeit. We had done it. It was over. We would all be going home soon.

We leaned against the truck and drank deeply of our remaining two liters of water. Juan and I had lost weight during the course of the survey. Manuel had not. I stood looking at them. I removed my fifty-dollar watch and trusty knife. The toadsticker was a U.S. Marine Corps Ka-Bar with an eight-inch blade that I wore on my belt during the job. I gave the watch to Manuel and the knife to Juan, smiling and thanking them. They were each quite pleased. I think that Juan said in Spanish that he "liked working for me." He wore a big, green smile on his defiant mug. I had learned to like them both. I considered that Manuel's new watch would be useless once the battery died. No watch batteries for sale in Nancarauintza. Even so, it would still be correct twice a day and look nice. That's how Manuel might look at it anyway. It was all about finding the silver lining if you lived in the Chaco.

⌒

"Gentlemen, a toast...to Falcon!" I raised my drink in the air.

"To Falcon!" came the response. I put a large plastic cup to my lips and downed a couple glugs of the powerful clear liquid therein. It was cold *singani*, served neat. Zane raised a Paceña, and Logan and Jack orange plastic cups filled with the same booze and lemon soda.

"Let's put the 'sí' back in singani!" said Chunk, who was possessed of an overriding and contagious glee. We all laughed. This was clearly going to be a rigorous training session for the Alcoholympics. Our *macheteros* were variously back in Nanca, at their homes, or off somewhere turning their newly earned money into piss after a two-hour afternoon farewell party at Felipe's house on the plant road. The three cases of Paceña we purchased ran out rather prematurely. We all said our good-byes, and the four of us drove to Tiguipa. We were at the restaurant and watering hole of the meretricious and locally famous Maria Teresa.

We had at some point started calling her Maria Chorizo, or "Mary Sausage." My three colleagues had made her acquaintance during their Chaco job of a year ago. She likely would have taken a tumble with any of us had we wanted, but was slightly too old and plump to be considered a candidate for such by me or my colleagues. Her huge breasts struggled with one another to escape from her tight, revealing white blouse. Her abundant curly hair, which was almost orange, appeared to share certain of its properties with those of steel wool. Her big hazel eyes were lined with copious black makeup, and her lips slathered with red. She might have been a knockout when she was twenty, and still acted like she was a hot commodity, but that was part of her charm. She flirted relentlessly with Logan and Jack. I enjoyed the immunity my inability to speak Spanish afforded me.

There were two long wooden tables and some well-used, white plastic lawn chairs outside the restaurant under an attached sheet-metal awning. We were seated at one of the tables, and a group of orange jumpsuit-clad Southwest Geco employees, all Latinos, were seated at the other. They numbered seven, were working on a seismic program in the area, and were growing louder as the evening progressed. Two bright floodlights swarming with bugs illuminated the area beneath the rusted, corrugated metal roof where we all sat; Maria brought food from inside a small cement building. The ground beneath us was very well-swept brown dirt. The Land Cruiser was parked on one of Tiguipa's sleepy side streets just a few dozen feet away. One of us would be driving back to the plant, which was twenty miles from Tiguipa, with a big buzz. But drunk driving was all right in the Chaco if done with care and at reasonable speeds. For most, if you had the good fortune of owning a car, you certainly weren't going to crash it into anything.

"So we had almost eight hundred total samples, and we only lost four. Youse guys did a bang-up job." Logan used his finest Brooklyn accent. "I might not fire any of youse!" His brown eyes widened as he laughed. His face was now deeply tan. He wore a couple of fresh, deep scratches on his right cheek and forehead.

"Gee, thanks bwoss," was Jack's best. "We're not so bad afta all."

"We haven't had a team this strong since Michael Jackson was black," Logan added, laughing. Out came the coca and smokes. Even Zane, who generally didn't chew much, plugged in a *bolo*. He acted differently toward me now. He knew I could walk the walk. I liked Zane. He was one tough hombre. He had been a rock-solid team player, and knew his limits well. Jack and I got spanked a couple of times by the heat, but he seemed always to be in control of himself.

"You must be looking forward to seeing Laura," I said to him.

"Yes, I am. There will be much pleasuring." Suddenly the stereo came on, pumping some loud salsa into the air. "I need to sink it," he said over the music, pushing his glasses back up his bronzed nose and smiling. "You miss the States at all?"

"I miss being able to talk everyone's language. The States themselves? Not really."

"You know what the problem with the States is?"

"Tell me," I stated flatly.

"People there think that you get what you deserve. In life, I mean. It doesn't take being here very long to realize that that's not how the world works," Zane opined.

"I'll say this, I don't think I can ever feel unlucky again without kicking myself in the ass. These are some happy people here. And they've got pretty much nothing. Except each other."

"True enough. You have learned well, grasshopper." Zane smiled.

Maria yanked Logan off the long wooden bench seat and proceeded to dance with him, an inelegant and haphazard affair that drew the attention of the Southwest boys. One of them stood and approached our table. He had a little silver earring in his right ear and a neatly trimmed beard. He spoke at us for several minutes, explaining primarily to Zane that they were Colombians and that they hated Bolivia; in moments, Zane seemed to be suffering a barrage of macho banalities. He gradually tuned out of the conversation. I watched Logan and Maria dance. One of the Southwest guys cut in on Logan, stealing Maria. He returned giggling to our table as she danced with the man. Two other bellowing Southwest boys spewing curses moved to our table beside Logan. He was tipsy.

"Tenemos cojones grandes aquí, en el Chaco!" roared the guy with the earring, slapping Zane on the back with a little more force than I might have used. Earring man's cohorts likewise roared, standing on either side of him. Even I understood. He said: "We have big balls here, in the Chaco." I stood and laughed tepidly, shaking hands with our two new friends and privately sizing up the rest of the sloppy Geco blokes. Though I hadn't quite got my head around Spanish yet, I was picking up bits and pieces of the conversation. It seemed to be verging on belligerent, at least on their part. Suddenly three of the seismic guys were standing chest to chest with Logan, Zane, and Jack, and were spitting loud, staccato Spanish at them drunkenly with evil grins on their mugs. I looked at Jack, and he at me. Tension was mounting. I wondered where the other Colombian guys had gone.

Zane rallied us. We had to go. Things were getting weird. Maria had disappeared after shutting and locking the door to the kitchen behind her. She finally stuck her head out a window to wave to us as we piled back in the Land Cruiser. Logan fired it up and we drove slowly away. I asked Logan if he thought we should leave Maria there by herself. He turned to me and said, "Oh, she got a pistol!" dismissively. After a few dozen feet, Logan realized that something was wrong. He stopped the Cruiser and hopped back out. He got back in the truck quickly and put it back into gear as a great cheer came up behind us.

"They slashed two tires." Logan growled. The Southwest boys were hollering and laughing. I turned around to look back through the rear window. They were all flying the middle finger and jeering. A couple of them started walking toward us. One chucked a bottle. We rolled away on two flat tires. Logan drove slowly through the center of Tiguipa on the rims. We stopped at a farm on the Porvenir side of town and got out to assess the damage. We were lucky they hadn't got around to the other two yet. We woke up a farmer sleeping in his mud brick hut and asked him if we might crash somewhere under a roof on his grounds. We offered him coca. He happily obliged.

We laughed about it in the morning, hitching a ride back on the first truck we saw headed to the plant. Ricardo came down to replace the Land Cruiser's tires. The job was over. We bid farewell to the good doctor, Ricardo the mechanic, and the kind gentlemen of Porvenir in the parking lot before the mess hall under a strong Bolivian sun. I felt like we had been in a fierce tug-of-war with the Chaco and it had suddenly let go of the rope. The following day we were back in Santa Cruz. I had lost twelve pounds in the course of the project. The post-job party raged for twenty hours back at the Yotau before we wearily boarded another blue-and-white Lloyd aircraft at Viru Viru International and returned to North America. I would begin to miss my new Falcon lifestyle shortly after we landed and parted company. We each headed back to relationships and families, to English, and to America. Back to normal. I was about to find that normal had lost much of its appeal. I knew somehow that it would not be long before I returned to Bolivia.

3 INTO THE WASTELAND

Shall I not inform you of a better act than fasting, alms, and prayers? Making peace between one another: enmity and malice tear up heavenly rewards by the roots.

— Muhammad

I LOOKED DOWN between my legs, up at the troubled gray sky, and laughed out loud. It was beginning to snow. While this development would not necessarily cause problems for most engaged in a summer activity above timberline in Colorado's Rocky Mountain National Park, the backpacker or peak-bagger perhaps, it would tend to get the attention of those pulling up on the handholds of near-vertical, technical rock climbs that were about to become quite wet. I was doing just that, and was doing so without a rope.

The Petit Grepon is one of the most singular high mountain rock spires in the United States. It looks like the Eiffel Tower when viewed head-on, is about eight hundred feet tall, and is tucked neatly out of sight in a high cirque where only those who make a four-mile walk may behold it. Simply to gaze upon it from the shores of an opalescent Sky Pond justifies the hike. Though the Petit is the merest splinter to a hardcore alpinist, the outrageous spur has style. It is vertical on all sides for two hundred feet below its tiny summit, and its form is echoed by two higher, cruder towers, Shark's Tooth and the Saber, that stand brooding on either side of it like surly older brothers, ready and eager to pound anyone who tries to get on top of their lovely young sister.

Though I did not normally set about assigning genders to big formations of granite, I had decided that the Petit Grepon was female. She was most lovely in form, her right and left edges sweeping in great and perfect symmetry to meet at her airy summit, her beauty matched only by the ambition of her design. She simply begged to be climbed, this despite or perhaps owing to the fact that she seemed to have at best dubious structural integrity near her top. It appeared that the summit section, the top one hundred and fifty feet or so of the Petit, was well overdue for a great swan dive into Sky Pond a thousand feet below. The summit block looked more balanced in its airy position than it did attached. It just didn't seem real sturdy.

The tower could be a sassy "little" thing. She had vexed me once before, conjuring up nasty, thirty-mile-an-hour blasts of wind and spitting rain as my girlfriend and I tried to get off of her after a roped ascent. The brat of a rock twisted our twin two-hundred-foot rappel lines all the way around herself in a frothing, preadolescent tantrum of wind and spray. Apparently, she was about to toy with me again. I was just over halfway up the tower, this time by myself, and this time with no room for error. The only rope I carried was coiled in my pack. I would need it to get back down. But the Petit was for me no adversary to be overcome. She was actually much closer to being a friend. She was the only thing holding me up in the air. I paused briefly to catch my breath. I stood on a lunch tray-sized ledge and leaned into the cool granite, splattered here and there with tangerine-colored lichen and white pigeon shit. I stared down. The rock's nadir slipped into a field of talus five hundred feet below. Sky Pond turned from turquoise to slate gray as clouds barged into the cirque. I faced the rock and felt its coarse texture through my fingertips, reached high with my left hand for a big, sharp-edged hold, and continued up.

Only through many years of experience on the rock can one develop the skills required to climb high off the ground and responsibly without a rope. Many climbers never even develop a desire to do so. They're smart. But I started climbing on the myriad, hundred-foot-tall granite gumdrops around Conifer, Colorado, when I was thirteen, when ropes were just some distant adult concept to me. I fell in love with rock climbing when I was still a kid. I became obsessed with the sport after learning how to climb with a rope in high school, and for ten years did my best to distinguish myslef as a climber in Boulder, Colorado, where I attended college in the eighties. But earning "rock star" status in Boulder during that era was a very tall order indeed. Colorado was a free-climbing Mecca in the eighties with Boulder at its center, and had for twenty years produced some of the nation's finest climbers. Though I was considered very good by my peers and climbed some famously hard lines in Colorado and Utah in my heyday, I never quite had the discipline required to reach the elite level.

Climbing with no rope is now referred to as free-soloing. Free-climbing is distinct from this, and while the latter just as the former entails using only one's hands and feet to move up the rock, free climbers are protected in the event of a fall by a rope. This slightly stretchy nylon line, to which both the leader and second are tied at opposite ends, is trailed and threaded through various devices that the leader places in the rock as he or she climbs. These devices, referred to in a general sense by the climbing world as "protection," will not, if properly placed, dislodge in a fall. The lead climber inserts these metal devices into the natural cracks and crevices in the rock, and the second removes them on the way up. Some of the devices are simply passive pieces of metal designed to fit neatly into constrictions in the rock, while others are mechanical, and can hold in place even in perfectly parallel-sided cracks. Using said devices to gain ground is considered cheating in free-climbing, as is using the rope to rest. Unlike mountaineering and aid climbing, every vertical gain in free-climbing is earned through direct body-to-rock contact, and the honor system plays a huge role. It is sometimes easy to cheat, stand on an old piton here or hang on a cam there to get a rest. The same safety system that allows for safe, rope-protected falls in free-climbing often becomes the means by which less able parties ascend a route. But if you lied about your ability in Boulder, someone might call your bluff and ask you out to the crag for a wee bit of fun on rock you couldn't handle—you could suddenly find yourself in dire straits on an old-school, hard to protect line like Blackwalk or the Diving Board in Eldorado Canyon.

I looked down and back up. The Petit's summit was still three hundred feet above me, and was now embraced by dark, wanton clouds that coughed out great swirls of large-flaked snow. My hands were stuffed into a two-inch-wide, vertical crack in sharp-edged, still-dry rock at the level of my chin. I grinned tautly. I raised my right foot until my knee was near my right shoulder and placed my instep on a half-inch edge on the face to my right. I removed my right hand from the same dark crack into which my left hand was jammed, reached high, grasped a big, edge-of-a-bucket type hold, and moved my feet up. The rock was so solid and sure that I didn't bang on the handholds to test their soundness before I weighted them. I needed to move fast if I wanted to summit. I knew I could. Though the rock would be getting wet soon, it was not a difficult route, and most of the holds were large and sharp. I felt that I could top out before the Petit was really soaked and dripping. I would need to be more focused on the moves, but a bit of water wasn't going to end my day on the rock. Not after coming that far.

I think it was on the tiny, wet, and snowy summit of the Petit that day where I decided that all the things that I really needed to know in life could be learned in Colorado's high mountains. After climbing that final two hundred feet of drippy, vertical rock to its top, I felt that nothing would ever again shake my self-confidence. That was in 1994, three years before I started working for Falcon.

Boy was I wrong.

2

Yemen. It felt important. I could say without fibbing that I was an international project manager to someone seated beside me on the plane. No one had asked. But I had a laptop, and I knew damn well how to turn it on. Someone was even waiting to whisk me through customs and immigration, I was told. I was a *player*. Yeah, right.

Most on the plane wore business clothes and white skin, and did not appear to be Yemeni. I did not stand out. The city of Sanaa spun slowly below us as our big Airbus 320 descended to land. I had tried to learn a little something about Yemen before I left the States. I was sheepishly flipping through my Lonely Planet guide to said nation before falling asleep earlier on the flight, and found it between my feet when the aircraft's PA awoke me. A male crewmember announced our imminent arrival, first in English and then in Arabic. I replaced the guidebook in my laptop tote, chuckling to myself and ruing the fact that I had been unable to locate any written works that approximated my imagined title, "The Beer Drinker's Guide to Islam."

I put my seat up. I felt like I needed to know more. The mainstream U.S. media covered Middle Eastern politics in much the same way they covered an auto race. Only the crashes made the nightly news or the front page. I wondered what Yemeni people ate for breakfast and, more importantly, how they would feel about being trained and supervised by a Yankee. My first destination was the great Masila field, the site where I would sample some existing, producing wells as models. I would reach the Canadian-operated facility via a de Havilland Twin Otter, a dual-propeller, "short takeoff or landing" aircraft, at six in the morning after a nap at some heavily-guarded employee facility in Sanaa. It was 12:45 a.m. when we touched down. It was mid-September. High temps would be in the hundreds. I was alone, and the pressure was on. No Falcon luminaries would work beside me this time. I was the project manager, and Falcon's sole on-site representative for the big Maxom soil-gas survey.

⌒

I was led to the back seat of a black Land Cruiser. The other vehicles in our little convoy waited before and behind us, also SUV's. We were parked at the curb outside the airport. Two other white guys I noticed on the flight got in and sat on the bench seat on either side of me. I could see the silhouettes of automatic rifles with big clips in the vehicle before ours, pointed straight up, and hopefully in the arms of Maxom's hired security. We pulled away from the curb as soon as the last door was shut. A man in the passenger seat turned to us and spoke.

"OK, now you are kidnapped," he stated with a thick accent, smiling and laughing goofily, looking alternately at the three of us. He wore a white, turban-style head cloth. I froze with fear, looking at him wide-eyed.

"For fuck's sake, Saleh," the man to my right said. "This kid's never been here before." He indicated me with a sideways nod of his big balding head. He was very large and pink. His tie betrayed either a certain heterodoxy with regard to fashion or simple bad taste. I stared at the side of his head, still stiff with fear, noting that his left ear and a small part of the side of his face had been badly burned some time ago.

Saleh looked at me. "Is this true?" He smiled warmly.

I addressed the man to my right. "How'd you know?" The man to my left was already sleeping.

"You're young. You look nervous," he said. He smiled and offered his hand. "Larry Welk. Where you off to?"

"Masila first." I felt like a foot had been lifted from my throat. I looked at Saleh contemptuously as our eyes met. He laughed gently and patted me on the knee with a long and slender brown hand.

"You are OK with us," he said quietly, smiling sincerely.

I continued. "And then those blocks in Al-Mahra, to do some work alongside the seismic y'all are running, with that French GCS company." Stating facts was helping me calm down.

"Oh, where we're runnin' seismic! In the Rub' al Khali! I'm going up there on Saturday! That is something *else* up there!" He paused, grinning. "Hey, you know what you call a piece of sandpaper in the Rub' al Khali desert?"

"No," I exhaled.

"A map!" He chuckled heartily. "So you're not the Falcon guy, are you?"

"Yeah, I am," I said plainly.

"I heard you guys were coming over. So you're a geochemist, huh?" he asked with genuine curiosity.

I knew this would happen in Yemen, and happen a lot. My credentials. My education. Oh no. "That's what they tell me!" I offered with a laugh and my best attempt at oil cowboy confidence, wondering who the hell this guy was. He looked at me, paused for a second, and then laughed loudly, almost cackling. I could tell he was a drinker, and I smelled a drop on his breath. Lufthansa had served Dewar's to the Scotch drinkers during the flight, and while not my first choice, it was free. I had four. We neared the oil company's Sanaa compound in a scant ten minutes. Conversation over. We went inside and were each led to a spacious private room where we might nap for a few hours before our early flight east.

⌣

At first light I was awakened by the *muezzin*, the call to prayer, on a public loudspeaker in the street outside my room. Hearing the sound of the man's voice was for me something like seeing a new color. I sat on the edge of my big bed for five minutes listening intently, transfixed. It was 6 a.m. Our anxious little drive back to the airport through some part of Sanaa in the pale light of early morning gave me some idea about life here. Sanaa was very poor, even in the part of town where oil companies had apartments. Boxy concrete and stone buildings were raw shelter, hiding well any joy within them. The streets were a bed for many. The signs and stoops and side streets looked somehow wan, touched more by heat and decay than by the hands of hale people. It seemed like a city with more of a history than a future. The *muezzin* rang on.

I found out over coffee back at the airport at six that Larry Welk was the head of exploration for Maxom energy. Maxom was Falcon's client. He and I waited with six other ex-pats as the taxiing Twin Otter's propellers churned the already-too-warm early morning air toward our gate. Larry would, through some delightful coincidence, be in block 12 at the seismic camp to which I was headed when I was scheduled to arrive there. Larry was a PhD geophysicist who lived in Calgary, outweighed me by eighty pounds, and could likely have hit the moon with a football and swallowed caribou whole. Larry really was an oil cowboy. Geology was more like a sport than a science to Larry. He had presence, authority, and seemed to have a wild streak, but listened intently and treated everyone with great respect. I imagined that Larry probably made upwards of half-a-mil a year. Conversely, I was holding my breath financially after several months without Falcon work. I was going to pal around with him for a couple of days. In the field. Finding oil. Chatting about geochemistry at a deeply technical level. And reservoir properties. Perhaps he would even kick sand in my face in a playful manner.

At the moment, he spoke only in a cursory manner with me—Larry was more interested in a dialogue with an engineer about drilling in high-pressure, high-temperature environments. I stared at my coffee in its white Styrofoam cup, and then at the plane through the glass of the ground-level boarding area. Soon we had all walked out a propped-open door and across a broad swath of concrete to the plane and were handing our luggage to a pair of hired hands who loaded it on board. A guard stood near the small plane with an AK-47 rifle and a smoke. I nodded at him, and he nodded back. I was ready. I had a great rush according my first day in a new world. I sat near the rear of the plane and decided it best to sleep. Or at least feign it. As the plane left the ground, I convinced myself that Larry would not be entirely displeased if he discovered my distinct lack of scientific or even technical training. I still preferred that he didn't. But then and there, I resolved to be honest and up-front with him. I was good at my job, and my job was to install samples in the right spots and retrieve them without losses. I couldn't pretend to be the highly educated geochemistry guru he apparently thought I was. I fell asleep to the drone of the plane's engines.

I awoke upon landing, four hours later. We were at Masila. I grabbed my laptop bag and got off the plane. I was directed to a solitary tan building adjacent the runway as the other passengers boarded a white Ford van that would take them to their rooms. A big blue Maxom logo was featured on the driver's side door—it looked like a Superman logo, but with an "M" instead of an "S." I had to register, having never been to Masila before. Larry waved and said something about dinner as he got in the van. I walked to the building and through a heavy metal door into a small room where a man sat on a stool behind a waist-high counter. He asked for my passport. He was dark brown, seemed Yemeni, and wore a blue Maxom jumpsuit. His short, neatly-trimmed hair was tight curls, and he wore a thick, broad moustache. He placed a plastic, credit-card-sized badge with a metal clip on the linoleum counter before me. His badge said Khalid al-something. I couldn't quite process his last name in my tired state.

"We have been expecting you, Mr. Brown. For two weeks. Wear this badge whenever you are outside your quarters." He smiled. Though his accent was thick, his English was impeccably pronounced.

"And now I am here." I matched his smile, still groggy.

"You are in fifty-seven. The van will be back shortly to get you. Welcome to Masila." I thanked him, and stepped back outside the building to wait for the van and have a look around. Copious black crude flowed through Masila's veins. This was where the oil from the huge field, hundreds of wells and many thousands of barrels of production daily, was separated from the salt water with which it was inconveniently mixed. That's how the crude came out of the ground here. Maxom, upstanding company that it was, separated the crude from the waste water, responsibly re-injected the latter, and then sent the black stuff off to the coast to a terminal east of Riyan in an above-ground pipeline. There it was loaded into tankers, sailed to a refinery and cracked, and finally hastened in some form to end-users markets. Most stunning about Masila was that it was an absolute island, both geographically and culturally, in the desert cliffs and canyons outside of Say'un in the center of eastern Yemen. The small, essentially Canadian town stood alone in the scorched and formerly forgotten badlands south of the *wadi Hadramawt* atop a large, broad complex of mesas. *Wadi* meant roughly "seasonal stream" in Arabic, but any water ever caught in the *wadi Hawdramawt* was too scant to reach the sea.

The white van returned and stopped. With me and my kit inside, the Econoline was conducted toward number fifty-seven by another local-looking fellow speaking demonstrative English and smiling brightly. I gazed at the impressive facility with mild wonder. Dominating the grounds were two massive separator buildings; great pipelines converged upon and disappeared into their pale yellow, corrugated aluminum walls, their hulking four-story frames the size of large aircraft hangars. Two huge gas flares sported twisting orange flames in the morning heat near the separators. It was ninety-five degrees at 9:15 a.m. A huge fenced yard with stacks of drill pipe and tubing and all things oil shimmered in the heat. We rolled past a headquarters resembling a modest high school and finally into the employee housing. The lodging looked comfortable, and the grounds reminded me of an affordable subdivision somewhere in Utah. The identical little houses were all tan with brown trim, and were familiar, U.S.-style wood-framed and vinyl-sided structures with tar-paper shingle roofs and cement sidewalks leading to each door. We rolled up to the guest houses. Neatly trimmed lawns and slightly roasted flowerbeds attested to a certain overabundance of fresh water enjoyed at the facility. Water wells were a simple side effect of the real hunt.

I hopped out of the van, walked to number fifty-seven, and unlocked the door. My chauffeur shouldered my largest bag inside for me and then showed me where to turn on the air-conditioning. He put it on full blast and smiled, looking at me, noting that I had broken a sweat just carrying my smaller bag to my room.

"Hot," he said.

"Sí." I paused and caught myself. "Yes. Very hot." I had defaulted to Spanish. I chuckled to myself, thanked him, and pulled the door closed. I plopped down on the bed after grabbing the remote off the nightstand. I fell asleep to Dan Patrick and Sports Center. I wanted to catch a couple more hours of sleep before lunch, when I would meet with someone named Ali. Ali was to direct me to the three production models for the survey.

We had lobster for lunch. Little ones, but awfully good. Ali told me that they were common in Yemen's coastal waters. Some five dozen guys had shown up for lunch, but Ali and I sat alone at one of a dozen rectangular white tables in a spotless mess hall. I listened intently to my official Masila guide and recently graduated geologist. Ali smelled rich. Though he wore a blue Maxom jumpsuit, as did almost everyone but me, a gold chain and a fancy gold ring announced a certain level of prosperity to those not close enough to enjoy his cologne. He looked strong and was tall among Yemenis, had light-brown skin, and might remind a Westerner, if only physically, of a clean-cut Sadaam Hussein in his early twenties. Ali was affable and funny. He spoke great English and had a significant black moustache. He told me proudly that his father was involved in some way in politics in Aden, far away on the southwest coast. Ali was about to be married. He showed me her photo. She was stunning, a real beauty. I said "nice catch" to him, and he laughed heartily. We quit the mess hall and walked to the parking lot. He replaced her photo in his wallet, and his wallet in the rear pocket of his jumpsuit.

"Nice catch?" He smiled, eyeing me, a bit nonplussed.

"Yeah, good job. She's gorgeous."

"But it is not a job, love," he said with a grin.

"Not yet!" I said.

Ali laughed even louder. "Ah, you understand relationships! But she is a good one. I met her at the university. In Aden. She is from an excellent family."

Ali drove the Toyota pickup very slowly and politely out of the front gate of Masila, waving at the gatekeeper in his glass box. I thumbed through some well location maps to his right in the passenger seat. The broad asphalted road that led out to the myriad wells rumbled with the traffic of heavy equipment. Ours was among the very smallest of vehicles. Big semis heaved along the road carrying the down-hole lubricant, or "mud," that was used during the drilling process. Bulldozers were ferried about on flatbed trailers. Bigwigs drove here and there in white Ford pickups with tinted windows and Superman logos. The heat rippled off of the gooey-looking asphalt with a pronounced visual effect as I thought about hiking in such ruthless heat.

There was absolutely no vegetation. Not as a result of oil development—there just wasn't any. The ground was covered uniformly by limestone rubble. I commented with some excitement about the sweeping, two-hundred-foot-high limestone cliff bands that formed the sides of the mesa upon which Masila perched. Where the road neared the plateau's edge, we were afforded great views of the desolate, hardpan lowlands stretching away into the distance below us. There was a climber's treasure of top-quality limestone here. I told Ali I was a climber. He seemed amazed. I told him it was popular in the United States. After several miles, we turned off on to a smaller dirt road, leaving the traffic behind.

"So, can you drive to Masila?" I asked Ali.

"No. Everything and everyone is flown in. Maybe you can, but it would be difficult."

"They told me I would be working with a military escort."

"When you go north, yes. In the Rub' al Khali you will have this."

"But no one can get here. Without a plane."

"Correct. And so, we are safe."

We arrived at a well. In the span of a couple of hours, I placed fifteen samples in a great circle around the producing oil well. Ali watched as I drilled the holes for the samples and placed them within. We marked each site with a strip of orange survey tape tied around a rock. The well was atop a long arm of mesa that extended out from Masila's main plateau. The ground was strewn with iron-hard, cantaloupe-sized limestone boulders. Drilling a good hole was difficult. I was soaked with sweat by the fifth sample. Ali's brow furrowed. He seemed taken aback by the crudeness of our method.

"The magic happens back in the lab. I just put them in the ground," I said as I panted.

"And these samples around this well are used for comparison. Because you know there is oil here, you will compare this chemical signature with the larger survey north. If some samples there have the same signature, maybe they are over oil."

"That's it."

"Incredible. What a method!" He smiled and looked at me. "You have the best impressive sciences in the U.S.!" We hopped back in the truck and cranked the air.

"Yeah. It's pretty incredible," I muttered, leaning into the cool air blowing out of the dash.

Larry offered me the hot sauce. I took it. Dinner was tacos in the mess hall that night. Some roughneck with a mullet was standing at our table talking at Larry. "So I told him, if that goddamn sub is cracked, you better shut that shit down."

"Yeah, that's right. I'll go out there in the morning and talk to Jimbo," Larry said coolly. "I need to chat with this fellah right now." Larry nodded toward me.

"Yes sir. Sorry to bother y'all while y'all are eatin'." The man turned and left.

"Sorry, Tom. Now, where did you say you went to school? Mines?" Larry munched down nearly an entire taco with one bite.

"No, I went to the University of Colorado." I did. But I studied humanities and not geology, much less geochemistry. The cool dining room was for me getting warmer.

"Oh, yeah. That's a good program." He swallowed. "You must be good if they're sending you all the way over here. Got a master's?"

"No, just a bachelor's. But I've learned a lot in the field. I really just put these things in the ground, you know," I stated uneasily. "How'd you burn the side of your head?"

"What? Oh, that? Well fire, long time ago. Well…you sure are a modest guy." Larry chuckled jovially. "I like that. But anyway, I want to pick your brain about micro-seepage. I don't get to talk with geochemists very often. Not the ones who work in the field. You seem to know what you're doing."

I balked. "Well, I must admit that I didn't really..."

"Larry!" A booming voice came from the entrance to the big mess hall. A man nearly the size of Larry stepped toward our table.

"Russ!" Larry stood and shook the man's hand, slapped him on the back, and seemed to be on the verge of French-kissing him. They spoke with their faces just inches apart, both grinning broadly. "I didn't know *you* were gonna be here! I'll be damned!" Everyone's eyes among the fifty or so men gathered were on the two physical and geophysical giants. Russ was Maxom's head drilling engineer. "You gotta sit down. This here is Tom, our geochemist from the States. The Falcon guy. He says we don't need seismic!" Larry said that really loudly. Some eyes settled on me. Russ extended his hand. I stood and shook it. He then turned back to Larry and leaned toward his ear, speaking softly.

"Oh, you're kiddin'. OK, let's get outta here." Larry bid me farewell with a wink. "We'll talk later, Tom. Gotta go put out a fire." I wondered if he meant that literally. He walked briskly behind Russ out the swinging glass doors of the mess hall, abandoning his half-eaten meal. I raised the jagged edge of my hard taco to my mouth and glanced around the room. I liked Russ. Great sense of timing.

The following day I installed the two remaining model wells with Ali at my side. Larry departed for block 12 at 10 a.m., two hours by plane to the northeast, out in the Rub' al Khali desert—the Empty Quarter. I would not see him until I arrived there the following morning. I ran into him at breakfast. I was headed out the door when he was headed in. No time for that chat about geochemistry. We shook hands, and I asked him what misfortune had sent him hurrying out of the mess hall the night before. He leaned close to me and explained that it had not been a misfortune at all, but that his good friend Russ had discovered a bottle of fourteen-year-old Oban Scotch whiskey in his luggage, placed there by some prankster, no doubt, and that he needed to get rid of it quickly.

I laughed, and bid him farewell until the following day. Bottled booze was not allowed on the grounds of Masila, not for the grunts, anyway, and transporting it around the country was at the very least frowned upon by the Yemeni government. I had discovered, however, that the Canadians circumvented this unfortunate fact by making beer on-site at Masila. They brought in hops, malt, and yeast, mixed it all together, and let nature take its course, right under Allah's nose. The brew was served in a makeshift pub, on Wednesdays and Saturdays, to anyone who fancied a pint or four. The brew was even free, but donations were gratefully accepted by the house.

Ali and I discussed a number of things as we drove around the huge oil field that afternoon, among them alcohol and religion. Ali explained to me that he did not drink, like any good Muslim, but that he had tried the stuff on a few occasions. He felt confident that God wasn't too mad at him for this. He went on to explain that Christ and Muhammad were sent by the same deity. He was most eager to have me know that Christians and Muslims worshipped prophets from the same source, and that Muhammad was simply the latest. He asked me what beliefs I held, and rather than get into it, I told him that I had been baptized a Catholic. I did not tell him that the phenomenon of organized religion had been for me the rough equivalent of catching the chicken pox. They were similarly contagious, both preyed on the young, and once I had had them and then shaken them off, I would never again be bothered by them. But I was no enemy of spirituality. The pomp and pretense of the most gaudy and gilded of the world's great religions just seemed patently silly to me, even at a young age. I never stopped thinking that Jesus was a really great guy though, a true revolutionary who pumped up the people and made a loud noise. And paid the price.

I liked Ali. I bid him adieu after dinner. I returned to my room and repacked my bags. I turned on the tube. One of those "America's deadliest homicides" shows was on. The TV programming seemed to be coming directly from the United States. I clicked over to CNN and continued preparing for my imminent journey to the northeast, into the Rub' al Khali, on another Twin Otter. I thought about the U.S. I had spoken briefly with a Canadian expat in the buffet line at dinner; he said that he was disappointed to be working in Yemen during deer hunting season in

Alberta. It made me think of Colorado. The mountains of my home state were at that very moment undoubtedly full of people who with straight faces referred to themselves as "outdoorsmen" as they sprayed bits of lead and gallons of burnt gasoline into the bright mountain air by the tens of thousands. Deer hunting season would begin soon in Colorado as well, and off-roading season raged on. Fords stomped Dodges. Dodges stomped Chevys. Folks smiled and admired one another's toys. Music ranged all the way from AC/DC to ZZ Top. Even some dogs drank beer.

I further considered the U.S. as I glanced vacantly at the news broadcast. I turned the sound down and just watched the images. A housecat was terrified by a vacuum. New cars were available with televisions. Hollywood continued to challenge the limits of banality, churning out movies based on old cartoons, superheroes, and seventies TV programs. Baldness, sadness, and lack of hardness were fought tooth and nail by a particularly healthy pharmaceutical industry. Pro hockey season was about to begin. The presidential election was imminent. In two days I had placed forty-five samples in the rocky ground, fifteen around each of three wells. Not much work, but the heat was terrific. Walking more than a few miles would be brutal. The last light of day waned to darkness outside my window. The desert relaxed. The violence of the sun was gone again for a little while. I closed the curtains, turned the TV off, and lay down to sleep.

3

"Kayf halak?"

"Tamaam," I replied to the Yemeni man seated in front of me. These Arabic words meant "how are you?" and "fine." It was the third time he had asked me that during the flight. But it was all we knew how to say to each other. The Twin Otter was ready to land. It was Saturday. I read a copy of Newsweek I had picked up in Masila during the choppy, two-hour flight across the vast moonscape of broken rock and sand that was the southern edge of the Rub' al Khali desert. For the final hour of the flight, my regular glances out the round window to my right revealed not the faintest sign of man or beast. Dark brown tracts of talus and shattered stone ceded to uncommonly elegant and long chains of pale yellow sand as we approached the GCS seismic camp. Soon we were slowly turning above the mobile headquarters of a sizable French seismic crew at what I guessed was about a thousand feet. I made out ten boxy, turquoise trailers and an adjacent grouping of a few dozen large canvas tents in a wide valley of pure sand below us; the camp fell between two long, parallel ranges of four-hundred-foot-high sand dunes. As the Otter did a complete circle and began its descent, I noticed with a dropped jaw that yellow dunes extended as far as the eye could see in every direction except south. We were at the southern edge of a massive ocean of sand.

The Otter bumped rudely back to earth on a crude sand runway. We taxied to an abrupt stop. Doorways opened both aft and forward, the type that swung down to the ground and became stairways. Heat filled the inside of the small plane like a liquid. It was cooking outside. It was the last weekend of summer. Only seven other men were on the plane, and I hadn't really spoken with anyone. Larry was already in camp somewhere. I stepped off the plane. My first thought was that only through a great expenditure of money and effort could humans live in this place. It was one hundred degrees outside, and only fine yellow sand was visible in every direction. It all looked the same—there were no distinct landmarks, and any one dune looked just about like all the others. A man walked toward me. He extended his hand and smiled warmly; his aura was somehow regal and almost palpably irenic.

"You must be Mr. Brown." He shook my hand.

"Call me Tom. And you are?"

"Yasser al-Rashid. It's nice to meet you, Tom. Please call me Yasser. And on behalf of Maxom, I welcome you to Al-Mahra and the southern edge of nowhere. Let me show you to your quarters. These gentlemen will see to your bags. You are American, yes?"

His English was perfect, more British than American, and his manner of speech revealed a certain linguistic sophistication. He spoke rather slowly, almost as though it was physically pleasurable to him. Words left his mouth like polished stones. The smile beneath his precise and robust black moustache was disarming, and his handsome, almost boyish face was full of sincere warmth. He wore not a blue jumpsuit, but a nice looking brown kilt called a *futa* and a Western-style, button-up shirt in a nice shade of mustard that might have come straight from the Gap. His head was wrapped in a traditional white-and-grey checkered head-cloth. He himself had brown eyes and skin. He wore sensible shoes. Nike trail runners without socks. I hopped into the front seat of an air-conditioned Land Cruiser where a couple of other ex-pats waited in the seat behind me. Yasser got behind the wheel and put on his seat belt as our luggage and the four coolers full of my samples were crammed in the back by a couple of yammering locals. The doors slammed. I noted a group of large animals in the distance near camp.

"Camels?"

"Oh, yes, you will see them every day. They belong to the Bedouin."

"What do you do here?" I asked Yasser.

"I am, I suppose, a diplomat. I am from Yemen, but I work for Maxom. I make sure that everyone understands one another. The Bedouin, the locals, GCS, subcontractors, even the Saudis. I am the peacekeeper." He smiled wryly, glancing over at me.

"Sounds like you've got the most important job in camp."

"I think that this is true, from time to time."

"The Saudis?"

"Yes, Tom, both the seismic and geochemical programs run right up to and in some cases across the border into Saudi. The border, however, is not marked. It's quite nebulous, you see, and their patrols have become grumpy when we enter areas which they have deemed to be theirs. But no one really knows where the border *is*. It is imaginary, and shifts like the sands themselves. Even if you tried to mark it, the sands would eventually drift across the markers, burying them," he explained.

In five minutes we were in a surprisingly lifeless camp and in front of the door to my turquoise trailer. Yasser explained that most science types in camp napped in the heat of midday. Each trailer had three separate little rooms, and each of these was designed for two blokes, but I might get one to myself given the amount of gear I had with me. Yasser left me and my baggage before the door to my quarters and sped off again, saying that he looked forward to speaking with me over dinner. I opened the door, which was like that of a walk-in refrigerator, and was hauling the coolers of samples into my box of a room when a voice boomed behind me. I was already wet with sweat.

"Tom!" it was Larry.

"Larry!" I blurted out, panting. "How goes it?"

"Oh, just really well, Tom. Really well. Welcome to New French Yemen!" He pumped my hand with his much larger version, smiling and glistening with sweat. His head was like a big wet pumpkin, bright with sunburn. Clearly he was no fan of the otherwise popular and world-famous hat. "Hey, let's pop in your room for a sec and get out of the sun. I am just not made for warm weather."

"Um, sure. Come on in." I walked up two steel steps and through the door, and in barged Larry behind me. Barely. He was nearly too big to practically use the space. He sat opposite me on one of two skinny beds against each long wall of the eight-by-twelve cubicle. His knees nearly reached the bed upon which I sat.

"We found a pretty big counter-regional surface bump east of here today. You know what, Tom? We're not even sure about the source rock here." Larry was hot. He panted and smiled, his chest expanding and contracting like an accordion. He was acting like a fourteen-year-old who just found a peephole in the girls' bathroom and ran all the way to his buddy's house to tell him. "And we found a couple of old Russian wells. Both dry holes from the fifties, according to Yasser. We even brought home a couple of old Russian drill bits! I'll show 'em to you. I just love gettin' out in the field, Tom. It's history, real history. Hey, you know what I wanted to ask you? We got quite a bit of sour gas here. Is that going to affect your samples?" I actually knew what sour gas was. Hydrogen sulfide. It was a poisonous fume that was sometimes released from underground in the course of drilling for and producing oil.

"No, that's not an issue. We've worked around it many times before," I stated, pleased to know something about *something*. To my immense relief, a knock came at the door. I opened it. Four smiling, blue-jumpsuit-clad young men looked up at me with eager brown faces.

"You are Tom?"

"Yeah." I walked down the steel steps of my trailer and extended my hand. "You must be the geochemical crew. From Aden!" I grinned. Larry emerged from the trailer behind me, stepping down onto the hot sand and placing a hand on my shoulder.

"We'll talk later, Tom. I'll let you get acquainted with these guys." He walked toward a great canvas tent that was pitched in the center of the square formed by the trailers.

"So what are your names?" I asked enthusiastically. I met Yasin, Talib, Hamzah, and Kamal, slowing down my English and noting a wad of some green stuff in Yasin's cheek. It looked just like coca. I asked him what it was.

"Qat!" he said proudly. "You have try some. Is tradition here, in Yemen. You could like it. We get you Qat." Yasin's English was not quite awful. He had an honest, jolly face in the same shade of deep brown shared by most Yemenis, was clean shaven except for a moustache, and was apparently the only one of the four with whom I would be communicating directly. He said something to the others in Arabic. I looked at each of them, sensing true hospitality and trying to attach their names to their faces. Everyone seemed terribly pleased.

$\smile$

"Talib sure is quiet," I said to Yasser as we walked from his room to the mess tent. We had for some two hours discussed my helpers, our Bedouin drivers, and in general terms the logistics of the project. He explained that the trailer camp was called "senior camp" and the tent camp "junior camp." Only French guys and important subcontractors slept in a trailer, and both Yasser and I fell into the latter category. Junior camp was where the Yemeni and Bedouin laborers slept. The big tent at the center of the trailers was where meals were served to the seniors.

"I think that is because, as you say in the West, he is 'thinking out loud.'" I burst into a paroxysm of laughter as Yasser chuckled. "I have worked with Talib many times, Tom, and consider him a friend. He is a good man, and little deserves such derision. But I think even he would agree that he is not the most erudite among your assistants. If he has grown, it is because we have watered him." Yasser's wit had already endeared him to me enormously. "The French have something they like to do before dinner, Tom. I think you may like it. We will eat a little later. The north side of the tent is for dining. Let's go to the south side."

Our shadows and those of the trailers and the mess tent reached far to our east as the sun neared the horizon to set. Everything in this new world was either blue or yellow, it seemed, but as the sun descended, the yellow of the ubiquitous sand ripened to a deep, fiery orange. I followed Yasser through a flap of canvas into the tent. Two cheap plastic lawn tables stood side by side in the dim room, surrounded by matching white plastic chairs. Five men sat at these tables and stared at a big-screen television in the west end of the room, and other than a large cooler and a couple of long wooden boxes that might have been additional seating, the room was empty. The floor was some sort of tough black mat rolled out upon the sand. The canvas roof of the large tent drooped above us. Only the TV lighted the room. The men were drinking beer. Yasser introduced me to the guys in the tent as I absorbed the shock. Each of them nursed a Heineken, and some bottle of what was ostensibly booze sat on one of the tables. A cold one was handed to me as I sat down, reeling. I looked at Yasser.

"I don't believe it," I offered, stunned.

"This French tradition is also practiced in the States, is it not?"

"Yes." I opened the beer and tasted it. "And it is a very important tradition." A man introduced to me as Françoise laughed.

"Oui!" he blurted out. "You are American, yes?" Françoise was long, skinny, and tan, and had sun-bleached light-brown hair and bloodshot blue eyes. His manner betrayed a certain hedonism, even at first meeting. He wore shorts and a ragged red tank top. He was popular with the ladies, I guessed, though we were miles from any such. He sucked deeply on a cigarette. His accent was classic French.

"Yes. First time here in Yemen." I pulled on my beer with delight.

"You of course do not speak French," he muttered.

"Of course not." I smiled wryly. "But I do speak some Spanish."

"Ah, this is good. Jacques here speaks no English. Many here do not. But Spanish he speaks. Why do you know Spanish?" Françoise plainly appraised me. I think that he wanted to like me, but first he would find out just what sort of arriviste this American was.

"I've worked quite a bit in Bolivia."

"And what do you think of Bolivia?"

"I love it. I think I could live there."

"I just returned from a vacation in Cuba. I too love Latin America."

"And the women?"

"Ah. You understand, then. We have something in common, Thomas. Do you drink Pernod?" He reached for the tall glass bottle before him.

"Is there booze in it?"

"Yes, there is."

"Then yes, I do." Françoise and Yasser laughed. Yasser did not drink with us, but explained that he did have a beer or two from time to time. More men entered the tent intermittently until we numbered twelve or so. I met each of them, and most were very welcoming. I actually did speak some Spanish with a couple of them, which went a long way toward dispelling any suspicions of my living in cultural terms under a rock, as did some of my oil patch countrymen. Good cheer abounded in the soft saloon as we watched some French news program and each got through two or three beers, these punctuated by shots of Pernod. It tasted like anise. Larry did not join us, nor did any Yemenis save Yasser. After ninety minutes or so of merriment, dinner was served. It smelled lovely.

"Now you might get to meet Pat," Yasser said quietly as we walked to the dining side of the tent.

⌐

Everything that lived braced for the sun's return. It was 6:15 a.m., and it would be back again soon. The boys were all off praying before breakfast, kneeling on the sand in a big rectangle with about forty others just north of the trailers, led in prayer by some guy I had yet to meet. I watched from the inside of my trailer through my little plastic window as I prepared to head for the first time into the field. Today was training day. GPS and compass, maps, and other such fundamentals would be taught to my assistants. I held a compass in my hand as I watched the prayer ceremony. After double-checking and committing a number on my laptop to memory, I stepped outside. I walked toward the group of praying men and stopped about sixty feet shy of them where I would not be noticed. The centrally-peaked tips of the canvas tents of junior camp were on fire with the first wild orange sunlight of dawn behind the supplicants. The man who delivered the prayer boomed, his words colliding and careening off one another in a cadence most alien and a timbre most exotic, the effect of which was quite beguiling. He sang as much as he spoke. The group's collective responses were a rich chorus to their leader's verse. I looked at my compass.

Two hundred and eighty-eight degrees. The compass bearing, or azimuth, from our location to Mecca, just next door, in Saudi Arabia. You were supposed to face Mecca when you prayed. The boys were off by about thirty-five degrees. The group faced roughly toward three hundred and twenty-three degrees. I turned and walked back to my room. I wondered if their prayers were getting there. I imagined marching over and telling them that they were misaligned, giggling to myself and thinking of Jack Barnes as I stepped back inside my room. He had always enjoyed this type of silliness, and would have understood that I meant no disrespect. We simply made fun of almost everything.

I went to the mess tent for breakfast. Larry was standing just inside the entrance speaking with a serious Pat, the supercilious and widely disliked on-site representative for Maxom. I avoided them, grabbed a plate, and headed for the buffet. Fifteen men were seated eating breakfast. Yasser was speaking with Pete, GCS's safetyman for the camp and the project and the only Brit on their roster. Pete held weekly safety meetings, scolded men who failed to wear their seat belts, and generally stuck his nose into everyone's business. Fortunately, he possessed enough charm and tact to do so without offending anyone. Unlike Pat. I could barely hear Yasser talking as I piled eggs on my plate.

"When you are in the Middle East, everything goes back to Israel and Palestine. Britain began imposing the Jewish state on Palestine in 1917. The Balfour declaration. It still rankles. It always will. What if Iran had set up a Palestinian state in Staffordshire?"

"Even here, in Yemen, people are still upset about it?" Pete asked.

"For most, yes, and for others, less so." Yasser sipped his tea. "It is a wound until it is healed, and the pain of it is felt from far away and by many people. We remember Sabra and Shatila. We know who Sharon is. Israel occupies land that it recently took by force, as you know, with the full support of the U.S. and other Western powers. Israel violates UN resolution 242 every day, but the U.S. only notices when countries it doesn't like violate UN policy. This enrages many, and leads some to violence. But I am a man of peace. We know what war is like here in

Yemen. For us, it is not a television show that happens in some faraway place. It really screws up your day. We just had one here, in fact, about six years ago. A quiet little civil war..." Yasser paused to greet me as I sat beside him. "Good morning, Tom. Have you slept well?"

"Morning, gentlemen. Yes, quite. Are those our trucks by the radio tent?" I had noticed two diesel Land Cruisers and a HiLux pickup with what appeared to be a large machine-gun mounted in its bed just south of the trailers. It was time. My first foray up and across the great thighs and bosoms of compact yellow sand languishing outside of camp.

"Yes. Your fleet is assembled." Yasser smiled. "Let the games begin."

4 IN THE WASTELAND

While Clinton was promoting peace and democracy, the U.S. in the Yemen civil war was giving diplomatic support to the aggressor, the northern President Saleh. At the same time, the Assistant Secretary of State for Near Eastern Affairs, Robert H. Pelletreau, under the rhetoric of defending unity, was ensuring the demise of the YSP. These actions by the Clinton administration effectively eliminated the major democratic threat to the conservative ruling families of the Arabian Peninsula. While Clinton espoused slogans of "security, democracy, and prosperity" for all, the status quo on the Arabian Peninsula - the gap between rich and poor and exclusionary governments against the Arab people - was once again upheld. In a truly Orwellian way, the Clinton administration defined "unity" as "democratic" and "secession" as "anti-democratic." Using these definitions, Assistant Secretary Pelletreau sold President Saleh's victory as a victory for democracy. In reality, however, the opposite occurred: President Saleh's victory was a triumph of authoritarianism over democracy.

— "The silent demise of democracy: the role of the Clinton administration in the 1994 Yemeni civil war," Arab Studies Quarterly (ASQ), Fall 1994, by Carlos A. Parodi, Elizabeth Rexford, Elizabeth Van Wie Davis

EVERYONE WATCHED ME. The gaunt Bedouin drivers, the surly military grunts, the garrulous city boys from Aden—each of them sized me up privately and then discussed me discreetly with a peer. They smiled and looked sideways, nodded politely, and asked courteous and perfunctory questions of me through Yasin. We were rolling through the outrageous piles of sand north of camp in nice Land Cruisers. Mine had powerful air-conditioning. I rode shotgun, and Yasin, Hamzah, and Talib rode on the bench seat behind me. Tarik, a Bedouin, drove. Yasser rode ahead of us in another Land Cruiser with Kamal and another local driver. A Toyota HiLux pickup truck with an attended fifty-caliber machine gun mounted in its bed followed behind. Yasser knew the area well, and was showing us around. I spoke with him intermittently on a Motorola radio. It was midmorning in the Rub' al Khali.

"OK, Tom, I believe that this gap in the ridge above us, in the distance on the right, is the pass. I think they should have opened this one with a dozer. It leads over the top of the dune chain to the next valley."

We drove west, doing sixty across the gravelly bottom of a long, narrow valley between two ranges of four-hundred-foot-high, steep-sided, and effulgent yellow sand dunes, each one like the last. We needed to go north to reach the next line of proposed sample locations. The samples on this job were to be placed in a wide array of separate and roughly east-west lines, with ten to fifteen samples spaced five hundred meters apart on each transect. We would not install samples today. We instead performed some important reconnaissance and made sure that everyone knew how to use a compass and a GPS. It took us ninety minutes to reach the first line from camp. This was no small commute. I realized that we would need to get up real early to have full days here.

"OK, we'll follow you," I replied into my radio. I replaced it in its mount on the dash. I considered that I was the only one in my entire crew who could not claim Yemen as his home. Yasser, my four assistants, and our three Bedouin drivers were all Yemeni, and besides Yasser, only one of them, Yasin, had ever even met an American. I was pretty weird, they must have agreed. I wore shorts. I was single and had never been married at the age of thirty-three. Or so I said. I *could* be a scientist. I did seem to be smart. But I laughed a lot. And I had big muscles for a scientist. But I *did* have a laptop. I knew how to use a GPS. And I taught everyone else how to do the same. I must have been the real deal!

They each became very kind and hospitable toward me in their turn, and in the course of less than one white-hot morning and afternoon, I was accepted heartily by the city boys. The day featured a memorable picnic of sorts at lunchtime; we all ate flatbread and canned tuna, the latter rendered crunchy by blowing sand, and sat cross-legged on blankets spread upon the very fine, hot grit that was the ground. After lunch, some of the boys wanted to pray. It was midday, and we were taking a break—why not? I wondered silently if this would become a way of excusing much-too-frequent breaks during the day in the weeks ahead. Before they knelt, and as a test of their newly learned compass skills, I asked my assistants to point out the direction to Mecca after telling them the exact bearing. Fifteen or twenty seconds passed as they fiddled with their compasses. With a smile and a fully extended right arm, Yasin proceeded to point out the way to Mecca rather accurately. The other city boys quickly did the same. A strong breeze tugged at their matching blue jumpsuits. They looked like a boy band dancing in-sync on the hot sand. Yasin was clearly the go-getter of the crew from Aden. We were all laughing when someone behind me grumbled loudly. It was Tarik, my driver. He was disputing the direction to Mecca as he stood near the trucks with his kinsman. He indicated a heading some forty degrees to the south, looking fierce as a falcon and stating "la!" over and over again with extreme gravity. *La* meant "no" in Arabic. Yasin and Kamal raised their voices to match that of the increasingly indignant Tarik, pointing at their compasses, at me, and shouting down the much older man. He was adamant, so much so that I checked the bearing again. Yup. Two hundred and eighty-eight degrees. I had it written in my field book. I grinned at Yasser as he stood from the lunch blanket.

"You've started quite a row, it would seem!" he said, grinning back at me mischievously.

"*I* have?! What do you mean *I* have?" I protested, laughing. I walked toward Yasser and stood near him, placing a hand on his shoulder. "Hey, what's with the daggers the Bedouin guys are wearing?" Each of our drivers wore a curved knife in a stylized sheath, and each was roughly the size and shape of a banana.

"Ah! Good question. These, Tom, are 'jambiyas.' They are not for fighting, nor anything practical, really. They are a symbol of one's clan and status." Yasser said "status" like a perfect Englishman.

"Are they made out of expensive stuff?"

"These you see here, no, but others, very much so. Your helpers from Aden likely have very fancy ones in drawers back home. Or even back in camp. I have one too," Yasser explained.

"So what happened here in ninety-four?" I asked.

"The war? The south, with its center in Aden, resented the abuse they suffered at the hands of the more powerful and conservative north in Sanaa after the nineteen-ninety unification. The new Republic of Yemen was formed on northern terms. The south was more liberal, wanted democracy, a two-party system, and so forth. They charged that the old guard autocrats in Sanaa were stealing all the oil money from the country and the people."

"Imagine that," I quipped.

"And this was when quite a bit of new oil had just been found. In the south. The Saudis and the U.S. backed the north. The Yemeni socialist party in the south obviously lost, and the south's reformist-minded leaders were removed and scattered. Now it's business as usual as far as the U.S. is concerned, and all of Yemen's oil wealth goes into a few pockets. Yemen is just like most countries with oil. It's poor."

We finished lunch, the lads prayed, and we continued. The Bedouin seemed none too eager to make friends with their southern countrymen, and were clearly going to need more time to get comfortable around me. Not so my assistants, who were all geology students at a university in Aden, on the west coast, and all in their late twenties. Before long, I was regarded by the city boys as a true authority on geochemistry. The fact was that none of them really knew *what* I was, educationally speaking, but they were much too polite to ask, and I knew enough geology that I sounded credible. At least to someone who didn't speak English particularly well. They asked instead *where* I attended college. My self-confidence went a long way to dispelling any doubts about my credentials. While I was slightly amused by this little charade, I had also considered that these guys might feel a bit insulted to be working for someone who studied not textbooks but novels by Nabokov at the university. Yasser agreed. I explained to him that morning that I was just a skilled outdoorsman with an unrelated college degree, a good memory, and no girlfriend to miss back home. He had laughed and smiled deeply when I told him, quietly saying "you are shitting me!" in his regal English. He seemed to respect me more for telling him. He had never asked. He understood quickly, however, after tagging around with our giddy little crew for a few hours during basic training, that a background in geology was not something I needed to do my job well.

⤳

"OK, guys. Y'all are fast learners. Good job today. We'll start installing samples tomorrow, working in two groups out of two trucks. And remember, no cologne, and no sunblock." They all wore the former. We had just hopped out of the trucks after arriving back in camp.

"Yes, Tom. No cologne. Too many chemicals," replied Yasin.

"Right. We'll leave at dawn. I'll see y'all at dinner."

The boys walked toward the trailers. Yes, trailers. They were, much to their delight, being put up in senior camp alongside the bigwigs. Their spirits were high. Yasser and I strolled to the mess tent for a cool drink. I was salty with dried sweat, though we hadn't walked much at all.

"It appears that your team should be able to more or less drive to most of the sample locations. At least in this block," said Yasser.

"Thank God. Or in sh'Allah, I mean." This meant "god willing." I had heard it at least a dozen times already. "Those walks we do encounter will be tough."

"Yes." The day waned around us. Yellows changed to oranges as the breeze eased. A few figures strolled about camp, and some vehicles carrying water and workers entered through the main gate. Camels loitered near junior camp outside the camp's barrier. A five-foot-tall berm of sand surrounded the entire camp, pushed into place by dozers—it prevented any unwelcome vehicles from driving right into the compound unchecked.

"Now, what is this Qat?" I asked Yasser.

"Ah, Qat! I will be getting some tomorrow evening, in sh'Allah. You must try some with us, Tom." Pat emerged from the mess tent as we neared the entrance flap. He walked briskly toward us, intent upon a meeting with the new American in camp. Yasser uttered a curt greeting to the small man and continued to his trailer. Pat and I shook hands and returned to the mess tent.

"Larry left this afternoon. He had to leave early. Now, me and you need to get some things straight. This is a seismic camp, and you gotta follow rules," Pat stated seriously. We seated ourselves beside one of the long tables where dinner was served, facing one another in white plastic lawn chairs.

"Yeah, absolutely. Where are all the shaker trucks?" I had seen only one of the ten-ton behemoths, and that one was being worked on outside the mechanic's tent. This was a vibro-seismic program. Instead of using dynamite to create the sonic energy that would echo off of structures deep underground, huge trucks with great hydraulic shaker units built into them vibrated the surface of the ground at all of the "shot" points. The sound they produced was recorded by great lines of geophones, electronic listening devices placed on the ground and connected by thousands of feet of cable; the highly sensitive microphones heard the underground echoes of the vibrations as the trucks generated them. The echoes were recorded and analyzed back in camp, and a three-dimensional map of underground formations and potential oil traps was produced. The lines of geophones and cables themselves were laid out and constantly redeployed along the dunes by a corps of Yemeni laborers who worked on foot from dawn until dusk. We had seen some of them earlier that day. They were the jug hounds, the foot soldiers of geophysical oil exploration. Their jobs were not enviable. But unskilled work for hard cash was very hard to find in Al-Mahra.

"The trucks stay at fly camps at night! They can't be driving all the way back here every night!" He guffawed, making fun of my question.

"Of course," I said flatly, looking into his eyes and idly rotating my half-full plastic water bottle between my thumb and fingers. Pat was Asian ethnically, and spoke with a pronounced accent to match. He said "fry camp," not "fly camp," which meant a very basic satellite camp, likely just a couple of big tents and a small generator out there somewhere in the infinite sand. Pat was a resident of Calgary, a citizen of Canada, and was a gruff man with dark eyes that flashed from behind wire-framed glasses. He was short and skinny, and his unkempt black hair was untouched after sleep. He wore an old Calgary Flames T-shirt and blue polyester shorts. His thighs were white and hairless. He was the on-site client rep for Maxom, and was also a highly respected geophysicist who assessed all the daily seismic data. He was plainly annoyed at having to deal with me and the geochemical program.

"You really a Flames fan? I love hockey."

"Never mind that. Listen. You never drive. You are always back by dark. You do not get stuck or damage vehicles. You give me a progress report every day. And don't make me come looking for you. And do not ever make the mistake of crossing the border into Saudi. You will be sent home. You are on thin ice here. Larry and I don't even think your little samples work."

I bristled, but kept my cool. I knew damn well that someone back in Calgary behind a big desk and above Pat's head had decided to do a geochemical survey in these blocks months ago. I also doubted that Larry thought it was a total waste of time. But no matter. I was actually a bit relieved to hear that Larry had departed, though I rather liked the big oil cowboy.

"No problem. I'm excited to bang this thing out. It's pretty exotic here. I kinda like it," I said, unperturbed.

"Give it a couple of days," he quipped. "I'll be watching you." He stood and left.

I walked to my trailer, disrobed, and re-emerged barefoot and naked but for a small white towel wrapped about my waist. I padded across warm sand around the mess tent and toward the shower trailer. Now I knew why almost everyone in camp quietly cursed Pat.

2

We all heard the gunfire. Though we were rolling along the flat gravel of a long valley floor with the windows up and both the air and stereo on, we all heard it, and all our heads jerked to the left in unison. Tarik sped up as more shots pealed through the hot, shimmering mirage surrounding us.

"Get down, Tom!" Yasin pushed me forward into the foot well before the front passenger seat as he jumped into the shotgun position from the back. I scrunched horrified on the floor of the Toyota in a ball, the cold air of the air-conditioning blowing straight into my right ear.

"Stay down. Stay!" He placed his hand on my recently shaven head.

"What's happening? Where is Hamed?" I shouted. Tarik slowed the truck down urgently, pressing me forward into the foot well. We stopped. So did the gunfire.

"Nothing. It's not OK! You are safe! We will worry later," Yasin stammered bizarrely.

"What? What is happening? Let me up, goddamn it!" I roared. I pushed out of my fetal crouch and stuck my head up, looking out Tarik's window and turning off the stereo and the Clash. Yasin seemed shocked that I had so raised my voice at him. Two vehicles were motionless about three hundred meters away on a bright ridge of pure sand above us and to our left. The miasma of heat reflecting off the midday sand turned the minatory trucks into twisting, wagging metallic specters of unsure shape and size. But they were doubtless the ones who had fired on us. I froze with fear. The fabric of my being grew taught. I felt sick, nauseated, like the feeling one gets after breaking a major bone.

"Who are they?" I asked Yasin, my voice quavering.

"I am not sure, Mr. Tom…but…"

"Well who could they be?" I demanded, whatever sangfroid I had quickly evaporating. "Are they warning us, or are they just bad shots?" I sputtered. Yasin quacked something to Tarik and looked back at me.

"He thinks they are not Bedouin." As yet another vehicle appeared on the ridge, one of the trucks started slowly down the steep wall of sand below it toward us.

"Fuck. Fuck!" I grabbed the radio from the dash, sitting between a stoic Tarik and a panicky Yasin. "Kamal, do you copy?" Kamal did not respond. He was installing samples down valley somewhere to our east in the other Land Cruiser with Hamzah. The army boys had no radio. We were thirty miles from camp and fifteen from the nearest seismic crews. Too far for our hand-held radios. "Fuck!"

Suddenly a vehicle appeared in the distance behind us, following our tracks and hauling some serious ass. It was our escort, the gun truck, and its three nominal soldiers, Hamed, Jamil, and their reticent rear gunner. They had been lagging behind, as usual, as their HiLux lacked the prowess of the Land Cruisers in the sand, but now it closed quickly, issuing behind it a great plume of white dust that rose through the desert air like the smoke of hell. Before it was within a kilometer of us, it veered from our path and tore up a burning apron of yellow sand toward the gunmen. Hamed was flying straight toward the unidentified trucks that had fired upon us. As the HiLux drew into profile, we barely made out a familiar figure in the back of it, ready to unload that big fifty-caliber gun on our assailants. The vanguard mystery truck that had begun moving toward us stopped. I felt both relief and terror, gratitude and crippling helplessness as our escort closed on the group. My throat was dry. Our escort truck closed to within six hundred meters of the offending posse. I held my breath, wanting to watch but not wanting to, hoping that somebody recognized someone, and hoping that our boys could prevail if hostility had truly found us. The truck sped up the slope, closed on the three mystery trucks, and no shots were fired. The HiLux finally slowed and approached the lead truck, doing so in a rather leisurely manner. We watched, frozen. I realized that I had a death grip on the dash with my right hand and on Tarik's seat with my left.

Our escort lingered near the vanguard truck for a few seconds and then sped urgently toward us. I motioned to Yasin to get out of the passenger side door so that I could as well. We hopped out. I walked in the direction of the truck as it approached and stopped. The rear gunner with the difficult name gave me the thumbs-up. Hamed smiled widely at me from behind the wheel. The little Toyota pickup truck had no door on his side. I noted an AK rifle resting barrel-up between his right leg and the truck's transmission housing. It pointed, roughly, at Jamil's head.

"Thank you, Hamed," I croaked. I was relaxing a bit, but I was deeply shaken, and scarcely noticed the crushing heat. It was well over one hundred degrees. Hamed spoke surprisingly adequate English.

"Hello, Mister Tom. The Yemeni military camp, on the hill on there, wish to say sorry for firing you. This, these, was as warning," he said. "And I cannot give them fault." Hamed's face was dark brown and was covered with black hair seemingly everywhere but his nose and forehead. His skin glistened with sweat. No air-conditioning for him. His voice was coarse.

"What?" I retorted, still dazed.

"Well, they maybe not…" he struggled for a word, "they maybe not usually fire on unknown about trucks fast coming this camp from Yemen side. They would say, or think, these are oil company. But you do not come from Yemen side."

"You mean…"

Hamed paused, savoring the moment. He spoke. "You are in Saudi!" he bellowed, his eyes watering with hilarity. The two other grunts laughed heartily.

"Let's go!" I hollered hoarsely. "We're right behind you, Hamed!" He turned the HiLux around as we jumped back in the Land Cruiser. We followed him toward the place on the ridge where the three Yemeni military trucks waited for us. I closed my eyes and hid inside myself for a few seconds, breathing deliberately. My heart was pounding and my mind was seared. For the first time, I had tasted what it might be like to have someone attempt to control or destroy my life, and despite it all being a case of misapprehension, I realized as we rolled up the sand that none of the self-imposed fear and danger of climbing could ever feel as oppressive.

Driving up the steep headwall of the big dune where the army camp sat would be all our Land Cruiser could do, despite the special sand tires it wore. Hamed and our escort left us and drove off to the east in search of some easier way up to the encampment. They worried me. Tarik had learned to drive up the steepest dunes with some speed and head-on, never at an angle, for the latter could result in a rollover. I wasn't convinced that Hamed understood this. The three Yemeni army trucks that began to stalk us spilled their occupants as we burst upon their hilltop post with an explosion of sand. They approached us smiling, most wearing checkered head-cloths and one sporting a black beret. They numbered ten or so, and were clad in tan Yemeni Army fatigues. They formed a circle around the Land Cruiser as we came to a stop, their camp visible behind them. The man with the beret, the clear doyen, greeted me as I hopped out of the Land Cruiser.

"As-sala mu 'alaykum."

"Wa 'alaykum as-salam," I responded. He spoke no English, but was most cordial, and shook my and Yasin's hands. He looked wan, even sick, but his tired eyes smiled above a straight brown nose and a salt-and-pepper moustache. Everyone exchanged pleasantries. Suddenly, he took a few dramatic steps backward, still facing me and looking directly at me, and planted his black-booted feet in the sand as though to box. Everyone ceased talking and watched him silently. He raised an invisible rifle to his shoulder and pointed it at me. He pulled the imaginary trigger. Everyone held their breath.

I realized that this could be nothing other than a simple attempt at levity. It recalled me from my darkness. I clutched my gut and chest with my hands, feigning injury and falling on to my back upon the hot sand. Everyone roared with laughter. The doyen said something loudly, stepped forward, extended his hand, and helped me to my feet. The sand was painfully hot. He threw a skinny arm around my shoulders, and we walked toward their nearby camp chuckling. All I could think was that now that we had met, the only bullets he might fire at me were those that could do no harm. That was what this captain had said to me, without using words, and that somehow redeemed me from my dread. The strange charade had relocated me in my proper self. The army captain's name was Mahmoud. He said something to Yasin.

"We go to eat lunch with them," Yasin translated.

I looked into his eyes. "Sorry I yelled at you, Yasin. I was pretty damn scared. Thanks for trying to protect me. You are very brave."

"It is OK, Mr. Tom. I was scared too," said Yasin. We walked with the captain toward a single large canvas tent adjacent a poorly made, twenty-foot-wide, six-foot-tall cinder block barrier. The cruel black barrel of a fifty-caliber gun mounted on a tripod poked through an opening in the wall. Three trucks, a tent, some cinder blocks, a big machine gun, and a seriously injured Yemeni flag on a fifteen-foot metal pole. This was the equipment that the Yemeni government provided to these dozen men who were to patrol and protect about fifty miles of the country's nebulous northeast border.

Mahmoud's encampment was squalid. Placed on the labile sands at the edge of two nations to guard Al-Mahra, Yemen's governorate of dust, an area the size of Massachusetts with fewer than a hundred thousand inhabitants, the camp was like a graveyard for the living. The view was essentially the same in every direction. Endless dunes. Empty tuna cans and cigarette butts were strewn across the flat sand behind the wall, and a discernable trail of waste paper and soda cans driven east by the wind stretched away down the side of the dune. There was a cache of fuel in dozens of jerry cans half-covered by drifting sand below us, beside a little two-track road leading back to GCS camp. The antennae for the outpost's SSB radio was deployed on the sand near a large, tired-looking brown canvas tent. Some cardboard boxes of bottled water stood near the tent's entrance, a simple flap that was held closed against the wind by an old, formerly black leather belt. This was home for these guys, at least for a few weeks, I imagined.

"How long are their shifts here?" I asked Yasin. He asked the captain.

"Two, maybe three months," Yasin translated. I winced sympathetically, looking at our host. He laughed. Mahmoud undid the belt to the tent, held back the flap, and beckoned us inside.

It felt hotter inside the tent than out. I had nearly forgotten the temperature, but realized that my T-shirt was nearly soaked through with sweat. Mahmoud handed us all a warm, one-liter plastic bottle of water. Our group took a seat on the oft-trod sand that was the floor of the tent beside Mahmoud and four of his men. I looked around. It seemed dark after being outside all morning. Salt-encrusted T-shirts and fatigues hung from the metal frames of the eight cots arranged along the tent's walls. Cans of tuna were opened. Smiles were worn by all, and we chuckled easily together as though assembled with old friends.

After lunch, we decided that we would drive straight back to the main camp. We would call it a day. Kamal and Hamzah met us at the army encampment in the other Land Cruiser after we told them what happened via radio from the outpost, a high point with good reception. I think each of us was doing a risk and benefit analysis of our current employment situation. What if we had been found by Bedouin bandits or worse still, an organized anti-West group fond of abducting oil workers? That was, after all, why we had an armed escort. I felt that among the seniors, only Yasser should learn of the event. My four assistants felt this to be prudent as well. We had crossed the border. We had, without meaning to, violated the prime directive. Above all, Pat could not know.

The world burned around us as we started back toward our town of turquoise trailers. We waved farewells to the army guys. No one spoke, and my mind settled into a dull thoughtlessness. Sand and sky. Blue and yellow. Up and down. I rode in the front seat like a child on a carnival ride. Some lonesome camels appeared in the distance on our right.

Not thirty minutes later, my radio crackled. "Hamed have accident, Mr. Tom. Come back," came Kamal's frantic voice from my two-way. My stomach knotted. Hamed had finally rolled his truck. I knew it.

"Turn around and go back over the last big ridge. Hamed didn't make it. Fuck!" I barked at Yasin, who then spewed some staccato Arabic at Tarik in the driver's seat. I punched the dash. I didn't have to tell Tarik how to take a ridge anymore—he had become an adept driver in the big dunes. He wheeled us around and sped back up the shimmering crest of sand we had just traversed, gassing the truck hard. I braced for what I was about to behold. Our Toyota burst back across the lip of the unusually sharp dune ridge with an explosion of tan sand. The front wheels returned to earth, and Tarik brought us to an abrupt halt facing straight down a steep slope. I flung my door open, jumped from the vehicle, and broke into a full sprint toward Hamed and his inverted vehicle.

"Get the med kit, Yasin! And set up the SSB antennae!" I screamed over my shoulder as I tore downhill to the upside-down HiLux pickup.

Hamed was on his back on the sand. Jamil was still inside the truck. The third soldier was seated on the sand behind the truck, head between his knees. The front wheels of the HiLux were still spinning. He looked up as I approached. Dazed, but all right. I dropped to my knees at Hamed's side.

"Hamed! Hamed!" I felt around his torso for injuries, careful not to move his head—a spinal injury was to be expected. I found no obvious damage, but pushed sand around and up against his head and neck to stabilize them both. By the time my sand pile reached his right ear, his eyes opened, and he sat promptly upright.

"Why you try bury me, Mr. Tom? I am not dead. You fill my ear with sand." He poked a finger into his ear, looking at me with disdain.

"Holy fuck, you're OK! I wasn't burying you, Hamed, I was stabilizing your neck," I said loudly as I moved to the truck. I got on my knees and peered inside.

Jamil smiled goofily from his position on the ceiling of the cab. His black futa was hiked up around his waist, answering a question that had been bothering me for some time. The answer was no, the men do not wear underwear in the al Rub' al Khali.

"Are you OK?"

"Yes, thank you, OK!" He gave me the thumbs-up, or down actually, and the triage, to my enormous shock and relief, seemed to be complete. Bumps and bruises. I sighed deeply as a terror-stricken Yasin came running up with our silly little first-aid kit. Two AK's, a two-liter bottle of water, some ammo, and a tuna sandwich lay in the sand beside the truck. Jamil crawled out of the cab and stood up.

"They're all OK, Yasin. It's OK. I can't believe it, but they're all OK."

"I have never seen a dead man, Mr. Tom," Yasin stammered.

"Me neither. Got the radio set up?"

"Yes, Talib has set it up."

"Better call camp." Hamed, Jamil, and the third soldier were all standing now, looking a bit stunned, but returning slowly to their senses. I gave them each a hug. "No better place to be tossed from a truck, I guess. The landing's nice and soft," I said to no one in particular. "Now let's flip this thing back over."

"What a day you've had, my friend. Just don't tell Pat about the border." Yasser reflected. "Do you believe in god, Tom?" he asked.

I paused, thinking, and settled on a mischievous response. I knew Yasser would ask me this sooner or later. "I haven't been quite that scared yet," I stated, carefully watching Yasser's serene face change. He looked vaguely miffed. He knew after six weeks around me that I was not given to pondering the next world. He knew that I didn't much believe that there was one. "But if those Yemeni military trucks after us today had been the local Manson family with AK's, I would have probably asked him, or her, or it, for help." It was getting late in the afternoon. I wanted to shower before dinner. I finished my coffee and stood to leave the mess tent.

"You should try talking to him when you don't need a favor," Yasser stated.

"Yeah, I suppose. You know, Yasser, you're the first really religious man I've met who I haven't dismissed as an intellectual amputee." I placed my empty coffee cup in the bus tub.

"Well, thank you, Tom, that's very kind." His words dripped sarcasm. He grinned and started giggling.

"Sorry—no, look. What I mean is that you are not dogmatic. When it comes to religion. You have strong faith, but you don't think basic human functions such as sex are somehow dirty. You aren't squeamish about being human. You can have a beer or two. You respect other beliefs. You haven't turned off your brain. And you are truly against war. When someone like you tells me to talk to God, I just might try."

Pat suddenly pushed through the entrance flap and walked purposefully toward us. "Hello, Pat. What can we do for you?"

Pat ignored Yasser and handed me a sheet of paper. "Seems there has been an incident in the Gulf of Aden. American warship attacked and badly damaged. Maybe you should pack your bags, Thomas. This could be some big deal." Pat turned around and walked back out.

The memo was succinct. It read:

From: L. Jordan, Maxom Energy, Yemen 10/13/00
To: all ex-pat employees and subs in Yemen

Re: USS Cole

All ex-pat personnel currently working in Yemen should be prepared to evacuate on short notice. The USS Cole, an American destroyer, was attacked by an unknown group in the Gulf of Aden yesterday, and casualties were suffered.

Pending any further developments, all in-country operations will continue as usual. Just be ready to leave if we need to move you out.

Leo Jordan

I handed the memo to Yasser, and he quickly read it. "We should go to the beer tent and watch the French news. Do you really think we'll get evac'd?"

"No," Yasser said simply. "We are used to this sort of thing. The company has to say something when these incidents happen. You're not going anywhere. But yes, let's go watch the news."

I sucked on a Heineken as the French news showed file footage of some U.S. destroyer, probably not the Cole, sailing in some waters, probably not those of the Gulf of Aden. Yasser and I realized that we were not likely to gain much insight into the attack, and resumed conversation. He was actually having a rare beer.

"You will be leaving soon anyway, Tom. You have six days of retrieval left, yes?"

"Yeah, six." I felt a strange detachment from the Cole attack. Yasser left the tent on some errand. I walked to my room, undressed, and proceeded to the shower trailer.

3

Yasser placed some tender green leaves in his cheek. The Qat had arrived. A two-foot-tall water pipe that I would have called a hookah smoldered on a metal ammunition chest before us. In Yemen it was called a *shisha*, and it was for tobacco. Sweet, apricot flavored smoke issued from its four flexible tubes when you drew on them. Six of us were seated in a circle on a large, purple cloth placed across the sand inside a tent in junior camp. Yasser smiled benevolently. His face looked like Dizzy Gillespie's from where I sat, bulging as his right cheek was. My Qat was kicking in, and I liked it. The *shisha* was forgotten as the cigarettes came out. The tent's interior was soon thick with smoke.

Three of the men gathered were unfamiliar to me, and I was having trouble remembering their names. They spoke rather quietly in Arabic among themselves and sometimes to Yasser, asking at intervals if I liked my Qat by pointing at their cheeks and smiling broadly at me, at which point I would nod and smile back. Another Westerner had joined our little party, and sat opposite me across the chest and the water pipe. It was Françoise. His longish, tan face was beaded with sweat, and his smile revealed horsy teeth covered with loose bits of leaf. It was clearly not his first time. My head swam a little as my saliva turned into a thick green broth around the tender young leaves. They were not at all bitter, and the buzz they produced was euphoric, not unlike Bolivian coca, but less intense and a bit more like that produced by marijuana. Françoise spoke.

"So, you had a little misunderstanding on the border, eh?"

"Yeah. But you don't know about it."

"Not to worry, mon ami. I'm no friend of Pat. You are from the center of your country, yes?" Françoise sucked some bits of Qat from his front teeth and pushed them back into his cheek with his tongue.

"Yeah. Colorado." My emotional pendulum had swung the opposite way. I was as relaxed as I had been panic-stricken earlier.

"Do you miss it?"

"Not really," I paused, "I miss my friends. I miss climbing. And football."

"I imagine you don't miss getting tossed in the jail for driving home after a couple of beers?"

"What?" My eyebrows raised.

"I have lived in Boston for a while. They gave me a DUI. They were going to deport me. For a drive around a block after just these two beers, I tell you. Some land of the free that is, you have." Françoise scowled, watching my reaction.

"That is ridiculous. I know what you mean. Same with weed," I said dryly.

"That's right! It's a plant on God's green earth, yes? How can you outlaw this *plant*?"

"I don't know." I rolled the plug of leaf in my cheek over with my tongue. "I don't even know if we elect our presidents anymore. The post is bought and sold."

"You are right! Democracy? It is not just that." Françoise sat upright, his voice becoming a bit louder, his blue eyes slitting. "It's a crime what your government does just south of your border! Look at poor Guatemala! They make a mistake of thinking that the government's job is to help the people, and boom!" Françoise clapped his hands loudly.

Yasser cleared his throat. He spoke slowly. "You are correct, my friend. You have only to read what America's National Security Council has itself stated and written time and time again with regard to its foreign policy, post-World War Two."

"What did they say?" asked Françoise.

"Well, one very high-ranking Mr. George Kennan of the U.S. State Department wrote in a Policy Planning Study just after World War Two, number twenty-three, I believe, that the U.S. had some 50 percent of the world's wealth, but only 6 percent of the world's population. He said this would result in great resentment of the U.S. He went on to say that the nation must strive to preserve this disparity and should cease to consider unreal objectives such as human rights, raising living standards, and democratization." Yasser paused, pulling on his cigarette. "He said that the U.S. should deal in straight power concepts, unimpeded by noble ideologies like those espoused in the Constitution and your Bill of Rights. You can look it up. It has been declassified." Yasser spoke evenly in his deliberate and smooth English, a subtle smile on his now glistening face. The Qat was making me sweat as well.

"But that was in the late forties," I countered.

"You would be naïve to think that this policy has changed, Tom. Look at Nicaragua's attempts at reform, or simply to remove Somoza, and how they were met by Reagan's administration. Look at your government's close alliance with Saddam Hussein throughout the eighties. They sold him the gas he used on the Kurds. They cared little about his murderous ways until he got 'too big for his britches,' as you say. Turkey, a trusted U.S. ally, has killed many thousand Kurds too, but no one in the U.S. speaks of their atrocities. Your government does not spread and defend democracy as it claims to. It makes sure that reformist, populist governments in the third world do not threaten access to resources and raw materials like oil, cheap labor, vast markets, and most importantly, unregulated corporate license. The U.S. installs and props up regimes it can do business with on its own terms. Your government regards Latin America as its own private turf. It feels the same about the Middle East. It will become worse if your second George Bush wins next month."

"Yes, I think this is true, Thomas. The Monroe Doctrine. That is right," Françoise concurred. "The French government is the same. But we have not so much power as you."

"Yes, the Monroe Doctrine extended to the Arabian peninsula. To the world, in fact. I'll give you another example. In 1992 Dick Cheney instructed Paul Wolfowitz, who was then undersecretary of defense, to draft a Defense Policy Guidance document that called for a second military intervention in Iraq to assure vital access to raw materials like Persian Gulf oil. You can look that up too. If Bush and Cheney win, they may invent some reason to go back into Iraq."

"How did you find out about that?" I asked.

"The Internet. I find your nation's politics to be worth following."

"You are a smart man, Yasser," said Françoise.

"Well informed, at least," Yasser said quietly. We all lit smokes. I considered Yasser's words, again impressed with the breadth of his education. My Qat buzz grew still greater and more narcotic. As the tent and our lungs filled with smoke, I wondered how well I understood my country, if there was indeed wool over my eyes, who had put it there, why, and if so, how I might remove it. And whose sheep had provided the wool. I smiled at Yasser.

"You seem to know more about the U.S. than I do. I don't think I even really know what the NSC does."

"It is not an easy thing to come to terms with, that the men who lead your country may be doing something other than what you've been told they do. With your tax dollars. With your military. Your whole life you have been told, by your parents, your friends, the media, that your country is a great force for good in the world. But who shall watch the watchmen?" Yasser pulled deeply on his smoke. "You are a decent person, Tom. Most in your country are. But that resentment Mr. Kennan spoke of will, sooner or later, manifest in action. Like the Cole attack. I never condone violence. But many other decent people in the world have serious, legitimate reasons to resent and even despise the U.S. government."

I sucked my leaves and ruminated. I would not sleep at all that night.

"They always forking me."

"What?" I stammered.

"Forking me. They in junior camp always forking me."

"Uh, you should go talk to, uh, Françoise. He's the party chief. That trailer, right there. That's his office. I'm the geochem guy. Not GCS," I uttered, pointing at myself.

"Oh, geochem guy. OK, thank you." He smiled, continuing gracefully to the trailer I had indicated, bare feet protruding from beneath a flowing blue *futa*. I continued to my trailer after my shower in complete shock. Did I hear what he said? I opened the door to my room and stood staring at the back wall of my small quarters, door ajar. Always *fucking* me? I wanted to laugh and scream all at once. I dressed quickly and walked over to Yasser's room, knocked on his door, and went inside.

"I think his name is Karim, Tom," Yasser said quietly. "He is going to need a room in senior camp soon. They won't leave him alone."

"You mean he's getting raped over there?"

"Ah, well, rape may be too strong a word. I believe that Karim now has more than one, ah, boyfriend, shall we say. I think his situation has worsened by degrees, changed from something he once accepted or even enjoyed to the point where his, well, affections are being coerced…yes, I mean, you are right. I suppose it should be called rape, yes."

"You can't be serious."

"Tom, for some men in Yemen, women are for babies and men are for pleasure. I do not agree. I am a big fan of my wife's vagina. But there are those in junior camp who find relief in one another." Yasser was more serious than I was used to, his ubiquitous subtle smile replaced by a gray solemnity.

"That doesn't offend me. Surprises me, but I don't care what people do. But rape, I mean, somebody's got to help that guy out."

"I was becoming aware of this situation. But the fact that Karim has marched straight to the party chief means we have reached some impasse. I will go to Françoise's office right now."

"That seems best. Poor fellah," I muttered.

On the last day of retrieval our ears, noses, and hair were filled with sand by a windstorm of Patagonian force and relentlessness. The world was a gray miasma, the horizon lost in teeming, hurtling shadows, the day as dark as twilight. The cacophony of rushing air easily cajoled the sand into flight; once outside the trucks, any exposed skin stung with the impact of a thousand specks of earth. It was like a nuclear winter or an afternoon on

Mars as we drove back and forth to our samples. The wind fired broadsides of sand and gravel into the metal skin and glass of the Toyota with sharp pops and hisses that for me recalled the sound of bacon frying in a pan. We would stop, gird, and then one of us would hop out, holding on to the truck's door so it wouldn't be torn off or pushing on it with all of one's strength just to get out. The interior of the truck would fill with a great roar of sound, the door would shut, and relative quiet would return. A figure would disappear up some flank of sand like a ghost and return moments later, and at once, we were off to the next location.

It was my turn. I borrowed Yasin's head-cloth and had it wrapped around my face and head. He helped me tie it in place. A slit allowed for vision. I hopped out, GPS in hand. I forced the door of the Land Cruiser shut. The wind pushed me over. I found my feet and turned toward a steep hillside of sand, following the instructions of my little black box. Sand crunched between my teeth as I clenched my jaw. I fought uphill toward the sample site, legs burning, sliding backwards a little with every lunging step forward. I couldn't see the truck once I was twenty meters from it.

I kept walking. Two hundred meters to go. We hadn't figured out how to drive any closer to this one on install. One hundred fifty. I was beginning to hear voices in the gale. I even thought I heard the truck coming toward me from behind and turned to see nothing but gray. And then I saw a camel. It was dead on its side, but it didn't smell. It wasn't so much rotting as it was drying out, and a fair amount of sand had piled up against it on the lee side of the wind. It stood a good two meters high when it lived. Its eyes were closed, and it was, without a doubt, smiling. I thought of the Grateful Dead. I continued, leaning into the wind. In a few moments I had the sample inside its bottle and was back in the truck. In another hour we had the last sample of the survey in hand and were headed blissfully back to camp along a freshly plowed seismic line, oblivious to the storm, all of us laughing, each of us looking forward to a change of scenery.

⌣⌐

The goat biryani had been excellent, replete with turmeric, coriander, and fennel. The wine, though no match for the aforementioned stew, was a welcome surprise—GCS apparently reserved a cache of cheap *Vin de Pays* for special occasions. After our meal the Qat appeared, and it was abundant. We sat in a great circle, twenty of us from seven nations, on a richly embroidered jacquard of violets and burgundies spread upon the sand beneath the stars, the wind departed, candles and cigarettes lit, and the night air cool in the wake of the storm.

I sat on Yasser's left and Yasin's right. The former was positively flying on Qat, his round, brown face now asymmetrical and glistening with perspiration, the filter of his cigarette wet and green with juice. He would begin levitating soon, I imagined. I took a swig from the green bottle of French red that was passed clockwise around the circle. As did Yasser. Even Yasin tasted the wine, but apparently had no stomach for it. My four assistants from Aden sat side by side, speaking happily amongst themselves. Françoise and Pete the safety guy were seated beside one another on Yasser's right, locked in conversation. Yasser and I spoke about nothing intermittently. The others gathered were less known to me, but all the faces were familiar—it was a rather small town I had lived in for nearly two months.

"You know, Tom," Yasser started mischievously, tonguing his wad, "you recall what you said to me earlier, about how you normally have little respect for the intellect of the religious man?"

"Yes," I replied expectantly.

"Well, it occurred to me today that you are the first person I have met who does not," he lowered his voice and continued, "who does not believe in god who I do not consider to be a spiritual cripple."

"Oh, my." My eyes widened. "I don't quite know what to say. Thank you?" I stated, sincerely shocked.

"You needn't say a thing."

"It has been excellent to work with you, you know, Yasser. You're one of the great ones."

"Well, let's not get carried away, Tom." Yasser smiled. The next morning I did get carried away, hungover and sour-blooded, by the same Twin Otter that had delivered me to the wasteland. I returned to the United States a changed man, in no small way owing to my excellent friend Yasser al-Rashid.

5 WHISKEY AND ICE

I am sure that in Canada the people...and the general intelligence which prevails over that country is such that I am sure there is no danger of a reactionary policy ever finding a response in the hearts of any considerable number of our people.

—— Alexander Mackenzie

JUST AFTER CROSSING Flat Creek in Canada's Yukon province on the Klondike Highway, the westbound motorist arrives at an historic intersection, historic, at least, in the annals of remote highway construction. If the driver carries on straight ahead for a while, he or she will pass through Dawson and on toward the Alaskan town of Chicken, but branching to the right is a two-lane highway heading, of all places, farther to the north. The intersection is already sixty-three degrees north of the equator, but an improbable ribbon of asphalt nevertheless lunges confidently toward the pole, plunging through boreal spruce forests so full of life that they regularly spill their fauna into the places of humans.

But such places are few in the Northwest Territories. The winter and summer in the north behave like bitter rivals, and their battles test what human constructions, machines, and minds that can be found there with frequency and vigor. In the wintertime, the ground beneath the road freezes into iron. In the spring, the muskeg bogs beside it become completely impassable by man or machine, and water fills every low place. In the summer, when the long days and the flies and mosquitoes return, the highway's thick gravel pad keeps the permafrost beneath it from melting and turning the highway into a canal. And in the fall, the road is crossed by a majority of the great Porcupine herd, more than seventy thousand caribou heading west, off to winter in Alaska.

The land is undeniably one of extremes, and of beauty no exception is made. If it is the fond duty of an Argentine to behold Patagonia, it should equally be that of the Canadian to visit the northernmost latitudes. Since 1979, it has been possible to make such a journey in one's own automobile. The road has been called the "road to divorces" by the men who built it, a road "from igloo to igloo" by Canadian politicians opposed to its construction, and the "road to nowhere" by many, when the first oil wells drilled in what were formerly prohibitively remote areas came in with either very poor shows of oil or none whatsoever. The road was not built, after all, so that people from Inuvik and Aklavik might drive to Edmonton when the notion struck them. It was built so the Mackenzie delta might fall under the bit, for it was believed that a great deal of fossil fuel waited beneath the NWT's permafrost, muskeg, and its dense, deadfall-choked forests.

The road, numbered Highway 5 in the Yukon and Highway 8 in the Northwest Territories, is the Dempster Highway. It is over four hundred miles long. In the summer it ends in Inuvik, which in the language of the indigenous Inuvialuit tribe means simply "place of people." In the winter, when the mighty Mackenzie River and the very Beaufort Sea itself freeze, one may drive eighty more miles across the ice, all the way to the village of Tuktoyaktuk, three degrees north of the Arctic Circle and very near the top of the world.

A big, ruddy Albertan with a head like a battering ram and the fine blond hair of a baby surrounded a pale pint of beer beside me. George wore a pair of black leather brogans and a red cheviot jumpsuit that smelled vaguely of diesel. We were at the Mad Trapper, the town of Inuvik's watering hole for the rather more accomplished drinker. Inuvik sat shivering in the dark of winter or sweating and insomniac during the summer months on the banks of a large channel of the Mackenzie River.

Water from the Great Slave and Great Bear Lakes passed by in somnolent duty, as well that from myriad smaller bodies like Lake Thutade, all the way down in British Columbia, the river's ultimate source—all of these waters eventually mixed with the brine of the ever-chilly Beaufort sea.

It was late February when I arrived. All manner of trucks and a few cars plied the frozen Mackenzie north of Inuvik, which had become, once again, an ice highway. There were only a few populated places to which the ice road could lead you: Aklavik, all the way up to Tuktoyaktuk, or to one of about five oil camps. Most went to the latter. All things oil happened in the winter in the Mackenzie Delta. Until the muskeg bogs and the endless network of river channels were frozen solid, there was no traversing them, but now, the Mackenzie's ice was strong enough to support fully loaded semis. Special crews in pickup trucks drove the length of the ice road every day towing sleds fitted with specialized sonic equipment, their task to constantly monitor the ice's thickness, and hence, its strength. The Mackenzie was, according to George, good and frozen that year, despite a relatively mild winter to date. The lowest lows had only been around minus forty-five Celsius, he explained. Now, the Mackenzie's arctic char and Dolly Varden trout swam slowly beneath a full four feet of milky white ice.

"Oh, he could stand on his hind legs and talk, but he wasn't much of a cook," George mumbled. "Anyway, he froze to death walking home from Frosty's. Drunk. That bar across the street. He only lived about ten minutes from here. Passed out while he was walking home, for fuck's sake. Probably dead in an hour. It was forty-below that night. The last part of freezing to death's supposed to feel good, you know that?" George spoke slowly and deliberately.

"Yeah, I've heard that." I was trying not to stare at one of the guys playing pool. The Trapper had a few tired and well-used tables, one of which seemed to remember a bit of gunplay with three circular wounds to its cheap laminate and particleboard leg. "What happened to that guy there?" I asked George.

"Oh, Isaac? He's got FAS," he stated quietly, turning his flat face and boxer's nose toward me. George's green eyes were bloodshot, and burst capillaries massed on his cheeks.

"FAS?" I asked.

"Fetal alcohol syndrome. Some gals up here can't stop drinking when they're pregnant," George explained quietly. I sipped my Molson. George sipped a Kokanee. Isaac's right eye was in the middle of his right cheek, and was shaped not like an almond or football, but something more like a strawberry. He was engaged in a game of pool.

"It's not all physical. Their brains are all twisted up too," said George gravely. "They come unglued sometimes. I've seen it. Seen it happen to him. Messing with him is like going down on a whore. Just isn't something you would ever do."

I considered George's simile. "I suppose that booze is the key factor when that happens?"

"Oh, yeah. They had a bottle shoved in their mouths before they ever saw the light of day. For them booze is the devil and mother's milk all in one, ey?"

I finished my beer and bid George farewell. I stepped outside the bar into the gray twilight of midday and walked back to the Mackenzie hotel to catch my ride north to Tuktoyaktuk.

Hugh Johnson was a small and lean man with an eager intelligence lighting his pale blue eyes. He had a chapped red face, was in his late forties, and his short, straw-colored hair looked like it had been beneath a tight hat all day. He was uncommonly hale. He had an aura of mirth and a quick smile. His sharp beak of a nose was scabbed up from its tip to just below his brow. It was healing up after some bad frostbite. Hugh and his snowmobile had the misfortune of plunging through a weakness in the Beaufort's ice cap at a pressure ridge. A pressure ridge, I learned, was a long fault in frozen waters, a place where great plates of expanding ice met and were forced upward as they ground into one another. Cracks and hidden holes were to be expected near these. Hugh drove soaking wet some twenty clicks back to camp after he and his second somehow got his snowmobile out of the water. Hugh's anecdote had served to illustrate to me why one never worked alone in the Arctic. But he wore his frostbite proudly.

Hugh and I sat drinking coffee in the huge mess hall inside a cozy, bustling seismic camp headquarters just east of Tuktoyaktuk. It was three in the afternoon, and the cafeteria was empty. We had just returned from a truck tour of the survey area. Hundreds of men and a few women were working in the dim moonscape outside as we spoke; they would all return, hopefully, to the shelter of the camp's yellow aluminum walls at the end of their shifts. The camp was really a large building the size of a big U.S. high school. It was two-stories-high and well-heated, and was a bastion of modern comfort in a frigid wasteland, complete with satellite TV, video games, and pool tables. It even had libations for a lucky few, I would discover.

Out in the frigid fields east of camp, a dynamite seismic program was in full swing. The camp and its mobilized forces resembled a military operation. Gentle hills and thousands of frozen ponds were traversed by full-size Caterpillar bulldozers; as these plowed access roads across the tundra and through drifts of deep snow, drill crews followed behind them and bored shot-holes many meters deep through the permafrost with highly mobile, truck-mounted drill rigs. The powder monkeys in turn followed them, carting tons of TNT here and there, placing charges in the bottom of the holes, wiring them up, and standing by to fire them until the recording crews had their geophones deployed and were ready to record. The geophones and the cables that connected them were laid out across the ground, on foot, by some tough grunts who resembled penguins, bundled as they were in matching dark parkas. They made about thirteen Canadian dollars an hour for their trouble. Their jobs were made worse by the fact that there were no trees to slow the wind down. Just wide open fields of snow, beneath which slept cranberries.

A company called Northern Seismic of Edmonton was executing the geophysical program. Donair Energy of Calgary was the client, the company that held the lease and would finally drill for product after the exploration was complete. Hugh was their on-site rep. He was the eyes and ears of his company. Donair started small as a wildcat, but had grown large after many successes. Some said it was ripe for a takeover bid by one of the really big players. Hugh liked his company's chances of finding oil outside of Tuk.

"What about shallow methane? We've got quite a bit here. The shot drillers hit it once in a while. Sometimes it actually blows up on those poor bastards," Hugh explained.

"The lab can tell the difference between shallow methane and deeper signature. It's not a problem." I paused. "So, am I going to work from a snowmobile?"

"Yup! I have two sleds waiting for you. I hope you brought a down parka and pants." Hugh smiled, his chafed red face full of a rare enthusiasm. He clearly loved the Arctic. He was the type who was made greater and more alive when leaning into the winds of a northern winter.

"Oh, yeah. And a full-faced motorcycle helmet."

"Good. I'm glad they didn't send a city boy up here. You're going to do just fine," he said. "Actually, how you gonna put those little things in?"

"Battery-powered hammer drill. With a really clean bit."

"Ah. That should do it. What's the survey design they gave you? A regular grid?"

"Yeah. Regular grid, three hundred meters between sites. It covers about the same ground as the seismic grid." We fell silent and our sipped our hot coffees contentedly. Our attention drifted to a large television high in a corner of the mess hall. Some new drug was being advertised. It was unclear what malady it was meant to treat, but its side effects seemed rather dire. Hugh giggled and spoke.

"Ask your doctor if cyanide is right for you." We laughed.

2

Ezekiel's brother Jacob had a condition that I would have called "hot dog fingers." As soon as I noticed them, I asked him what had happened. Jacob froze his hands on a hunting trip when he was just nine years old. His fingers looked like those of a blow up doll, sausages without clear knuckles, nails set deeply in swollen white flesh. Thankfully, his fingers still worked—had he frozen them as an adult, he likely would have lost them. Jacob put his gloves back on, said "good luck" to me and

Zeke, and left the building. Jacob had delivered the rented snowmobile from Tuktoyaktuk that I would ride.

Zeke looked a good deal like his brother. He had a round, white face, deep brown eyes, and the east-Asian features I had always associated with Eskimos. But Zeke was Inuvialuit, and I had already learned that the word Eskimo likely meant nothing more than "speaker of another language," and not "eater of raw meat" as many believed. We were standing in the hallway near the coffee lounge in the busy Northern Seisco main office, sipping hot coffee from Styrofoam cups. People walked briskly in and out of the main entrance. Steam leapt out of the door and into the cold morning with each swing of the double metal-and-glass doors. Boots were to be removed upon entry. Some fifteen pairs sat on low metal racks on either side of the entrance. It was 8:45 a.m., and still dark as midnight outside. When the sun did rise, it would not be coming up much at all.

Zeke wore a subtle smile and a handmade parka of beautifully brain-tanned caribou hide. His gloves were of the same material and workmanship.

"You live in Tuk?"

"Yeah. With my mom. My dad's dead." Zeke's speech was very deliberate and round. "He died in the river. Crushed by ice. In a canoe," Zeke offered.

"Oh. That sucks," I said, feeling a bit ambushed by his quick candor.

"It happens," he said plainly. Looking toward the entrance, I noticed that almost all the boots on the low rack were black Baffin brand boots, the same that I wore. Hugh told me to pick some up during my layover in Calgary. They were like the "moon boot" of the seventies, soft-soled and not very supportive, but apparently the warmest thing going. Hugh emerged from some storeroom or other down the hallway in his socks, walking briskly toward us. The office was very warm once you got away from the door. I zipped out of my big black jacket and hung it on a peg in the lounge next to several blue Northern Seisco outer shells. Their standard issue parka was warm, fireproof, and quite heavy as a result of that second feature. I would wear my goose down mountaineering parka and a bib instead.

"OK, here's your radios. Did you sign out yet?" Hugh smiled, handing me a Motorola. "Wear it inside your parka, or the battery will freeze."

"OK. Yes, we did. I guess we're outta here."

"Good luck. I'll come say hi to you guys after lunch. You're starting in the south, right?"

"Receiver lines one and two. That way we get closer to camp every day."

"But you've got a big commute today."

"Yeah."

Zeke chimed in. "We can't get down to one and two in much less than an hour on sleds, ey?"

"Nope. And don't forget, they're shooting to your north today. Lots of shot-holes blow out here. But you know how they're marked. Don't get blown up out there. We can replace you, but that's a nice Ski-Doo you're driving." Hugh giggled like a guanaco.

"Damn, it is really cold up here, Hugh. Really cold."

"Good luck. I'll see you two in a bit." Hugh walked back down the hall to the main office. I put on my parka and walked toward the entrance and my boots with Zeke. I slipped into them and grabbed my burgundy motorcycle helmet. We checked the temperature on the office's external thermometer as we stepped out. Thirty-six-below on the Celsius scale.

"Oh, warm morning," Zeke said quietly.

⌒

The brittle eggshell firmament was Bible black and starry above us, but a timid sapphire light clung to the horizon to our south, growing tentatively and spreading subtly. My breath left me and went through my balaclava in great plumes of white steam, dissolving into the darkness enveloping us. Ice filled my beard and moustache. I was standing near my snowmobile, swinging my arms back and forth like pendulums hung from my shoulders, trying to get blood back into my hands. The pain was great as the centrifugal force of my motions pushed warm blood back into my snow-white fingers. I screamed.

"Oh, yeah, it hurts, ey?" Zeke giggled beside me.

I had removed my down gloves in order to place the first sample of the survey in its freshly drilled hole, and had subsequently made a note of its location in my fieldbook. That's all it took. My hands were numb.

Deep breaths taken through my nose hurt my sinuses. My eyelashes were freezing together and I had to pull them apart. A mini-thermometer that I had attached to my parka zipper had bottomed out at forty-below. It could go no lower.

"Zeke," tears were freezing on my cheeks. "It's forty-below now. Fahrenheit, I mean," I choked.

"Oh, that is where Fahrenheit and Celsius meet, ey! Forty below is the same for both. It's always warmer in camp than out here." Zeke smiled, completely unperturbed by the cold. A round ring of fur framed his face. I wondered how old he was. He turned and put the hammer drill back in the sled that he towed behind his snowmobile after handing me the battery. I unzipped my parka hastily as my fingers returned to partial functionality, placing the cumbersome thing into an inside pocket where it barely fit. It simply had to be kept warm.

Though my core was warm enough, I had to stop three times during our commute to the southern lines to rewarm myself and clear the ice from my helmet's visor. I was pretty sure that my cheeks were frostbitten where the frigid air had come knifing through the teeny crack between visor and helmet during our ride. Our two Ski-Doo sleds didn't want to idle and were hard to restart, but we had to turn them off at every sample site to ensure that each module emerged from its bottle into clean air before going into its hole. I was wondering if we at Falcon had bitten off more of a survey than we could chew. The lights from snowcats and pickup trucks and bulldozers were ghostly whites and oranges in the distance to our north. The snow beneath our feet squeaked and crunched like Styrofoam. We stood silently for a moment. Though it was about a kilometer away, we could hear a D-9 bulldozer straining across the permafrost. Sound traveled extremely well in the cold.

"Here, eat this. It's caribou." Zeke handed me a round piece of jerky. It had been inside his parka and was not frozen. It was incredibly delicious.

"Goddamn that's good. Did you make it?"

"Well, no. I just killed it and dried it out," Zeke said without a trace of sarcasm.

"Oh...well, I suppose that's what happened. Can I have one more?"

"Oh, yeah...here." Our words turned into great puffs of steam and disappeared into the dull blue air. First light had come. The sun would rise soon, but it wouldn't rise much. We fired up the sleds and moved off toward the next sample site.

___

"It was so cold that winter that I almost got married," Zeke chuckled. "This winter really isn't bad, ey." I was rewarming my hands, again by swinging my arms. The sun hovered feebly above a fuzzy gray horizon in the south. It had provided no perceptible warmth during our little outing. My mind prepared for another nauseating wave of pain. Hugh had not been out to visit us, instead occupied with a D-8 bulldozer that had gone through the ice on a frozen lake. He said something over the radio about having to get it out quickly lest it freeze in place. Our day had proceeded with a gnawing monotony, and now, my core was getting cooler.

"OK, Zeke. I think I gotta go back," I mumbled. "I'm gettin' cold now." We pointed our sleds north and headed for Split Pingo and for camp. Split Pingo was the second-largest permafrost hill in all of northern Canada. It was a pimple of sorts, a place where ground ice expanded upward and formed a large mound in a landscape otherwise devoid of any pronounced features. Split Pingo was most famous locally. I was going to suggest that they sell it to Arizona, just to be funny. That seemed funny to me. I think because the front of my brain was cooling off. My forehead and cheeks were painfully cold and would soon go numb. We were heading north at forty-five miles per hour. I couldn't see Zeke. I couldn't see shit. Suddenly I was airborne. I came back to earth in a white explosion, heels over head, snow up my back and down my pants. I stood, dazed, breathless, and colder still. I lifted my visor with a crack of ice. No injuries. My sled was quite thoroughly augered into a deep bank of crusty-skinned snow. I sluggishly produced my radio from within my parka.

"Zeke—Zeke, I'm not behind you anymore."

___

The whiskey was flowing like wine. It looked as though Hugh and I would kill a bottle of Bushmills before the evening was through and solve most of the world's problems in the process. We were in his room, seated in comfortable armchairs and facing a TV perched on his dresser. Hugh had a room reserved for the brass. The queen bed took up much of the room's space, and upon it rested an orange and brown nylon bedspread dating from the 1970's. The television featured hockey, Calgary's own Flames versus the Los Angeles Kings. The Flames led by a goal. The sound was turned down on the tube. Steve Earle's guitar issued tinny and thin from the tiny speakers of Hugh's laptop, and his orange-carpeted, fake-wood-paneled room was most cozy and warm.

I had scabs on my cheeks to match those on Hugh's nose from the frostbite I had suffered on my first day of work. It was snowing outside, more horizontally than vertically. A low-pressure cell spun like a debutant in a trance over the Mackenzie Delta, bringing colder temps, poor visibility, and a stiff westerly wind. The shot-hole drillers had gone on what was essentially a temporary strike. They complained that the conditions were too extreme to work in, and had refused to go back out until things warmed up, this despite a modest offer of extra pay by Billy Rawson, the drill-push and top dog at Big Pike Drilling. Zeke and I had continued working, but out of a snowcat rather than snowmobiles; Hugh borrowed one from the surveyors so that we might continue the geochemical survey without risking serious frostbite. The storm would pass soon, but until it did, the seismic program progressed sluggishly at best. Hugh was none too concerned. "It's the Arctic," he would say, raising his eyebrows in resignation.

"So if you guys hit something here, how you gonna get it to market?" I asked.

"Good question. Most likely on the backs of wooly mammoths, which we plan to clone using the DNA from some frozen remains we've just discovered." I chuckled. He returned to seriousness. "We will have to have a pipeline, eventually. From Tuk down to somewhere near Edmonton."

"That'll be fun to build."

"Oh, yeah. There's lots of capped wells up here just waiting to be put on line. They're already talking about it, and talking to the natives about land settlements and compensation, where it'll go, and all that."

"Do the Inuvialuit stand to make much money out of this?"

"Oh, Christ. They have the best deal with the oil companies in the country. Maybe the world. They settled back in eighty-four for hundreds of millions, and they have absolute title to about ninety thousand square-kilometers here. The Gwich'in got a big settlement too. They're all doing just fine, thank you. Some don't even have to work," Hugh explained, tilting his tumbler back and forth and clinking his ice.

"Which isn't necessarily a good thing," I responded.

"Right. Too much free time can lead to some serious boozing up here. For fuck's sake, it's dark all day for three months, anyway. Some of these boys up here don't just have a few drinks and head home for supper."

"Yeah, I've noticed."

"So, you think you can work out of a pickup truck starting day after tomorrow? We can get you one that'll hold two sleds, and you can at least drive out to your starting point without freezing, ey? The surveyors want their snowcat back."

"I don't see why not. But how do you get a Ski-Doo in and out of the bed?"

"Just back up to the snow on the side of the ice road. The plows make perfect piles to load and unload your sleds from."

"Sounds good," I uttered. I was the owner of a delightful whiskey buzz. Of course we could work on sleds again.

⌇

"Well, do they give more milk?" Zeke was trying to understand breast implants. I put another sample into another freshly drilled hole, repacked the hole with dirt shavings half-thawed by the action of the bit, and stood up. I grabbed the snow shovel we now carried and made a pile of snow about three feet high atop the sample, into which Zeke jammed a four-foot section of wooden lathe. He tied a piece of pink survey tape to the stake.

"No, they don't. I don't know what's gotten into these women, Zeke. I guess they'll be able to make our Johnsons bigger soon too." The sun was about twenty-five degrees above the horizon, and it actually provided some warmth for the first time since I had arrived. The storm was gone, and a fine haze of ice hung in the air, a frozen fog I had never before seen the likes of. It gave the sun a distinct yellow halo, complete with sun dogs on each side.

I dropped the shovel back in the tool sled with a cold aluminum clang.

"What is a Johnson?" Zeke asked plainly.

"You know. A pecker. A willy." I smiled, steam leaping from my mouth into the sparkling air of midday. It was only fifteen-below out, and I had left my helmet in the truck, preferring instead a pair of ski goggles and a windproof balaclava that Hugh lent me. It really was warm enough to work from sleds again.

"Why would you want a bigger willy?" Zeke wondered aloud, genuinely nonplussed, trying his best to understand the contemporary proclivities of the mysterious people from that country just south of his own.

"I guess for the ladies. I don't think...well, maybe some guys have real little ones. Too little for...hell, I don't know."

"How big is yours?" Zeke asked casually, as though we were discussing truck tires or Thanksgiving turkeys. I chuckled, putting a hand on Zeke's shoulder.

"Average, Zeke. Average."

"But how big is that?"

"Come on. Let's start the sleds." I laughed. It really seemed a lot warmer than it had a week ago. Zeke wasn't even putting his hood up between sample sites, which were three hundred wickedly wind-chilled meters apart.

"Mine is like..."

"That's OK, Zeke! I don't need to know how big your unit is!" I sped away to the east on my sled laughing, standing on the balls of my feet with my knees bent, absorbing the shocks from the uneven ground I traversed. Standing up on one's snowmobile was the best way to see ahead and prepare for what was coming. With a great concussion of sound like a thunderbolt, a shot-hole blew out just twenty feet to my left. I was stunned. I swerved wildly to my right. Fifty pounds of dirt flew high into the air and came raining back down around me. I had seen the red piece of wooden lathe that marked the shot-hole, but I hadn't the slightest idea that they were shooting the line we were working. I slowed to a stop. Zeke quickly caught me.

"Did you see that? They're shooting this line!" Another blowout fired into the air a hundred meters to our west. It seemed like we were being shelled.

"Oh, yeah, ey! We should be quiet!"

"What?" I blurted.

"We should be quiet. They are recording."

"Oh...Hugh said our sleds don't make enough noise to interfere with recording. The truck might, but the sleds are OK."

"Oh, is that right? OK, so let's keep going then, Tom."

"Yeah. We could get over thirty in today at this rate. Let's be careful though. You never know if one might not be marked." I gave my sled the gas and veered away to the east, taking a course south of and parallel to the shot-line across untouched snow. Zeke sped behind me as I followed the map screen of my GPS. Two hundred more meters to the next little hole in the ground. Fifteen more samples until dinner. I hoped Hugh still had Scotch.

3

"This is Swimming Point. This is where that girl died a week ago. Froze to death when her car broke down. Did you hear about that?" Hugh asked.

"Yeah—that sucks. Best not to drive home late here, huh?"

"Especially if you drive a friggin' twenty-year-old Impala with a bad main-seal. Engine overheats, driver freezes to death." Hugh and I were humming down the ice road to Inuvik in my rented F-250 across the frozen Mackenzie River. The floating and now ice-bound barge-*cum*-oil camp called Arctic Star appeared to our right like a ghostly tomb, its feeble yellow beacons twinkling through the blue and gray half-light of another overcast midday. It was twenty-five-below outside, and probably eighty in the truck. We had the heat cranked. Trucks whizzed by us heading north every few minutes, but the road was wide and well-maintained, and we could safely do sixty when not in the curves. Hugh had run out of whiskey, in no small way thanks to me, and needed to resupply. Install of the geochemical survey was complete after over two weeks of work, and I would not return to Tuktoyaktuk with Hugh that night. I craved a bit of time outside of seismic camp. I could not begin retrieval for three more days, not until the first modules I placed in the permafrost had full exposure. I was bound for the Mackenzie hotel for some rest and relaxation. Hugh had recommended it as the only place in Inuvik with what one might call a sense of comfort.

The sky was light for eight hours a day now. I drove the truck. Thick willows massed on both sides of the road, ubiquitous along the terminal channels of the Mackenzie where it entered the Beaufort Sea. Black spruce trees grew here and there, stunted and tortured at first, but soon aligned in tight legions along the road's edge and atop the river's steep banks.

"You know what? I fucking love it here. We're not off the beaten path. We're at the end of the goddamn world," I stated.

"That's right. I love it too, ey? It's like another planet. I've always wanted to go to places where no one else has been, since I was a kid. There aren't many left. There's a few here, though. If you stopped the truck here, got out, and walked due west for twenty miles through the pines, you would at some point be walking across ground never trod by man." I considered the grizzlies sleeping beneath the sugary snow and tangled spruce branches in the forest on either side of us. They must have had really bad breath when they woke up, I imagined.

"You know what I've noticed Hugh? It's really hard to keep from getting beer and whiskey in your mouth in the Arctic."

"So true, my friend. So really, you're an English major, right? I mean, I know you said humanities, but that really means reading lots of literature more than anything else, right?"

"That's right. Some music and art, but mostly literature."

"So there's this line from some book that goes something like 'Two paths diverged in a yellowed wood, I took the one less traveled, and it has made all the difference.'"

"That's Robert Frost," I indicated.

"It's so goddamn famous, and everybody thinks it's so great. I've always hated that line."

"Really? Why?"

"Two paths? Fuck the paths! Go straight into the woods! Whoever wrote that was a poseur!" Hugh laughed. In twenty minutes we were in Inuvik.

~~~

At least a few of Inuvik's formally educated citizens were regarded as quislings by their more feral and numerous brothers. Those individuals considered infected with book smarts were generally not held in the highest esteem by some of the area's backwoodsmen. Normally, if you hunted white bears and could set a trap line well, you drank at Frosty's or the Mad Trapper, whereas if you wrote environmental impact assessments and read Jack London in your spare time, you drank at the Brass Rail, inside the Mackenzie hotel. On any given evening, the first two bars could prove culturally hyperbaric to the well-heeled, the college graduate, or even simply the stranger in town.

I was drinking a Molson at the bar at the Brass Rail. It was a cozy and nearly elegant pub wrought of brass and glossy blond wood. A large, u-shaped bar and a dozen tables with wooden chairs were all shiny with lacquer. Patrons were seated at five of them, among them a couple of seeming oil bigwigs. The grog was poured by one of the prettiest gals in town, through some odd twist an Australian; even more bizarre was the fact that she was in possession of a seeming midsummer tan. She had a mischievous gleam in her big green eyes as she moved from table to table in the happy orange light of the barroom with pints of beer and cocktails. Outside, the air was bitter and still. A steady trickle of vehicles crunched by in the darkness on Inuvik's two main thoroughfares, snow-packed ribbons which converged at a forty-five degree angle just outside the bar's big main window. A number of vehicles were parked in front of the hotel. Those not issuing plumes of white exhaust as they idled were plugged into electrical outlets on wooden posts sticking out of the ground, these provided by the Mackenzie. If you turned your truck off and didn't plug in the block heater, the anti-freeze within would do exactly the opposite of its expressed purpose and freeze solid in a matter of hours, cracking the engine block and ruining the vehicle utterly.

I had just finished listening to the exaggerated woes of someone named Niles who got nosebleeds and wore some sort of beads from Fiji around his slight neck, the type of guy who took two or three showers a day—Niles seemed to feel that the Arctic was closing around him with the death grip of a boa constrictor. He was an electrician, and took a job in the frozen north without knowing exactly what he was getting into. Niles was from Regina. He might not last much longer. Perhaps he would be eaten raw by natives in some secret clearing of the black spruce forest sprawling away from town into the breathless, brittle night. I was sick of the Rail. I decided to go to Frosty's. I finished my Molson, paid my tab, and left a generous tip for Mary. I zipped up my parka for the five minute walk.

Frosty's was packed, almost exclusively with natives. I squeezed between tables and chairs toward the bar; no one seemed too eager to get out of my way, and whatever smiles were worn on the faces of the bar's patrons uniformly dissipated into sour objurgations as I entered the bailiwick of Inuvik's most profligate set. I sat on a stool at the bar, the last available, and was sandwiched between two parka-clad blokes stinking of booze. The air inside the bar was cold and full of smoke. The aging barkeep wore enough black eyeliner for three women and looked spent and blandly disgusted with her station. Her face drooped like a Basset Hound's and she was no native, the only other person in the bar besides me who wasn't. I ordered a double Johnny Red rocks, flush as I was with cash. Falcon had already deposited my pay for install in my bank back in Colorado.

I had just tasted my first sip of the pleasantly fiery Scotch when it began. A man with a wrinkled mug and a crooked nose turned his head to stare at me. His brown eyes were heavy-lidded with drink, and he wore a homemade, red wool cap with earflaps. He drank a Labatt's. He was smallish, and his feet did not reach the round footrest near the base of his stool.

"White people suck," he said toward me, slurring his words.

"Are you talking to me?" I asked.

"Yeah. You white motherfuckers should leave our town, ey?" he continued. I looked him in the eye. I cleared my throat.

"I'm not 'white people.' I'm a person. My name is Tom." I extended my hand to him.

"I'm not shaking your little city boy paw, you little pussy," he slurred slowly.

"OK, whatever." I sipped my whiskey, looking straight ahead and bristling quietly. The two blokes on my right and left wore big grins and chuckled quietly. The one to my left spoke.

"Where you from, little boy?"

"Where do you think?"

"Faggot land."

The three of them laughed. Adrenaline began entering my bloodstream. I took a big swig of whisky, finishing the glass, and hailed the barkeep. "Gimme another double. Save the ice." Many pairs of eyes around the big rectangular bar were settling on me. The fun had begun for them. Pushing strangers' buttons was apparently a popular pastime at Frosty's.

"We used to kill little faggots like you, ey? Cut you up like a seal. You should go back to the Brass Rail," said the small man who had initiated our discussion. He was so lit that he was barely able to sit on his stool without holding on to the bar. Still, he did his best to stare daggers. I guessed that I outweighed him by a good forty pounds, and wondered if I ought to invite him outside to resolve the matter.

"I came here for a drink. Let's just behave like adults, all right?"

"Don't you tell me what to do, boy. I'll cut you up so bad your bitch mother wouldn't know you."

"Is this what you guys do for fun? Act like fucking assholes?" I muttered, staring him down and feeling more than a little steamed. I wasn't really sure how serious this was getting.

"How'd you like me to cut off your little cock and stuff it in you mouth, you little white piece of shit."

"Your skin is whiter than mine." This much was true. Asshole and his two buddies didn't much like that comment. "Why don't you and I step outside and settle this right now," I said seriously, my jaw set and my hand finding the lighter in my right pocket. I would require a knuckle-backer in the event of a fistfight. A broken hand was not something I wanted with three more weeks of work ahead of me.

"Let's go," he mumbled drunkenly. I stood from my stool, quickly downing my fourth whiskey of the evening. Asshole's friends were grinning broadly on either side of me. The bartender looked at me like I was completely insane as she picked up the telephone, doubtless preparing to call the law. Or an ambulance. Asshole pushed himself away from the bar and slid off his stool, placing his feet on the bar's filthy red carpet. He couldn't have been more than five-foot-seven, and my fourth whiskey had made me stupidly fearless. I was sure that I could break him in two.

No sooner had my adversary stood to walk outside than he fell completely over, onto his back, and onto the deck. I heard his head hit the carpeted wooden floor with a thud as his cap came off. He lay there like a corpse for a couple of seconds before his eyes reopened, at which point he rolled over onto his belly and pushed himself into a crouch. He tried to stand. His two friends grabbed him by the arms and lifted him upright. Though I was standing six feet from him, he lunged forward and took a wild and looping swing at me, which I easily stepped away from. He did a complete face-plant and proceeded to flop about like a Dolly Varden out of water, trying to grab my feet. I backed away, leaned into the bar, and ordered another drink.

The bouncer at the entrance to the bar, a strapping Inuvialuit, came over, put Asshole into a headlock, and proceeded to remove him from the bar. I waved my middle finger above my head during the fifteen seconds it took to get the drunken freak outside. I felt fortunate that a fight was no longer on the evening's itinerary. I returned to my stool. The barkeep approached me, scowling.

"Do you have any idea where you are? Don't you ever pull that kinda shit in here again. I should kick your candy ass out of here too. This ain't California, you fucking dummy. Those guys will fucking kill you. You just better hope you get back to your fancy hotel room without a blade between your ribs. For fuck's sake. You're on real thin ice, mister. I just hope you can get around these two, 'cause they're gonna wait for you outside. Your only hope is that they get too drunk to walk. You are a fucking fool to mess with these boys," she hissed. She turned and stomped back to the cash register. Shortly thereafter, Asshole's friends were seated on either side of me at the bar again.

"You just got our friend kicked out Frosty's," said the man to my right. "That means for good. He can't drink here no more. 'Cause of you." He spoke slowly, staring me down. Asshole's friend was big.

"What the fuck did I do? You saw what happened! He was being way out of line, not me!"

"This bar closes in three hours. We'll be waiting outside for you." The man to my left produced a large hunting knife within a scabbard and placed it on the bar. "You got Benjamin eighty-sixed from Frosty's. He can't go to the Trapper, either. You're gonna pay, white boy."

I realized that my sole recourse was to out-drink these two. I ordered three double bourbons from the barkeep, feeling fortunate to be carrying a c-note. I could buy rounds all night. Eyes had settled upon the three of us. I felt sure that they would not try anything in plain sight. The bouncer watched closely from his stool near the door.

"Well, I ain't stepping outside this bar until I drink my fill. I suggest you guys let me buy you a drink."

They did not refuse my largess. Booze was their weakness, and was therefore my chance to save my hide. They would have to out-drink me if they were to have a real shot at fucking me up. The barkeep seemed to approve of my plan with a skeptical but hopeful wink. These were not the type of thugs who would pass up free bourbon. It was my ability to drink that might save me. The cocktails followed quickly, one after another. I managed to move our conversation away from vengeance and more toward topical banter. I asked about their families, hunting, whaling, and what kind of sleds were the best. They were getting drunk and I, while not without a hefty buzz, was clearly handling the strong Tennessee whiskey better than they were. My plan was working.

Their eyes began closing intermittently. Their speech was slurring. The minutes ticked by uneventfully until it was midnight. My two companions slumped into the bar to keep from slumping off their stools. I was feeling no more than nicely high, and no longer very nervous. The scene had become almost comic. The man to my right began rambling about hunting and white bears until he finally fell silent and put his head down upon his folded arms on the bar. His partner could barely walk to the bathroom, and lingered therein for some time. The coast was clear. My assassins-to-be had the coordination of toddlers. I left without incident, crunching quickly across the hard-packed snow back to the Mackenzie.

⌣

"Nice job, Tommy boy. They really might have stuck you, you know. Those boys are loco. They got nothing to lose." Hugh bit off a chunk of caribou jerky and chewed it strenuously, smiling, looking sideways at me, his left hand on the steering wheel of my rented Ford pickup. I chewed some as well. It was my new favorite food. Hugh had just picked me up at the Mackenzie hotel. We were driving north back to Tuktoyaktuk after my memorable two-day vacation in Inuvik. He laughed. "You know that one with the knife? I'm pretty sure from your description that that was Joshua. Mighta been anyway. Joshua is widely thought to have killed his brother. Over a snowmobile."

"For fuck's sake. I guess I was lucky."

"Well, you did the right thing. You played to your strengths. I've seen you put away some whiskey, my friend!" he said, laughing.

We fell silent. Black forest ceded to brittle desolation as we neared the ocean. The comatose open lands of the Mackenzie's terminal channels looked so painted with snow and dead that only a miracle could have saved them from this wizard's spell of endless winter. The ice road turned northeast and left the land behind—now, we rolled steadily across the frozen Beaufort Sea. Gray winter light hung in the air like a soporific vapor beneath a solid bank of high clouds. The arctic waited for that miracle, sleeping. I was pleased to be once again in the company of a friend.

"A shot-hole driller got killed while you were down here pickin' fights, ey?" Hugh stated darkly.

"What? Killed?" I asked heavily.

"Got caught in the cowling around a spinning joint of drill pipe. Grabbed his parka and hair first. He had real long hair, ey? Then it grabbed him. Shredded the poor bastard. Shot drillers haven't worked for two days. They're supposed to start again today."

"Holy shit. Was he native?"

"Yeah. Eighteen years old. From Aklavik."

"I guess death's never far away."

"Oh, no. It's with us right here. Right now. Just gotta be comfortable with it. What did Shakespeare say? Readiness is all?"

"Yup. Hell, if we plunge into the ocean right now, I couldn't complain about a single damn thing. I've had a good life."

"Me too, my friend. Me too. So, you think your boys are gonna go into ANWR soon?"

"The wildlife reserve?"

"Yeah. In Alaska."

"I reckon so. The whole Bush cabinet is ex-oil. Cheney, Rice, Rumsfeld..."

"And George himself. His company was called Arbusto. In Texas. He's an oil patch flunky. Couldn't cut it," snapped Hugh.

"What's that mean, something in Spanish, right? Shit, I ought to know," I trailed off.

"It means bush. Like a shrub. And guess what? They are busto. Bankrupt."

"Yeah, I guess we'll be drilling there in Alaska soon. There's not much oil there though, is there?"

"Somebody at Donair told me there's enough oil to power the whole U.S. for about a year. Seven, maybe eight billion barrels or so. No, not very much. If they were smart, they'd save it for manufacturing. Not burn it in cars."

"But they're not. I hate the fucking neo-cons. The U.S. is gonna spill a lot more blood for oil as the world starts to run out of it. I'd be mighty nervous now if I were Chávez in Venezuela. Or Iran."

"Hell, you guys might even invade Canada! That'd be a hoot!" Hugh said with a smile.

"Well, y'all do have oil. That's the main thing. I don't think the U.S. government is beholden to big oil companies anymore. I think it *is* a big oil company," I said, glowering through the windshield.

"Oh, yeah, that's it. But the U.S. has been trying to take over the world since World War Two. Same shit, different president. Just be glad you're on the right team."

"Yeah, I guess so."

It was twenty-five-below outside and windy as well, but a bright sun shone above. Retrieval was almost complete. Zeke and I returned to the truck on our sleds. Once we got close, I could tell that someone was sitting in the cab. They were three, and their machines were parked just beside the truck, which it had never even occurred to me to lock. As soon as I killed my sled's engine and removed my helmet, I could hear loud music coming from inside. One of the men sat in the front passenger seat, and two others sat behind him on the rear bench seat of the crew cab. Zeke stopped his machine beside mine and turned it off.

"Who are these guys?" I asked Zeke, removing my goggles and tonguing the ice on my moustache.

"Wildlife observers. They keep an eye on Donair."

Whoever they were, they liked loud rock and roll. They had started the truck with a set of keys I had left on the driver's seat. To my surprise, the stereo was cranked up and blaring one of my favorite tapes. The band, from Oslo, Norway, was Turbonegro. "Humiliation row," sang Hank von Helvete, "where are the hollow kids glow, puzzled panthers in the dirty snow."

I opened the driver's side door. "Hi, guys!" The man in the front turned down the volume.

"Oh, hi, ey? Just popped into your truck to warm up and eat a little lunch, ey? Kinda cold out today."

"Yeah, it's a breezy one. I think we'll hop in and join you," I stated, grinning and nodding a greeting to each of them. They all knew Zeke. "So, you guys found my Turbonegro tape, I see."

"Oh yeah—they're real good, ey? Real powerful. I can't tell what they're singing about, but you should listen to them loud."

"You might not want to know. But, yeah, loud, for sure. They're from Oslo. Way up north too. I'm glad you like them!" I hopped in the driver's seat as Zeke hopped in the back of the crew cab with the other two observers.

It was bliss to be out of the wind. I turned the music back up, staring vacantly through the truck's windshield as my face and hands rewarmed. The whole world was caught in a spider's web of frozen sunshine. I munched on some chocolate. We sat quietly as the music raged inside the truck and the wind without. Retrieving our samples had been difficult out here. I had even peed on a module a couple days prior in an effort to melt the permafrost surrounding it. It worked, but the lab might not appreciate my methodology. Zeke enjoyed that immensely, and got to assess my unit after all.

6 TO GREENER PASTURES

Further, the process of transformation, even if it brings revolutionary change, is likely to be a long one, absent some catastrophic and catalyzing event—like a new Pearl Harbor.

— Section V, Rebuilding America's Defenses, "Creating Tomorrow's Dominant Force," Thomas Donnelly et al., Project for the New American Century, 2000

No one has the least doubt that you are the economic leader and the military leader to the world, but I have heard a lot of doubts regarding the moral and political leadership of the United States.

— Lech Walesa

I HAD JUST arrived in Warsaw. It was the sixth of July, overcast and muggy. Everything was green or concrete gray. I drank from a cold can of beer in a speedy cab with an attractive woman named Beatrycze seated beside me. Beatrycze spoke like a proper British schoolmarm. She had a pretty, freckled white face, a cute figure, and a productive cough. Long black hair draped over her slender shoulders and down her back. She was more than a little aloof. She smoked a lot. Though she did not appear to disapprove of my 8 a.m. can of beer, it likely did nothing to improve her first impression of me. But we were in Poland, and I needed an eye-opener. As I would discover, many successful men in Poland drank. Too often and too much.

The city rattled and clanged around us. Things were being made. Large-scale industry rose to the level of messianic ideology in the oft-invaded, belittled, or simply ignored nation caught between east and west both geographically and culturally, a nation that longed equally for acceptance and puissance. The steel machines whirred away in Warsaw and in Lodz, creating all manner of goods and rivaling even mighty Deutschland in productivity, while in the countryside a bucolic silence reigned, and one might hear an apple drop from a tree or sip sweet water from a nymph's gurgling brook.

Our taxi slowed to a halt before one of the largest hotels in the center of Warsaw, some thirty stories; while busy, Warsaw never felt cramped. It actually seemed to me to have been designed for a larger population. The city's housing resembled that of Moscow, identical, twenty-story gray structures splashed here and there with the colors of drying laundry hung on balconies. Cars hissed by in a damp drizzle as we stepped out of the cab. Beatrycze looked at me in her detached fashion and told me in her considered English that I needn't tip the cabbie. He wore a face that drooped like that of a Chinese shar-pei. He produced my two large bags from the car's trunk as though he was removing sacks of garbage from his ride. I tipped him anyway, which only served, it seemed, to make him more envious of my relatively excessive Western wealth. He smelled a bit of booze and a lot of tobacco. I put my empty beer can in a nearby wastebasket and shouldered my bags beside a rather bored-looking Beatrycze as the taxi rolled away. We walked into the lobby.

Soon I was checked in. I would meet Beatrycze three hours later at a big powwow at Geofysika Warsawa's office, a seismic firm that would supply local labor for the large geochemical program. She was a receptionist, and met me at the airport to facilitate my passage into a town where very little English was spoken, where an American might spend hours attempting to explain why he was bringing a bunch of GPS's and two hammer drills into Poland. But no such difficulties had arisen. My room was austere, but the large windows revealed commanding views of the city's downtown. I imagined Panzers rolling through the broad boulevards. The sky was a uniform gray that pilfered joy from the day like a hard rain might from a parade. But Warsaw plodded steadily forward in a trance of purpose.

I lay on the bed and stared at the ceiling, wondering if I would be sleeping beneath asbestos. I nodded off.

⌒

"You should not try learn Polish, Tom. Even we do not understand it. It is very hard language." Jurek was a very large man. He wore delicate, wire-framed glasses with round lenses that looked rather small on his big globe of a head. His dark brown hair was thinning on top. His face had been shaped and creased by laughter and drink, was pink on the cheeks, and his blue eyes hinted at some subtle mischief. I guessed he was in his mid-thirties. He reclined in and dwarfed a black office chair as he spoke, tapping his fingers on the large glass tabletop that our group surrounded. We were about a dozen, all Poles except me, and I was the smallest guy in the room. Apparently, Poles were large people.

Jurek was not the group's doyen, but was the most proudly affable of them, and had decided that he should be my tutor and guide to all things Polish, for to understand his country was no simple matter. Jurek's English was somewhat poor. The leader and president of Geofysika Warsawa was Aleksy Stefanski, and he was about to speak. Aleksy's English was better. His big beard was as white as the ceramic mug from which he drank coffee, the only one worn among those of us gathered in the high-ceilinged conference room beside my own. He stared at some papers upon the table before him through a pair of thick-rimmed spectacles with the air of a head of state, oblivious to all around him. Though Aleksy had the manner of a displeased suzerain, a smile flashed occasionally across his weathered face. He had a bit of a lacuna between his yellowed front teeth, and his thinning gray hair had not been paid any attention post-slumber. I imagined him sitting with children on his knee in a Santa outfit in a shopping mall a few days before Christmas. He would have fit the part well, but all that secondhand smoke for the kids...

Aleksy looked up, cleared his throat, and squashed out a smoke. Beatrycze entered the room and walked over to Aleksy's side. She whispered something into his hairy old ear and strutted back out of the room, closing the glass door behind her and drawing several unabashedly covetous looks from the lads. Most of them were married with children.

Aleksy's average employee was in his late twenties or early thirties, was college educated in geology or perhaps surveying or engineering, was polite to a fault, spoke some English, and rarely missed a meal. He also wanted to shag Beatrycze.

Aleksy spoke. "All right, gentlemen," his English was coarse and thickly accented, something like that of a Russian, and his voice was gravelly. He took care to make eye contact with each of us as he spoke. "First I like to say welcome to Mister Brown from all us at Geofysika Warsawa." The group looked at me and to a man either smiled or nodded. "And now to the job. Mister Brown has already explained you about the, how do you call them, modules? And now I tell how we work. We have four trucks. We will be four groups of two man each. This is big survey. Big area. For first six weeks we stay in Opoczno. Then we move at Klesczkow. One week off between two parts of job."

I balked. "Excuse me, Aleksy, but we are taking a week off mid-job?"

"Yes. We have some rules about, how you say, overtime? These men want go home to family after this six long weeks."

"But I can't go home. It's a fourteen-hundred-dollar flight," I stated.

"This no problem. You go to Krakow for week. You love it there."

I love it there? I bit my tongue. Aleksy's plan made no sense. I knew we could complete the entire survey in eight weeks tops. Aleksy's estimates of daily production were absurdly low. And then I realized what was up. This was a time-and-materials bid, and not a "lump-sum." Had it been the latter, it would have made sense to hurry up and finish the survey for Aleksy, for his costs would be less—fewer man-hours to pay out of his fixed amount of job revenue. A T&M job meant he and his boys would make fatter cash by going just a bit slower and doing a wonderfully thorough, painstaking, and languid survey for the beloved client. Aleksy was milking the job and the German client alike, one Deutsche Koenig, but no one was bitching about it. This was not my style, but when in Rome...

"You all worked seismic before in this area. The Polish Basin. This area you know. We do no permitting yet. You talk to people on your way. As you work."

My jaw dropped. I had been told quite the opposite stateside. "It's not permitted?" I gasped.

"You not worry, Mister Brown. Polish people you not know. You tell them big company need do something on their land, they too scared say no," Aleksy stated dismissively. I was beginning to wonder why I was even *there*. I settled on the obvious answer. I needed the money. And maybe Beatrycze would like to discover more about this newcomer from across the pond. But I was clearly not in the driver's seat. I had been told I would be by Logan before I left. This meant one thing. If the job went well, Aleksy would take all the credit. If it went poorly, I would take all the blame. Aleksy finished his briefing. The lads variously stood and went to the coffee machine or resumed chatting. Jurek turned to me with a question.

"So, Tom, I must ask you this. Does this method really work?"

"Good question." I paused, considering my response. "Yes, often it does. But even seismic, what you guys do, doesn't always work. As you know. Seismic is still the best method for exploration, but geochemistry definitely helps. For example, we did find something in the Arctic this last winter, actually. But they had seismic going too, and I think there's gas pretty much everywhere in the Mackenzie delta. In northern Canada. I think it's like anything. It's about how you spin the data. And geochemistry is way cheaper than even the most basic seismic program."

"Spin?" Jurek puzzled.

"Interpret the information to suit your needs. To suit what you already believe."

"Oh." Jurek looked disappointed. "Are you a scientist, Tom?"

Once again, the inevitable query. I paused and spoke. "I've spent a lot of time with rocks." Jurek looked at me strangely. I returned to a tentative seriousness. "Science is like a religion. And I am an agnostic." I hoped this was sufficiently cryptic to end Jurek's line of questioning before it truly began.

"Ah, agnostic! You study volcanic rock!"

2

Milosz was a man of limited intelligence and boundless convictions. He was the eldest of our group at fifty-three, and had finally crossed the threshold to drunk. He had a hatchet for a face and eyebrows like salt and pepper moustaches; he was tall and skinny, but he carried a sizeable beer gut around with him that poured over his belt. We were checked into our modest but comfortable hotel in Opoczno. We arrived at night after driving two hours from Warsaw, and the town had been difficult to discern. I cut my last cheese and potato pierogie in two with my fork, placed half of it in my mouth, and chased it with some Zywiec beer. Milosz was ranting. I listened to him as though listening to a televangelist, simultaneously amused and offended.

"The woman should be at home! She is to help the man, not be equal with him!" he spewed. I looked at Jurek. He rolled his eyes and smiled subtly. His was a much later generation than that of Milosz. A big bottle of Dubrovka vodka was being passed clockwise around our large table. Everyone took swallows straight from the bottle. It had a bison on the label, and was infused with some form of sweet green grass. It was anything but smooth, but tasted pretty good. The boys drank like there was no tomorrow. I was bringing up the rear as far as consumed volume, but I had a mighty buzz.

"You not drigging enough, Tom!" Milosz boomed. "You learn to drink like Pole!"

"Oh, I'm feeling no pain, my friend—vodka's just not my specialty. I drink Scotch."

"You not in Scotland now!" Everyone laughed dutifully. The bottle was handed to me out of turn. I took a deep pull. "That is better! Now I tell story. About the war!" I thought of excusing myself and heading to the rack, but considered that it might be seen as rude. Milosz was annoying nearly everyone, it seemed, but I resolved to suffer through his upcoming soliloquy nonetheless. I soon discovered why he commanded such rapt attention. His story actually proved to be fascinating. It concerned his father, and the resistance to the Nazi occupation in the Warsaw ghetto. After five minutes I was listening intently, my imagination putting faces on the players in his tale, delivered for my benefit in English.

They ate rats, spat Milosz. They lived like dogs, he explained, bristling. They cared for their children without hot water or proper sanitation. Mostly they starved. They would rather die than give in. I considered that our client was German. Milosz's story ended some twenty minutes later, a respectful solemnity replacing the crew's former mirth. We all returned to our rooms and our own thoughts at just past midnight.

⁓

The morning sunlight shattered through the outstretched arms and fingers of maples and pines above and around us. I easily plunged a meter-long, stainless steel drive tool to its hilt in the soft black soil under my feet. We would not need the hammer drills I brought. I put on a pair of blue nitrile gloves and screwed the top off of a sample jar. I removed the module, placed it on the insertion rod, likewise made of stainless steel, and stuck it in its new home in the bottom of the hole. I pulled out the rod and refilled the top of the hole with a fistful of damp dirt. Jurek then put a nearby chunk of rock atop the hole, this to deter curious animals which tended to dig, chiefly rodents and the like. I marked our position with my GPS, which was getting very good signal. Jurek tied a strip of orange flagging around the closest tree.

"That is all?"

"Yup. We'll be back in three weeks to get it." I removed my gloves. Jurek looked at me like I was trying to sell him a pair of photography shoes or tickets to the 2000 Olympics.

"But how can this work?"

"Microseepage, Jurek. If there's oil down there, it's been there since before humans walked on their hind legs. It's under pressure. Teeny bits of it, trace hydrocarbons, make it all the way to the surface, even through perfect top-seal like salt. The samples can pick up C-2 through C-18." The nomenclature referred to hydrocarbon compounds like methane and toluene. By the time the Poland job began, I had become quite adept at explaining geochemistry. After lots of reading and discussions with Logan, I was an expert on the theories behind exploration soil-gas testing. Now I could play the advocate.

"But this is so simple—how can this work?" Jurek's brow was furrowed.

"First oil well in the world was drilled on a site with visible surface seepage. Most reservoirs seep. You just can't see it, usually. But we're not trying to see it. We smell it," I offered confidently.

"OK. That is something I may understand."

"What do you do for Geofysika? I mean what's your job during a seismic program?"

"I am on the recording team."

"Ah." We walked back to our little Hyundai SUV across a spongy forest floor strewn with dead leaves and dotted here and there with mushrooms, many of them edible. While the countryside around Opoczno was sparsely populated, what forest we had encountered between the farmed fields of sugar beets and alfalfa and wheat seemed devoid of all animal life. It wasn't really a forest, just a bunch of trees. We emerged from the woods and onto a narrow dirt road, an east-west ribbon of tan separating the trees behind us from a sea of ankle-high emerald grass where a group of Jersey cattle grazed. We walked down the road and back to the car. Poland in the summertime was nothing if not richly green.

***

"Tom, what happened to mud wrestling? Foxy boxing? You know this thing, from America, where the girls do this fighting, but they are no clothes."

"Good question. Don't see that much of that anymore, do you? I think it got replaced by foxy knife fight. Violence is big business in the U.S., you know. Movies, video games, sports—violence is great. We love it. So long as it's not happening to us. You know. Like a bully."

"Ah, yes, bully. I know this word bully."

Jurek was driving. The summer foliage throbbed with emerald vigor under a strong sun and after a night of constant soft rain. Pink, yellow, and ruby-red roses thrived along fences and in the front yards of farmers' homes. Most of these farms maintained truly vicious dogs, these kept in cages the size of pup tents—they were not shown the remotest kindness, and were expected to attack anyone but their owner and his family when released. I suspected that he might not actually be exempt from such treatment either.

There seemed to be no such thing as trespassing in the farmland around Opoczno. It was just as Aleksy said it would be. We simply informed the closest warm body of our intentions and proceeded without a care, plodding through backyards, jumping fences, and disappearing into the sterile forest with mysterious purpose. The survey was a regular grid with five hundred meters between sample locations. Most of these could be practically driven to. We were getting to know the area quite well. Opoczno itself had a modest and dingy grocery, three or four restaurants, and a few bars. It had a football pitch and a third-league team, a little river gurgling through it, and one could walk from one end of town to the other in fifteen minutes. Many who lived there worked at the large ceramic tile plant just outside of town. Some who lived there remembered September of 1939.

It was hard for me to picture. I was in my shower at the little hotel. I stared at the back of my shampoo bottle as pleasantly cool water ran down my back. It read: "Waterfall Mist shampoo combines the fragrance of a refreshing, tropical waterfall and water lilies in a formula with gentle cleansers to enhance fullness, restore shine, and bring out the beauty of all hair types." I tried to imagine Messerschmitts buzzing around overhead outside the hotel and storm troopers marching around town. It just didn't seem possible that such a scene could have transpired here. The German client representative would be paying us a visit soon, one Werner Kopp. He was to arrive around dinnertime. I sat before my laptop in my white hotel towel looking at a digital progress report and map of the first phase of the survey I had prepared for Werner. They first part of the survey was, after three short weeks, almost fully installed. The guys were doing well, and they took the job seriously. They had to a man made me feel welcome. Milosz was the clear jackanapes, but I had learned to like him. All the boys were heading back to their homes in two days, mostly in the town of Torun, and I had already decided to ride back with them and spend a week in the capital, a better alternative to seven days alone in sleepy little Opoczno.

3

I was back in the capital in the early evening. The city sparkled and purred, a poor man's Prague, the scents of foreign foods and car exhaust and French cologne mingling along the black cobblestone streets and below the vaulting towers of Warsaw's fashionable old town. Restaurants bustled with patrons. Shop windows alight with baubles both precious and frivolous drew looks from passersby on the busy sidewalks. Lovers kissed on public benches. Poland's largest city was not at all without charm. I walked beside Beatrycze. She wore an elegant, strapless black dress cut just beneath her sharp white knees—the gown wrapped her slight but womanly figure just as its designer had intended. She looked lovely and smelled fragrant, the scent of cigarettes not quite lost beneath her perfume, a jasmine queen who commanded attention from the young men as we strolled down the street to our restaurant. We crossed a broad boulevard, walking quickly through a break in traffic.

"Why do you have no girlfriend?" Beatrycze's icy blue eyes flashed at me sideways as the heels of her pumps threatened to catch in the cracks between the cobbles of the street. She walked deftly on the balls of her slender feet.

"I'm always gone. And I love my job. I want to keep doing it. Where did you learn to speak such nice English?" I found myself stealing glances at Beatrycze's legs and breasts and butt more than I thought I would. She was lovelier than I remembered.

"I lived in England for a while. In Bristol. With my ex. I miss it terribly. I hate Poland."

"Yeah, me too. Too pretty and prosperous."

"Don't be mean."

"I wasn't trying to be mean."

"You're so sarcastic. Like my ex," she chirped disapprovingly.

"But really, how can you hate it here? I quite like it." I smiled, trying to make nice.

"If you must ask, you wouldn't understand. You don't have to stay here." She stewed like a little girl. Suddenly, I found her fetching beyond the physical. She hated something. It was a start. There was nothing less attractive to me than a girl with the personality and sophistication of a spoiled puppy whose backyard was all she ever wanted. We arrived at our restaurant. It served some interpretation of Tuscan cuisine. It smelled like fresh flowers and garlic. We were led to the sort of table reserved for the amorous. Beatrycze seemed displeased, and her smile was forced, even to

152

someone who did not know her. The delicate, almost translucent skin of her brow crinkled as she stared a hole through the menu, thinking about anything but what she wanted for dinner. I wanted real pizza. The pizza of Poland's countryside had been more like a large piece of circular wonder bread painted with ketchup and covered by a plasticky pseudo-cheese that melted poorly. I stared at Beatrycze above my menu. I placed it back down on the table.

"I really want to know why you hate it here." Beatrycze looked up from her menu and into my eyes with something approaching contempt. I hoped it was for my question and not for me.

"Don't you know? Mister world traveler man? I am stuck in a place where most people think that a trough of beer and a sausage is heaven. My parents think I am wrong for liking England. For wanting to see the world. For being bored, bored and sick of this."

"Fancy Italian restaurants?" I eyed her appraisingly.

"No! I am stuck here! I am stuck in Poland! I want to see Barcelona! I want to see Rio! I want Hong Kong! I want smart people who are interesting, and—you don't know how lucky you are, you're so smug, so satisfied, this month here, this month there..." Beatrycze realized how loudly she was speaking as some people at a nearby table looked coldly at the two of us. She continued more softly. "I could do your job. I am smart. I am tough. You make more money in one month than I make all year."

"I'm sorry. Look, Beatrycze, have you divorced your ex? If not, can't you go back to England?" I asked tentatively. "Did you get citizenship with your marriage?"

"Yes. But I can't afford it. And my mom is sick." She became quiet, looking again at the menu. The steam in her soul slowly dissipated through the cracks in her staid, proper, and practiced façade. A moment later, she spoke. "The risotto is good here," she managed to say evenly. Her eyes were wet. She lit a cigarette with a little black lighter, staring thumbtacks at me.

"You're telling me that there isn't anyone here you find smart or interesting? That Poland is your prison?"

"Pretty much," she spat sourly in her BBC British accent.

"Do you want some wine?"

"Sure." She ashed disgustedly, missing the little glass tray. Her face softened slowly. "Look, I'm sorry. I don't mean to be such a pain."

"No, it's all right. I am lucky, I know. I wish I could spring you. From Poland." I looked into Beatrycze's sapphire eyes, searching for something, maybe a sign that she was playing me. I found none.

"Would you ever hit a woman?" Beatrycze asked quietly.

"Would I ever hit a woman? Of course not. No good man would," I said evenly.

"Then my ex was not a good man," uttered Beatrycze.

"Oh, God. I'm glad you've left him."

"He was my way out of here," she said slowly, her voice quavering. "He was..." Beatrycze rose and went to the bathroom, passing a tall waiter bringing our wine. He opened the green bottle and presented the cork, which I approved with a nod. Beatrycze returned a moment later. She went to her chair and sat down. A slender blue vase containing a single iris stood between us on the little table. She looked at me coolly, having successfully fought off tears.

"Do you want to sleep with me?" she asked plainly.

"Well sure, if you were in the mood. But you're not."

"I'm not sure if I ever will be again."

⌒

Was I doing a dance? Did I do it well? Who could tell me? And were their opinions reliable? I *loved* the girl I danced with. That was all that mattered. Her name was Nadia. The skies had opened and were pouring forth vodka. It flowed down streets and into culverts, driving half-drunk rodents to higher ground and pushing maple leaves and candy wrappers spinning dizzily into gutters and eddies beside the liquid's rapid course. It pushed poorly-formed sentences and fiery outbursts from the laughing wet mouths of those whirling across the hardwood of the dance hall at the Hotel Kleszcow, our new base of operations, already proving better than Opozcno, already awash with mirth, in no small measure chemically induced. I had double vision, and could only barely discern Nadia's bobbing and diffuse features. But I knew that I had found her lovely when I had seen only one of her earlier. She kept referring to my still secluded cock as Piotr. I had never named my penis. It was, to me, like naming your left arm.

And then it all ended. It was morning, cruel and searing, and I still reeked of potato vodka. The world had apparently stopped spinning so that the sun might remain fixed in place and beam through my uncurtained window and into my face. I cursed all of existence. My head was in a vice. I was still wearing my clothes from the night before. The bedside clock said 7:45. I rushed downstairs to breakfast, not bothering to change. I fought vomiting as the smell of hot breakfast barged into my nose. I barely won the battle, but I would soon lose the war.

Milosz started in on me. "You have a little fun with Nadia last night, Mr. Vodka?" He grinned devilishly.

"Ah, no." I burped. "I don't think I could've managed a wank last night. I was polluted. Polluted."

"Ah, no matter. You'll have another chance with that one. She lives on her back, that one."

"Great. Just my type," I mumbled unintelligibly, stuffing something like hash browns into my mouth and gagging. I considered that Nadia's name was one letter away from meaning "nobody" in Spanish. My eyes watered. I clinched my ass and swallowed. My mouth filled with vomit, cheeks bulging like Dizzy Gillespie. I made the quick trip to the thankfully proximate loo, and then back upstairs to the shower. I went back to bed. Three hours later, I was bumping down the road again beside Jurek in the SUV, feeling a good deal better that when I had initially awakened. Poland smiled and shimmered at us through the car's windows. They were rolled up because the air-conditioning was on. I watched my GPS absently, feeling my headache. Jurek kept looking over at me and laughing.

"OK, take a left here. We're getting close. It's up on that hillside there. Near that silo."

Jurek stopped the car after a few hundred more meters. We hopped out into a field of snotty brown mud and coarse green grass that squished beneath our feet. A dozen piebald cows stared at us as though our sole mission that morning was to perturb them. They ambled away groaning. The ground was soaked from heavy rains during the night, but now, the sun shone brilliantly in an empty sky. None of us could know what was about to happen, and few were even properly equipped to understand it.

We would place ten more samples that day in a leisurely cruise about the Polish countryside, bantering with locals, staring at girls, eating blood sausage for lunch, and then, in New York City, where I had never been, more than three thousand people were suddenly murdered in the largest attack on American shores since Pearl Harbor.

"Tom, there is an accident in your country." Milosz spoke so quietly that I hardly noticed.

"Really? What happened?" I remarked absently, staring at the screen of my laptop. I was preparing yet another progress report to be e-mailed to our somewhat demanding German client.

"A plane has crashed. Into a building."

"Really. That's too bad," I stated as I finished adding the day's installed points to my fancy electronic map, one I hoped would impress.

"You should come watch television. Come." I looked at Milosz. I assumed that he was up to his normal mischief, or more accurately, his mildly amusing dysfunction. But his face looked different. His expression was almost grave. I shut down my laptop and stood up.

"OK, let's go watch TV." I walked behind Milosz to the hotel's dining room and its only television. It was late afternoon, and though we had all returned from the field, I was surprised to find our entire staff gathered there before the tube. I joined them, and together we watched what would become the most infamous images of the early twenty-first century. In Manhattan, the twin towers of the World Trade Center had been struck by two commercial jets with people on board and had subsequently collapsed. Three thousand people were killed on live television. I watched for some moments as my throat tightened and my heart recoiled. I went to the lobby to place an international call to my family. I fought to control many emotions as I dialed.

Eight hours later as America wept, another tower with the address Seven WTC collapsed. The forty-seven-story building likewise fell neatly upon its own footprint with a tidiness that would have made any demolition firm proud. But no plane hit building Seven. Three times in a row in one chilling and turbid day, asymmetrical damage had caused the perfect, symmetrical collapse of three massive New York skyscrapers. But we were all too far in shock to think that worth scrutiny. In fact, any scrutiny of that horrific September day's events would soon become uncool in a United States stricken with a frothing patriotic fervor. Someone somewhere was saying "mission accomplished." Perhaps some obscure zealots in caves in Afghanistan, yes, but others as well. Who else might benefit from a second Pearl Harbor-type event in this new American century?

7 INTERVIEW WITH STONE

The name "Anasazi" has come to mean "ancient people," although the word itself is Navajo, meaning "enemy ancestors." [The Navajo word is anaasází (<anaa- "enemy," sází "ancestor").] It is unfortunate that a non-Pueblo word has come to stand for a tradition that is certainly ancestral Pueblo. The term was first applied to ruins of the Mesa Verde by Richard Wetherill, a rancher and trader who, in 1888–1889, was the first Anglo-American to explore the sites in that area. Wetherill knew and worked with Navajos and understood what the word meant. The name was further sanctioned in archaeology when it was adopted by Alfred V. Kidder, the acknowledged dean of Southwestern Archaeology. Kidder felt that it was less cumbersome than a more technical term he might have used. Subsequently some archaeologists who would try to change the term have worried that because the Pueblos speak different languages, there are different words for "ancestor," and using one might be offensive to people speaking other languages.

— Cordell, Linda S. Ancient Pueblo Peoples. St. Remy Press and Smithsonian Institution, 1994.

T HE PEOPLE WHO lived in what would become the Four Corners region of the southwestern United States between A.D. 900 and 1300 cooked at least some of the food they ate in great earthen pots. The Four Corners are those of Colorado, Utah, Arizona, and New Mexico, and they are the only states in the United States that meet with such geometric elegance that one may hop childishly from one state to three others in a celebration of modern man's arbitrary boundaries. Better still, a newcomer can visit perhaps the most accessible and intact prehistoric ruins in North America, a mere half-hour drive from Cortez, Colorado, a modern town bearing the name of one of history's cruelest and most successful conquerors.

The Anasazi ate corn, squash, beans, rabbit, mule deer, antelope, and wild sheep. Their stews were cooked by placing a superheated cooking stone inside a great pot with all the ingredients, doubtless sending the aroma of the region's *haut cuisine* wandering up the nearby canyons between the pines and cottonwoods. A rabbit's bones would have fit neatly inside of one of these gurgling, covered pots, but those of a deer or an antelope were much larger. Owing to this, a certain subtle but readily recognizable change was brought to bear upon larger bones, a change we can observe to this day. When the stew was stirred, the often broken ends of the bones within it rubbed against the inside of the pot, and in the process of cooking became polished. Pot-polishing of deer and antelope bones is commonplace, a phenomenon well-known to the anthropologist. There is nothing odd, extraordinary, or troubling about pot-polishing when it is found on the thousand-year-old bones of animals. It is when one discovers pot-polishing on human bones that one is compelled to raise certain questions about just what was going on back then in the cliffs and canyons of what we now call Montezuma county.

⌒

Long before Hernan Cortez terrified Moctezuma's soldiers with the horse and sent them back to him with their hands chopped off, the Anasazi farmed the relatively fertile ground of river basins such as the Mancos in southwestern Colorado. During the latter period of their civilization, they moved into *jacals*, homes in the sides of cliffs, well above the valley bottoms where their crops of corn and beans grew or faltered. We have given these cliff dwellings names like Mesa Verde and Bandelier, and we have wondered why a people would choose to live in dwellings that were such a long walk from their crops and from the river, especially when carrying loads and infants. Though several theories exist, one explanation is that they needed to live in defensible places. While many contemporary scholars of the Anasazi have told us that they moved into the cliffs for the shelter from the elements they would have provided, others wonder if the Anasazi were under pressure, in a constant state of vigilance, and had to move into places where a few men could protect their families from assaults by groups of other men greater in number. For centuries they had lived in comfy, circular pit houses or beautifully masoned stone buildings on the open plains, but around 1150 A.D., the great stone city in Chaco Canyon and its extensive system of outlier communities experienced cultural collapse. Why this sudden sea change?

It is perhaps the most compelling mystery in the history of indigenous North Americans. One scholar of the Anasazi, Christy G. Turner II, has produced extensive evidence of cannibalism in and around the Anasazi territories, particularly during the Pueblo III phase from roughly A.D. 1150 to 1350. His evidence consists not simply of pot-polished human bones, but of human remains with severe skeletal and cranial injuries which, due to a complete absence of signs of healing, were the demonstrable cause of death. Turner has also found human long bones such as the femur or ulna both pot-polished and smashed in a manner that surely would not have resulted from physical combat, but from an effort to remove the marrow from within the bone.

Dr. Turner's writings do not purport that this was Anasazi-on-Anasazi violence, though he has been construed as claiming such by his sometimes shrill detractors. While the Anasazi likely faced pressure from Numic-speaking tribes moving onto the Colorado Plateau like the Ute, Paiute, and Shoshone, Turner's book *Man Corn* explains that another much crueler culture from the south may have exerted its influence on the Anasazi through terror and ritualized cannibalism. These were the Toltec, from what is now Mexico, a militaristic people who tended to dominate their neighbors. Whether true or not, it is a fact that the clever, thoughtful, and clearly hard-working Anasazi who lived in what we call Mesa Verde, the most impressive of their cliff-bound cities, quit their fine homes with apparent haste around 1280 A.D., leaving tools and valuable personal items sitting upon tables and lying on floors, abandoned, perhaps, in some flight before an irresistible foe. A majority of scholars explain the exodus as a simple and direct result of a period of intense drought that gripped the area around 1270 A.D. and continued for some twenty-five years. A prolonged period of meager precipitation may have stolen the crops, the game, and the will of the cliff-dwelling Anasazi, and could also help explain the presence of at least survival cannibalism. None shall ever know exactly what happened.

2

I braked my newly purchased, used Nissan pickup to a halt before the Best Western's turquoise and peach facade in the center of Cortez. I had bought the truck with some money from the Poland job and named it *La Poderosa* after Che Guevara's fabled Norton 500 motorcycle. It made the trip from Boulder without a hiccup. Cortez was home to perhaps eight thousand people, and made nearby Durango seem rather cosmopolitan. The motel admitted guests through a pair of swinging glass doors beneath a little teal roof where one might park in the shade while checking in. The whole affair was as welcoming as a pillow mint. It was called the Kokopelli Inn, its proprietors clearly loathe to miss out on any association with the local ancient culture. Better might have been the Rubber Tomahawk.

Seated beside me in the passenger seat was Scott. Scott was the FNG, the "fucking new guy" at Falcon. Scott was slight of build, short, and had a face as quiet as he was. He was young, in his early twenties, and he hadn't betrayed much emotion with his voice or his pale brown eyes during our ride to Cortez. He had short, brunette hair and wore a little blondish goatee, perhaps to offset his rather delicate nose and chin. I had my doubts concerning his future with Falcon. I opened the truck's door, shut it behind me, and ambled toward the entrance. SUV's ranging from modest to luxurious abounded in the motel's oversized parking lot. Scott followed me inside. We were soon checked in. I had chosen a relatively nice joint. My room had Internet access and two queen beds, a huge TV on which I might watch the Broncos every Sunday after work, and even a small refrigerator. Paradise. A knock came at my door. It was Scott.

"Sweet rooms," I stated.

"Yeah, I guess so," he muttered. Scott had not expressed much of anything without equivocation. "Are you hungry?" he asked blandly, looking not at me but at the garish, patterned wallpaper on the rear wall of my room.

"Not really. I was going to go across the street to City Market later and buy stuff to make sandwiches. Colorado is playing St. Louis tonight. I wanna watch the game."

"Football? On a Wednesday night?"

"No, dude, hockey."

"Oh. Well, I'm gonna go find some food."

"Good luck, then. I'll see you at 7:30 tomorrow morning." He pulled the metal door shut behind him. I wondered if Scott was a duck at a goose fight. He didn't seem like the type of guy who would enjoy working in some of Colorado's most rugged terrain in the snowy springtime.

Highway 666 was the one we would take to work every morning, the pavement of the Beast, the Devil's road, an odd number for such a lovely stretch of asphalt. The road ran northwest from Cortez toward the border with Utah through the expansive Dolores River Valley. As one might expect, some local Christian blowhards were about to demand a name change. They would get it. I could not drive this road, which ran so very near so many notable Anasazi sites, without wondering what had happened there eight hundred years before. Scott understood little of the Anasazi, but I spoke of them often, and had piqued his interest. We were about to learn a good deal more. We were going to meet our archeological monitors, Dean Marsh and Rhett Wilford, out at the jobsite. Our work could proceed only in their presence, and our client had arranged their services.

My newly acquired truck hummed with seeming glee. I took a left about thirty minutes outside of Cortez on to a dirt road that led to Whetstone Energy's oil wells. These had been carefully and controversially drilled in Hovenweep Canyon itself some years before, and now they wanted to drill a couple new ones. A geochemical survey would hopefully help them understand more about their partially depleted reservoir. Hovenweep Canyon was more of a broad and shallow valley than a canyon, replete with juniper and piñon pines, bobcats, cougars, and extensive, unexcavated, and sometimes completely undocumented ruins. With a great plume of brown dust behind us, the early morning sun in my side-view mirror, and a black coffee in a paper cup between my thighs, we approached perhaps the most extensive and least-visited Anasazi ruins and accidental big cat preserve in the world. The Dead Boys were on the truck's stereo. I exalted. Scott toyed with his GPS.

While Mesa Verde National Park waited for its latest herd of visitors, we were given the combinations for every single one of the six padlocked gates that barred vehicular descent into Hovenweep Canyon and to the wells that comprised the client's modest field. Some guy who worked in the main collection facility on a mesa top above the canyon gave them to us with a welcoming smile. He seemed to know what a breathtaking place we were about to enter. In guarding access to their wells, both in their own interest and that of public safety, Whetstone Energy was also guarding the valley's ruins from those vandals and thieves who were unwilling to make approach hikes of more than a couple of miles. Although Hovenweep was on public land and open to anyone who sought to visit it, the average group of drunk high-schoolers were deterred by the oil company's gates, and souvenir seekers assumed that the gates meant the canyon was off limits. But anyone could park outside the gates and walk in.

Few did. The cougars were doubtless thankful for this. So were the archeologists. Following the directions provided us, we drove to the northernmost of the gates, and there they were, both waiting in the cab of an old, sun-bleached Ford F-150. Rhett's old pickup had a camper in the bed, and I knew at first sight that he was living in his ride. He looked like he was already at home. His Jack Russell Terrier emerged from the trees as I slowed my Nissan to a halt. Scott and I hopped out. We walked to either side of the formerly blue and now turquoise Ford.

"Hey!" said Rhett. He had not emerged from the truck to greet us as he was preparing a joint in his lap. Dark green and shwaggy pot was being de-seeded on the cover of an old *Mother Jones* magazine by Rhett's weathered-looking hands. Dean was pouring coffee from a filthy-looking French press into two plastic mugs seated on the dash. It was not for lack of politeness that they had not gotten out to greet us.

"Good morning, gentlemen. Glad you could make it. Did you bring enough to share?" I quipped, only half-sarcastically.

"Oh, yeah...I just got this. I have an ounce!" Rhett smiled. Dean looked at me appraisingly.

"Nice. I would love to puff a bit after work. We'll get the beers."

"Perfect," said Dean.

I rolled a Drum cigarette and accepted a black "cough of cuppy" in a plastic mug when Dean handed it to me. I offered him my bag of Drum, but Dean didn't smoke tobacco. It was "pushed" by "the Man" to keep the working class sedated, he explained. I already liked these guys. They both remained seated on the truck's wide bench seat as we puffed, drank, and chatted. Scott returned to my truck and grabbed his GPS.

"Hey, wanna see something?" Dean opened the Ford's glove box as I watched. He tentatively placed his hands on some mysterious object within, almost as though he was handling a live crab. He produced a yellowish rock the size of a croissant and dropped it on the dash with a gritty clunk as though it was red hot. Rhett looked both amused and annoyed, sucking on his coffee and looking at me wryly and sideways. He rolled his piercing blue eyes below his wild gray and blond eyebrows. "It's uranium!" Dean declared gravely and absolutely. Dean had the eager energy of a reckless teen, an adolescent who had tried his best to resist adulthood and had finally failed. He was as tan and parched-looking as a sun-dried tomato, had a keen, longish face, and gray hair growing from his ears. He looked like his Ph was off just a bit. Judging from his facial stubble, one might have guessed that his bathroom lacked a mirror, but I knew that he just didn't give a shit. His eyes were also blue, but unlike Rhett's, a certain weariness was in them. His graying brown hair had retreated from his forehead a fair bit, and what remained was long and tied into a ponytail. He wore a red and black T-shirt that read: "Save the Earth—Kill Yourself." His skinny shoulders slouched forward as he stared at the formidable rock.

Rhett seemed to me the happier of the pair of archaeologists. Though he did indeed live in his truck, his short brown beard was neatly trimmed, and upon first meeting, Rhett had an aura of cleanliness and order. He wore a denim button-up shirt, and his jeans were nearly the same color. He smiled a lot, which had wrinkled the tan skin around his eyes into deep crows' feet. His recently trimmed but unruly hair was caramel colored where it wasn't gray. His round face was tan, his cheeks and nose a deep red, and his kind blue eyes were bright with intelligence. Rhett would have been perfect playing Robin Hood, and even had political tendencies to match. Both Rhett and Dean were in their mid-forties. Dean lived outside of Cortez in a home he owned, was recently divorced, and had meticulously imagined apocalypse fantasies, I would soon discover. Rhett orbited Cortez in his truck with his dog Boogie, his pot, and his smiling disdain for American culture. We were soon walking in pairs through the low pines and the shining morning air, strangers for the last time.

⌒

"So you were in Poland during 9-11?" asked Rhett. We walked deliberately through some piñons uphill toward the rocky canyon rim. It was noon. I had placed only six samples so far, and these were only two hundred meters apart, but we had been given a mandate—go slow and be careful. Translation: Whetstone wanted no trouble with environmentalists or the many friends of Hovenweep's amazing ruins. Of course they didn't. But they also wanted more oil.

"Hold up, Tom. That's a midden above us." I looked uphill. There was a vague pile of dirt resembling the tailings of a miniature mine directly above us on the hillside. Rhett walked ahead of me for several steps, stopped, bent over, and picked up something. He beckoned me with a twitch of his hand. I approached eagerly through the checkered light and shade of mid-morning.

In Rhett's right palm was a piece of a shattered bowl. It was corrugated and gray on the side facing up. He flipped it over. The slightly concave inside was smooth. It was the size of a saltine cracker. He handed it to me. Looking down, I noticed that the ground was strewn with pot shards, though all smaller than the one Rhett had found. I looked at it closely. Whoever made the thing had pressed tight, coarse, latitudinal ridges into the damp clay of the pot's exterior with a piece of wood or some such so as to give it a rough texture.

"That is too cool. Why the texture?"

"For better grip. This was a container for carrying water. It got wet when you filled it up in the river. Could get slippery. So they made them corrugated."

"Fuck me."

"I'd rather not," quipped Rhett. He nodded toward the ground. I understood. I put the shard back on the forest floor. "There's probably some old dwelling above this midden. A midden is essentially a garbage dump."

"They still have them in Latin America," I stated absently.

"You've been down south?" Rhett's attention focused on me.

"Yeah—Bolivia. Amazing."

"Me too! I love it. You speak Spanish?" asked Rhett.

"Yeah, not too badly."

"You know that Íngrid Betancourt just got kidnapped by the FARC?"

"Yeah, I heard. She's awfully brave. The FARC have become what they say they fight against. Wouldn't they rather have her in charge than Uribe?" Betancourt was a reformist presidential candidate in Colombia who enjoyed a good deal of public support. She had insisted on a meeting with the Revolutionary Armed Forces of Colombia in an illusory demilitarized zone as a part of her 2002 presidential campaign. She had paid with her freedom and perhaps her life. We walked uphill. Rhett was right. There was a low-ceilinged cave, about five feet high and fifteen feet deep, and within it were several partially collapsed stone walls. Only in a couple of places did the old stone blocks of the walls reach the cave's ceiling. We entered, crouching. I noticed something in the powdery reddish dust on the cave's floor. It was an arrowhead. I picked it up and smiled at Rhett. He approached and spoke.

"Nice point. But it's not Anasazi. Much later. Looks Ute. Other tribes camped in the caves and ruins they found in this canyon while they were here hunting. I always wonder if the Ute knew more about the Anasazi than we do. They knew they were long gone." I put the point back where I had found it despite wanting very much to keep it. We quit the cave and walked once again uphill toward the canyon's rim. I was astonished. It was only our first morning. "So anyway, you were in Poland when the towers came down?"

"Yeah." I was already looking around for the next group of ruins.

"What do you think about that? I mean 9-11," Rhett asked coolly.

"Sucks. Horrible. But there's a lot to understand. Some people have every right to be mad at the U.S., and they sure can't fight the world's mightiest military. They can't get the ear of people here, either. But I don't approve of that method."

"Oh—you get it, then. People who died there didn't deserve it. The government's violence and war-making make it pretty expectable, though. People in this country ought to be scared of their government. Scared of the fights it picks. Scared of what it would do to get its way. Those planes in 9-11 were not enough to bring those towers down. The towers were designed to take an impact like that. They fell straight down. Uneven damage does not cause perfect, total collapse. Neither does a fire. 'Pancaking' my ass. Somebody put bombs in those buildings, and they really knew what they were doing."

"And what about building Seven?"

"Exactly." Rhett's tone had grown hard. "It's tempting to just believe that 9-11 was the price of empire. But it was actually the means to more."

3

The blocky red numbers on my nightstand's alarm read 7:12 a.m. I sat up and tossed aside the blanket and comforter. I threw on my jeans and T-shirt and walked barefoot out the door of my motel room. Three inches of fresh snow sat quietly atop the Best Western's rooftop and upon the manicured grass surrounding the now-covered pool. Leaden clouds hovered low above the motel, and a light snow continued to tickle noses around town.

After an anemic continental breakfast at the Kokopelli Inn, we discovered that the left rear tire on my truck was flat. It would have been foolish go out on a morning like that without a spare, so we waited at the motel while the tire was patched. It would be an hour or so. The tire store was busy, but was a ten minute walk away. Rhett showed up at the motel. We had yet to be over a few minutes late during the first eleven days of install, and he had come looking for us, thinking my truck might have had some problem. Rhett did not own a cell phone. We talked in my room over coffee.

"I know your type. You don't break up with girls. You fire them."

"Why, whatever do you mean, Rhett?" I said drolly.

"You know. You gotta heart like a wheel. Where's the Mouth?" Rhett had chosen a nickname for the still-reticent Scott at some point during the job. Rhett looked older when it was cold out. He clasped his bony red hands around his steaming cup of coffee gratefully. His truck had no heat.

"How about we just go out in your truck? We're already late."

"Sure. Got a big cab."

"I'll get the Mouth."

Outside of town, the clouds had broken up and were sailing off to the east like radiant white schooners in an azure sea of ether. Colorado spun once again in its great arc through space, stuck to the side of the world, fixed in the blaring light of morning and slathered with a generous layer of wet spring snow. We drove northwest on the wet pavement of Highway 666 once again. The desert drank deeply all around us. The sage and piñon pines, the prickly pear, the damp cougars and sardonic coyotes all quenched their thirst. Wet, cabernet-hued sandstone cliffs dripped where they overhung, and the bright white snow at the bottom of washes bruised into gray as it melted into slush and absorbed water from the hillsides above. It was nearly forty-five degrees by 10:30 a.m. We all smiled behind sunglasses. Scott's were new-school, Rhett's cheap and well-used Ray-Ban rip-offs, and mine brand new mirrored state troopers, $5.99 at the Kum & Go. Scott sat in the middle. The smell of coffee filled the cab.

Rhett had become unabashedly polemic after discovering that I had a healthy contempt for U.S. belligerence. He loved to talk politics, and started up anew not five minutes outside of Cortez. "So you said that you believe there are lots of people who have a right to be mad at the U.S. Who?" He half-yelled over the constant strained roar of the engine.

"Oh, God. Well, obviously, people all over Latin America. For our meddling in their governments, for effectively choosing their leaders. Or killing ones we don't like. Like Torrijos in Panama. Guatemala was horrible after Arévalo and Árbenz. We made sure they didn't last long. That was truly awful," I said loudly.

"Yeah, it was. We didn't mind Montt cracking skulls in the countryside, but true reformers can't be tolerated."

"Right. Hell, Guatemala, Nicaragua, and Panama have all come close to having truly representative governments in the last fifty years. But the U.S. removed each one of those budding true democracies. Can't put the rights and well-being of Guatemalan people over those of U.S. corporations. They have every right to resist U.S. free trade bullshit and U.S. corporations. They should be pissed. Nothing's changed since United Fruit. But I think they're out of energy after thirty-five years of war and atrocity."

"Yeah. I think for now they are. But why do you think so many Arabs are mad at the U.S.?" Rhett raised his eyebrows and looked at me sideways. Scott seemed to be listening as he stared at the desert slipping by. The morning was simply resplendent.

"A market-dominant minority that makes its money in oil is quite rich, and most everyone else is fucking poor in the Middle East. But really, it's about..."

"Israel."

"Right."

"And who would like it if the U.S. was hit with the same kind of Arab-authored terror it faces daily? Who was quietly pleased by 9-11?" asked Rhett.

"Oh, man—that's—I don't know about that. Do you believe that?"

"It's true. But no one wants to say it. Wouldn't be the first time either. The Israelis attacked U.S. facilities in Egypt in the 1950s and blamed the Egyptians. To foment hatred between the two nations. The motto of the Mossad is 'By way of deception thou shalt make war.' You don't think that the hawks in the Knesset would be thrilled if we turned Afghanistan and Iraq and Iran into de facto U.S. states? You think we're really after bin-Laden? We are after crude, man! The U.S. has an awfully important pipeline route in Afghanistan. Slowly but surely, our military and Department of Defense is being turned into an oil grabbing and guarding service. The U.S. doesn't fight for freedom. Get real. It fights for power and oil. Fighting's not making anyone free."

"The freest country I've ever been to is Bolivia. And they don't do much fighting," I stated. Scott looked a bit ambushed by all this. We sat quietly for a moment as it sank in. The truck rattled and strained along at sixty. Much to my surprise, Scott spoke.

"I would leave it to you to wonder who did 9-11 and why. How quick this country is to accept war as a first option is what gets me. War is a TV show in the U.S., a video game. It's OK, even good, even at the grassroots level, the same people who send their kids over there think it's not appropriate to even think twice about it. We have some kind of cultural virus in this country." Scott looked straight ahead through the pitted windshield as he spoke.

"That's right, Scott." Rhett's tone was supportive. "Folks here have never seen war up close. On their soil. Not for a hundred and thirty years anyhow. All images of all bazillion U.S. wars were brought to you through a camera or a pen. A filter. People here have more compassion for animals than for other people," Rhett spat.

"Yup. OK, if instead of tens of thousands of civilians getting killed in Desert Storm, imagine that it was thousands of black labs, golden retrievers, and house cats that would be maimed and killed as 'collateral damage.' More or less public outrage?" I offered.

"More. Much more," Rhett stated darkly.

"Maybe that's the biggest reason they hate us. Us 'armed humanitarians,'" mumbled Scott.

4

I walked alone into a broad canyon filled with the low stone footprints of former Anasazi dwellings. We had finished work early after a light final day of install, and Rhett took off to go fishing somewhere. I walked around a few hundred meters from my truck, waiting for Scott and Dean. I let my gaze brush across the ground. It snagged on pot shards and spalls here and there—spalls were chips of chert left over from tool production. At some point my thoughts turned to cannibalism. Christy Turner's variously tedious and fascinating work *Man Corn* offered compelling taphonomic evidence of people whacking one another to death and eating human flesh during the turbulent years of the 13th century in the Four Corners area. But just who was eating whom, and was it a simple result of impending starvation? Could it also have been an integral part of a campaign of terror against the Anasazi, intended to "shock and awe" the people of a culture being victimized by raiders and bellicose opportunists?

Jonathan Haas of the Field Museum in Chicago turned some heads when he brought to light the remains of an Anasazi community near what is now Kayenta, Arizona. The small village actually relocated from its former home in a canyon to a remote mesa top, quite far from water and arable land. Haas concluded that this group's relocation could only have resulted from a need to live in a more defensible place. There was simply nothing that a community of farmers and hunters would have wanted and needed at the new site, especially water. The 13th century was quite possibly a time of sporadic warfare, unexpected raids, and social disarray for the Anasazi, exacerbated, perhaps, by the arrival of nomadic Numic-speaking tribes. Newcomers from the south and west may have encountered the ostensibly peace-lovin' Anasazi and decided to be less than neighborly. Pressure from a number of such groups could have sent the Anasazi into the sides of cliffs and finally out of the area with apparent haste sometime around the late 1200's.

The nature and the quantity of demonstrably cannibalized human remains discovered by Turner certainly suggest warfare and even deliberate terror. Rhett and I had discussed all of this at length. He told me about a body-length cape made of human hair excavated in the Hovenweep area. He followed by describing a recently excavated kiva he had visited; kivas were the wide stone circles sunk into the ground where the Anasazi lived and gathered prior to their move into the cliffs. The smallish kiva that Rhett visited had across its floor, from one side to the other, the complete but disarticulated skeleton of a human female. A little line of bones, too perfect to be authored by nature.

I sang a little Streisand to myself as I strolled around eyeing the ground in the slanting shadows of late afternoon. "People..." I began, "people who eat people, are the wackiest people, in the world." I imagined what it had been like in Hovenweep, the smell of corn roasting in hot coals, still-wet clay jugs returning from the river in calloused brown hands to their homes in the walls, and perhaps someone else, watching from the trees of a nearby mesa, waiting.

I heard Scott and Dean approaching just before they emerged from the trees. Soon we were rolling back to Cortez. All the samples were in the ground, and the archaeologists' jobs were done. We would do retrieval alone.

⌒

I carefully descended a crumbling cliff band on my way down into Yellow Jacket Canyon to retrieve my eighth sample of the day. Two inches of snow lingered in the shade from a little storm the night before. Scott worked off to my northwest somewhere, and our radios weren't doing so well in canyon country, so we walked alone, our thoughts uninterrupted all day now, silent where we had chatted with Dean and Rhett before. Now, we had a chance to behold some of the animals of southwest Colorado. I saw lots of mule deer, cottontails, and turkeys. I saw several bobcats. Bobcats were curious and bold, and would even approach a person or a vehicle just to have a look. I guessed that they had few natural enemies save the bigger cats, who could not easily catch them anyway. I also saw one of the bobcat's favorite meals, the impressively fast black-tailed jackrabbit. The big hare could leap fifteen feet in a single bound once it was running at full speed, this evidenced by their tracks in the snow. That morning, on a mesa top, I found the best and freshest tracks of the job.

Two adult cougars had walked by only moments before. Tiny grains of sugary snow still lingered in a crust on the rim of their prints, melting in the sun as I watched. They might still be only ten or twelve trees away, were surely aware of me, and were also probably aware of what I was— another slow and weak house monkey walking around alone. They would only show themselves if they decided to eat me, I reckoned, and though I might have smelled like an odd sort of lunch to them, I got the impression after three weeks in Hovenweep Canyon that they were pretty well fed. The numerous mule deer loitering in the area looked nervous. The cougar was doing just fine here. Eating a primate would have seemed a bit uncouth to these cats, I hoped.

I felt a little nervous too, but now I was out of the trees and out in the open on a steep slope of rubble and low brush where an ambush would be difficult. I regularly scanned the hilltop above me, however, as I hopped and skidded my way down to the bottom of Yellow Jacket Canyon just as I had three weeks prior. This time, I had a secondary objective. Rhett told me where I could find an extensive and important panel of rock drawing up a side canyon that wouldn't be far out of my way. After finding my next sample and returning it to its bottle, I headed north up a steep draw per Rhett's instructions. I remarked how remote and well hidden the site was, tough to get to without crossing private land on foot. But we had permission.

I rounded a bend in the two-track trail that I followed. The old road had become impassably rough for a vehicle after years of disuse. I knew I had found my goal when I saw a fifty-foot-wide, eight-foot-tall chain-link fence standing before the nadir of a section of red sandstone cliff. Someone at the Colorado Bureau of Land Management had at some point decided that the petroglyphs here deserved some protection. I approached the wall like a kid approaching a tree on Christmas morning.

I walked up and placed my hands on the metal fence. Ten feet behind it was a veritable explosion of rock drawing. There were crude men on horses wearing cowboy hats and wielding seeming rifles, initials and dates from the late nineteenth and early twentieth centuries, and older, more clearly Native American images of deer and men with bows. Just beneath a red patina, the rock was pale tan. By scratching away the red varnish with a harder rock, the lighter rock beneath it could be exposed, a perfect medium for lasting rock art. I walked to the east end of the fence and slipped easily behind it where it met the rock.

The panel was like a thousand-year-old bulletin board. The Anasazi had apparently started it, and were represented well by several images, the most striking of which was some anthropomorphic creature with something like beams of light emitting from its head. There were also more familiar Anasazi forms. A snake. A spiral. A man with a weird hat on. More recent images, ostensibly carved by the latter-day tribes of the area such as the Ute, included a large bird like a heron, some elk, and a human in a cape. Mixed in throughout were the simple names of settlers and travelers accompanied by dates. Some of them had tried their hands at drawing, and a large cowboy occupied a part of the wall, rendered by a hand less skilled but perhaps no less deserving of its chance at expression. It seemed to me that even the Spanish might have put a point to the wall.

After I got my jaw off the ground, I spent an hour looking closely, trying to decipher meaning, and wondering most about the Anasazi-authored humanoid with something beaming out of his head. His head beams were, beyond a doubt, very cool. It was tempting to draw conclusions about some of the scenes depicted that might not have been accurate, but it did look like there were some cowboys with thunder sticks after some natives. It occurred to me to draw two towers with two huge silver birds flying into them, but I decided to leave that to someone else. Still, I thought that the tradition of depicting human life on the wall ought to continue. I took several photos and slipped back through the gap between the rock and the fence, continuing on my way.

The day waned. My boots sat tired on the dark green carpet of my motel room, their tongues dry and wagging. I was feeling capital, watching some hoops and drinking a glass of Johnny Walker on the rocks. I considered playing one-on-one basketball against an Anasazi point guard as Tim Duncan's image contorted and heaved across the screen. If there was anyone I would want to face, it was someone shorter than me. I would get in his head. I would school him. I would hand him his corn. I loved sports clichés. They were among the best and most widely used of all clichés, durable and rugged like the men who used them. I clicked off the tube and walked over to Scott's room. I knocked on the metal door and it opened.

"You ready?"

"Yeah, let's head over."

Rhett and Dean were meeting us at a brewpub down the street, one we could all walk back from. We had offered them the unused queen beds in our rooms for the night if they got too lit to drive home. Rhett would likely prefer his truck and a parking lot. Tomorrow was our last day of retrieval, and a small day at that. We were planning to whoop it up a bit. Cars hummed by as we walked down the main drag in the purple twilight. The air was soft and warm. Cortez could be charming at times.

"So what do you think?" I asked out of the blue.

"About?"

"Doing fieldwork. Working for Falcon."

"It's cool. I'd do it some more," Scott replied with characteristic blandness. We walked some three-quarters of a mile before pushing through the swinging wood-and-glass doors of the pub. It was packed with people and smelled like malted barley and hamburgers. I saw Rhett and Dean sitting off in a corner booth in a big, high-ceilinged great room full of locals and replete with old gray wood. Scott and I moved to the bar in the room's center, grabbed a couple pints, and walked over. We caught Dean in midrant.

"I dunno, she's probably selling lupus memorabilia on eBay or something, I mean," Dean paused briefly and nodded to us as he and Rhett slid across the vinyl bench seats to let us in. "I mean, she never *did* anything, you know what I mean? I will never get married again. Unless she is bootylicious." Dean finished talking as I nearly squirted stout out my nose with laughter. Rhett chuckled.

"The last one wasn't too freaky fly, huh, Dean?" I asked, giggling.

"No," Dean stated.

"She had lupus?"

"No, it was just her fondest wish."

I laughed. "So, glad you two could make it. Beers are on Falcon."

"Cool," Rhett and Dean said in near unison.

"Shit's gonna hit the fan soon anyway. She'll come crawling back after the worldwide infrastructure and economy collapse and the only safe place for her is my cave," Dean stated seriously.

"Your cave?" I asked, preparing for yet another "world according to Dean" soliloquy.

"One Ruger mini-thirty, two chests of ammo, six months' worth of canned food, storage for one hundred gallons of water, a five-thousand-watt generator, lots of gas for that, enough chocolate for three chicks, wine for a month or so..."

"Wait, you've got all this there waiting right now?"

"Well, not exactly—it's at my house."

"Where's this cave?"

"I ain't decided which one to live in yet, but I got my eye on a few. It's going to happen. The collapse, I mean. We're going to hit the worldwide Hubbert's Peak soon. When the world pumps out X amount of barrels and never puts out that many barrels in a day ever again. The halfway point.

The problem won't happen when we run out, it'll happen at the halfway point. World demand keeps going up. World production starts on its way down. Forever down. We might already be there, man!"

"I reckon you're right. I don't need to be convinced." I didn't, but I also didn't want Dean to feel it necessary to get too much further into his favorite rant. I wanted to talk to Rhett. Less dire.

"You know, your skin looks really soft and, and pretty in bar light, Scott," Rhett quipped. He wore a mischievous, beer-addled grin.

"Fuck you, Rhett," Scott said flatly, cracking a smile and sucking on his pint. Rhett had enjoyed ribbing Scott during the job. But we all knew that Scott was pretty tough despite his city-boy appearance and soft-spoken nature. Scott would be sea kayaking along Alaska's grizzly-infested coast in a couple of months.

"Well," continued Rhett, a taught smile on his face, "I hope you guys found us some more oil. And I hope you didn't. It's sure better to find it here than overseas. But when we do find more and burn it, the planet just gets hotter. Even if we didn't find anymore starting right now, and just burned oil that was already drilled and being pumped out, the planet's still gonna go into a coma from heat stroke. A financial one too."

"We'll just switch to coal when the oil runs out. And then it will all be over," muttered Dean, "just two degrees Celsius, man, just two degrees is all it takes."

"The day's gonna come when there'll be no gas in the pumps, no dough in the banco and not much food to eat." Rhett spoke with more than a hint of admonishment, almost as though he addressed a group of oil industry executives. I thought of the bumper sticker on his old Ford, one I had seen before in Colorado. It read: "I'm polluting the atmosphere."

We all had many beers. I wondered to myself during the evening if the brief history of humankind would go something like this: upon reaching industrialization, Homo sapiens collected every last bit of easily recovered carbon from within the earth's crust, burned it to generate heat and electricity, spewed the waste thereof into the atmosphere, and changed the climate enough to render the planet uninhabitable to them. Sounded like something that a virus would do.

Could it really be exit stage left for us, just like the dinosaurs, except that we arranged our own demise? How embarrassing. We set the house on fire to keep warm, and choked to death in the heat and smoke. We talked of less serious matters, drank our fill, and in the morning, Scott and I bid farewell to Rhett and Dean and polluted Colorado's lovely air some more on our way back to the Front Range.

8 THE CONSCIENCE OF THE KING

Judgment comes from experience, and experience comes from bad judgment.

— Simón Bolívar

D RY TROPICAL FOREST surrounded us. Thrashing and chopping through it was more like hand-to-hand combat with a quick and cunning foe than it was like hiking. A sample waited out of sight above us. It was midday, and the Venezuelan sun seemed the eye of some monstrous devil leering down at us, staring with the rapt glee of a child who for the first time has held a magnifying glass at that perfect height above an anthill. It was preternaturally hot. My body pumped out sweat as I leaned into the hillside before me, the steep, barbed, tangled hillside—my machete was already dull. I stopped. I could hear Logan panting behind me. The sunlight came lancing through the gaps in the forest's single canopy like laser beams, searching for us, always searching, turning our skin red and sustaining the legion walls of perniciously thorny low growth through which we whacked. Sweat dripped into my eyes as I stared uphill into the knotted vines and massed thickets of something very much like greenbrier above us.

"Almost there," I said, gasping for air. "There's the first cliff band." We had cut trail for only about a mile, but the resistance had been robust. "It smells hot," I uttered between breaths. It felt like a sauna.

"What?" Logan quacked from behind.

"It even smells hot here," I muttered dully.

"Oh fuck." Logan scanned the rocks and treetops above us with plain dread. "Listen!" he hissed urgently, lowering to a crouch. I held my breath and held still, also lowering. My heart leapt. I jerked my head up and scanned the white limestone cliff above us. There it was. I backed up, panicky and suddenly nauseous. "They don't see us, dude. Don't move fast. Be quiet."

"Right." We retreated carefully down the loose topsoil and scree of the same steep gully we had just fought our way up. We slipped behind cover, turned, and trotted quickly downhill, stopping some hundred feet below.

"Is there another way?" Logan asked quietly, his face close to mine.

"Yeah. We can contour across the hillside, off to the right here, and then we'll head back up a little cliff. It's like a twenty-foot section of steep rock," I was catching my breath, "but there's good holds all over it. Good rock. Roman even followed me up it on install," I whispered, glancing about.

"OK. Lead on. Let's keep quiet though." Logan grinned tautly, his brown eyes wide and full of anticipation. I traversed the irregular blocks and loose ground of the forty-degree hillside as quietly and efficiently as I could. Logan and I were both nimble in talus and unsure rubble, even with packs on. We soon stood below the little cliff I had described. It was hard white limestone, perfect for climbing. Logan stuck his machete beneath his belt and grabbed a hold on the steep rock.

"Mind if I take the point?" he whispered.

"After you," I responded. In twenty seconds of fluid and instinctive motion, we reached the top of the cliff. Standing atop it, I froze. I could hear them again. I dropped to all fours, pulling down hard on the back of Logan's sweat-soaked cotton pants. He instantly dropped to his hands and knees and snapped his head about to look at me. Though I couldn't see them, I pointed toward where their sound was with a slight jerk of my head, careful not to move. I figured they were about fifty feet away. Logan's mouth opened as he heard them. We held still for moment. They couldn't see us, and had therefore still failed to register our presence. We were only fifteen feet from my sample. Two long, pink strips of survey tape were now plainly visible. In another ten seconds, Logan clenched his jaw, turned his face from mine, and began crawling toward my sample through the claws and fangs of the underbrush. I crawled behind him for a few seconds until I was given pause by a hot, orange pain on my right bicep, worse than any a thorn would produce. Before my left hand had slapped my right arm, I knew what was happening. I knew that it was *on*. I also knew somewhere in my mind just what Logan and I would have to do very, very well for the next several minutes in order to avoid a most unpleasant death, but principally, my head filled with the tall flames of abject panic.

"Go! Go, go, go, go!" screamed Logan as I spun in place and sprung downhill to the cliff top. The air filled with a loud and evil sizzling around us. Pain exploded on my face and neck. I looked down and in the same instant jumped off the cliff. Before I hit the ground, Logan was airborne behind me. He hit the steep and rocky hillside beside me with a cry of pain and went into a roll, just as I had. They were well and truly on us. Hundreds of Africanized or "killer" bees had launched a vicious, deadly serious attack upon Logan and me and their numbers were growing fast. But we moved very quickly. It was imperative. If we broke an ankle or leg, though, it was death by lethal injection. I yelled coarsely to Logan, who rolled, slipped, and skidded down the hill to my right at top speed. He swatted at his head as though his hair was in flames. "Fuck!" roared Logan.

"We can do it! Keep moving! We're gonna..." Brown dirt and cactus slammed hard into my face. I had stopped. The plastic belt buckle on my field pants had opened during my flight from the hive and my pants had fallen, gathered about my knees, and completely tripped me. Bees sizzled furiously through my hair and around my eyes. I sat up and reached for the Ka-Bar knife that I wore on my belt, now panicky and nauseous. I yanked it from its scabbard. Pain erupted along every inch of exposed skin as I sawed my pants in half in a flash and launched back to my feet. I careened downhill, crushing bees against my arms, neck and face with my swipes, blood trickling into my eyes and mouth. For the next ninety seconds I was a cannonball, hurtling through cactus and cat-claw vines down the crooked hillside in a bloody blur, screaming and rolling, shoulders bunched, smashing through tight branches without losing speed, knees flying and ankles braced against that one footfall that might break them. My mind had turned off, and I was pure reaction. My heart had never beaten faster. I could taste the adrenaline, unlike any I had tasted before. Two minutes and a few hundred meters later, I was panting and wide-eyed beside Logan on a faint game trail at the bottom of the big hill, and not a single bee was in sight. My ass was a pincushion for cactus spines. I trickled bright red blood from most everywhere.

"Fuck that sucked." I gasped for air and crouched on one knee.

"You OK?"

"Yeah. Something really scary…about getting killed…by bugs, though."

"Yeah. There really is." Logan was drenched in sweat. His curly black hair was wild and full of coarse dirt, and his brown eyes were still wide. His light blue shirt had smudges of blood all over it. He looked at me, and we finally laughed. We hugged. I had never heard myself or Logan scream like that. Logan's right hand was deeply cut and bleeding. We poured a little water on the wound and threw a nitrile glove on his hand, the kind we carried with us and wore whenever we handled a sample. We escaped with around thirty stings each. We began walking back to the truck on the game trail. I walked in my underwear. Some dozen or so locals, mostly farmers and their wives and daughters, would get a big kick out of my lack of pants during our return to the Land Rover. Incredibly, after all that, Logan still clenched his machete.

⌐

Caracas seemed a little surly to me through the taxi's window. Hugo Chávez was digging in for the long haul, and Venezuela was still having spasms as it got used to the brash new president. Bush's "Operation Iraqi Liberation," or O.I.L., was in full swing, and held the attention of the United States, while throughout Latin America, reform-minded, left-of-centrists and populists were peacefully gaining positions of power. To wit, populist Evo Morales was expected to win the presidency in Bolivia. The privatization of the public water utility in Cochabamba had backfired in the face of the Lozada government and a certain giant U.S. engineering firm, precipitating mass revolts and hastening the ouster of now ex-president Gonzales Sanchez de Lozada, or "Goni." An interim president would have to do until January of 2006. Evo wanted to revise Bolivia's Law of Hydrocarbons, ensuring that Bolivia and her people made more money off of the huge new gas reserves recently discovered at Itaú and elsewhere. Bolivia had some darling gas fields, it was true, but Venezuela possessed more crude than all but five nations in the world, and maybe had more than even Saudi Arabia if you counted their unconventional, expensive-to-recover heavy crude in the Orinoco Basin.

Chávez was a self-proclaimed populist in a nation with abundant petroleum. A former Army paratrooper, the "Indian from Barinas" was unabashedly anti-Bush, seemed fearless, could give a mean speech, and perhaps most importantly was ethnically indigenous, a brown-skinned *pardo*, the first such ever to lead the nation. Most of the poor, who were three quarters of Venezuela's population, loved him. Those of the middle and upper classes were in collective shock. However ominously, a handful of anti-Chávez protesters had already been shot by police in the streets of central Caracas, leading to a sense that this new "people's president" might be nothing more than another Latin strongman, and could in fact be the very apotheosis of that tired archetype. He was alleged to be worth a great deal of money, measured not in millions but hundreds of millions, embezzled, many said, from the vast coffers of PDVSA, the huge, corruption-plagued national oil company that he gutted and was reshaping. It was thought that he would soon force all multinational energy firms currently operating in Venezuela to renegotiate their contracts with the state, taking a bigger chunk than former presidents dared. Most of them had been in bed with Big Oil and Washington, two camps that for all intents and purposes had been one and the same for decades. Oil flowed into politics in Venezuela like blood flowing into an erection.

But now Chávez would demand a bigger take from the Exxon Mobils and BP's of the world. Some foreign energy firms operating in Venezuela were paying as little as *1 percent* of their revenues to the state as late as 2004. Hugo would not abide outsiders who sought to bend Venezuelan policies to their advantage and shortchange the country. All this new money, as well as the windfall profits from the steadily rising price of crude, was to be spent for the people, said Hugo. The dough was earmarked for infrastructure, schools, medicine, anything needed by the neglected proletariat, hastened on its way by a revolutionary fervor

that might have made Che proud. Hugo was even talking about—cover
your ears, capitalists—land redistribution. That basic tenet of Marxism,
that property is theft, was threatening to make a comeback vis-à-vis the
encomienda, the large, profitable ranches with native labor and white or
foreign ownership that abounded in Latin America. The thought was to
take some land from certain wealthy landowners and corporations already
making tidy profits on their ranches and farms and redistribute it, hand it
back to subsistence farmers who had been pushed off the same land, land
they once used to raise crops and feed their families. The state as Robin
Hood or something like that.

What Hugo would really do was anybody's guess. Lots of money
had left the country in the wake of his first election victory, and the
international investment climate in Venezuela was stormy at best. Two
U.S. oil giants were about to pull out of the Orinoco. But Hugo would
first have to survive a recall vote, the results of which he had agreed to
abide by; his opposition insisted that this vote would prove conclusively
that most Venezuelans did not want Hugo in charge. Contention was in the
air in Caracas. One thing most Venezuelans agreed upon, however, was
that Hugo ought to stop pre-empting Sunday's soccer games with his often
hours-long homilies, called cadenas, in which he articulated his positions
and his plans for the nation. I learned of these on the flight. I was told
that even his staunchest supporters were no fans of this sort of Sunday
programming, but I could not be sure. One did not typically sit next to
Chavistas on international flights.

Logan and I rolled into the posh Altamira area of Caracas sometime
around 5 p.m. in an airport cab. We had gained several thousand feet
from the airport to the city, and Caracas was pleasantly cool in the shade.
Logan's father's apartment was near the base of a huge forested hill just
north of town called Pico Oriental; many stately deciduous trees had
quit the forest and wandered downhill to homes on the street corners
and in the lovely parks of Caracas' most upscale neighborhood. We were
buzzed through the gate of Carl's complex. Security was robust. People
in Altamira lived behind big walls. We unloaded our kits and hauled
them up a floor on a flight of wide stairs, rang the bell, and were soon
looking Carl in the face. He hugged his son and extended a big, warm hand
to me.

"You must be Tom! Welcome!" Carl was jolly. He wore a black dress shirt tucked into some black slacks, and his shiny black leather belt might have gone around my waist twice. He would have made a great Paul Bunyan had he let his closely shaven facial hair grow out. I followed Logan inside as a young man grabbed my bags. Carl's place lacked neither taste nor style—the walls of his spacious flat were covered with art, and sculptures loitered about his living room. He motioned me to sit on a black leather couch with the air of a man who loved to entertain guests, his bright, handsome face alight with the joy of seeing his son once again. He emanated health despite being so sizable, and his big brown eyes smiled. He had a touch of gin blossom on each cheek, slight jowls, and wispy gray hair that had not receded much and likely wouldn't. Logan was smiling ear to ear. He looked more like his dad when he did. He sat in a chaise lounge that matched the couch.

"What's your poison, Tom?" Carl spoke Spanish fluently and English with a perfect, middle-of-the-country U.S. accent.

"Scotch on the rocks, please, Carl. Thanks!"

"Did you tell him, Logan?" Carl asked mock-seriously.

"Tell him?" Logan asked, perplexed.

"Did you tell him that Scotch on the rocks is the official drink of Venezuela? Do you guys know that Venezuela used to consume more Scotch per capita than any nation in the world? Back during the big oil years," Carl offered. "Dewar's OK, Tom?"

"Yeah, great."

"Same, Logan?"

"Yeah, I'll do a Scotch. Where's Isabela?"

"She went to the store. Be back any minute."

Carl walked our drinks over to us on a silver tray and sat beside me on the big couch. He and Logan caught up as I rose to get a better look at the paintings. I knew that Carl had divorced Logan's mother in the States quite some time ago and returned to Venezuela, where he was born.

"So, what do you think of Venezuela?" Carl asked, looking at me warmly.

"I've really not seen enough to say. Your place is beautiful though."

"You enjoy the paintings?"

"Yes. Very much."

"In America, the man with a little extra money wants new things. In Venezuela, he wants old ones. Some of these pieces are over a hundred years old." Carl grinned at Logan. "You know what, guys? I've seen these walls too much today." He placed his Scotch back on the silver tray. "Let's step out on the town before my dearest returns. I could use a little time with the guys."

Soon we were driving. Carl was ever so pleased. He spoke with Logan about people and places that Logan had not seen for ten years, not since he was last in Venezuela. "Do you remember him? That guy saw every woman he ever met on her back, Logan! So, they've divorced, and she and Isabela like to play bridge, in a club, so we still see Patricia." I watched the people walking along the clean, tree-lined boulevards of Altamira as the afternoon turned to evening, a neighborhood where Hugo had few friends, I imagined. Nice clothes, nice cars, cute butts, French perfume, and shimmering black hair. The upscale neighborhood eventually segued into another less residential one, and we had reached our destination. "But no, we don't see Elian anymore, Logan. Nice place we're going, Tom. You two will like this."

We stepped out of the car as Carl handed the key to a valet. Evening descended on Caracas with the fond and familiar embrace of a lover. We walked across a wide sidewalk and toward the doorway of a freestanding stone cottage tucked amid much larger concrete structures in a seeming business district. It might have been a country pub in Wales. As we pushed through the heavy wooden entrance, Logan, Carl, and I were suddenly met by three Scotch-wielding young women of perilous physical beauty, all promoting some distillery across the pond that had clearly saved some money by cutting back on wardrobe for its sales staff.

"Quieres probar algo especial?" my girl asked, transfixing me with her emerald eyes. I had never seen a more physically beautiful woman.

"Ahhh—sí. Sí," I stammered. Did I want to try something special? Then I realized it was the name of the Scotch they were pimping. "Something Special" was emblazoned auspiciously on the label. I looked at Logan and saw the same giddy incredulity on his face that I wore on mine.

"Have you ever seen the like? And they're giving us free Scotch, bro!" He began chuckling uncontrollably in that special Logan way that made those around him laugh. This time was no exception.

"Oh, English! I speak! What is your name!" My Something Special girl uttered the question like a statement as she stared into the air above the tall, round bar table where the three of us sat. Aphrodite and Shakira could have walked in the bar holding hands and not one of us would have turned our heads.

"Tomas. What's yours?" I asked her.

"Me!" She giggled.

Logan clucked, looked at me sideways, and then back at her. What? She went to scare up some free booze for us as her friends moved to the next table. It was all I could do to keep from staring at them, and then I realized that most everyone else was too. I reckoned it was something like a Latin "Hooters" but for the brass beer taps, endless dark brown hardwood, the huge hams hanging from the ceiling curing, the old claret in the basement, the lead joints in the etched and smoky glass that diffused the reds and yellows of the street—so far, Caracas was doing a great impression of western Europe, and we were spending house money. Carl looked at Logan and me and chuckled.

"You guys just hate working together, don't you?"

"Yeah," we said in unison, bursting into more laughter.

"Do you both like caviar?" Carl asked without looking at a menu.

"Yeah." Also in unison.

"Well, where you are going tomorrow is surely not like this, but I have found a place for you to stay. I have seen the area, and to me, it looks a bit daunting. I have your vehicle arranged, and David will be at my apartment in the morning. You can make it to Cumarebo by 5 p.m. tomorrow, I think."

"Why daunting?" I asked Carl.

"Well, it is steep hills and lots of cactus and it's going to be hot. Now I don't know if the *mapanare* snake is there, but we should assume that, yes, it is."

"And you are partnered with Pinkerton, Carl, or how does that work?" I asked.

"You guys work for me, and get paid in *bolivares*. That way you don't get taxed in the U.S. I'm putting up the money that you guys need to do the field services, and making part of the money that Pinkerton will pay out for the survey. I'm paying for the field services, essentially, in exchange for the good-faith promise of future work, which Pinkerton has already got survey designs for. I would be happy to break even, this time. What's more important is that you guys do your usual good work. I want you to have everything you need, and to be comfortable in the evenings at your accommodations. Because I think this will be a tough job. Even for you two." Carl smiled.

David was chubby, and stood around five-foot-eight. The son of a well-off Caracas businessman, he attended college and was about to earn a degree in geology, but lacked a bit of the field experience that could add depth to both his acumen and resume. His big blue eyes were wide-open and thoughtful above his freckled white cheeks, and a tangled mat of chestnut hair rode atop his big, round melon. His dad was friends with Carl. David would be joining us in the forests south of some place called Puerto Cumarebo on a three-hundred-sample, five-hundred-meter-spaced regular grid survey, the kind that made a hungry field-worker's mouth water. David had the good or bad fortune of being invited to work on a very burly survey.

We were wheeling off to the west of Caracas on a twisting mountain highway. David rode in the back, and was the beer dispenser. After looking at the project maps the night before with Carl and Logan, I felt that this would indeed be a classic "tough guy" job, and David seemed less rugged than epicene at first meeting. He was a pleasant fellow, though, and I already liked him. But he was handing me beer. The fourteen-year-old Land Rover that Carl rented for us felt like it had hexagonal wheels once you got it up to speed on the highway, but the route was beautiful, winding steeply up and down through striking and verdant coastal hills until we had the ocean on our right. It would stay there for the last two or three hours of the road trip. The seawater was now brown with silt some hundred yards out from the narrow, dingy beaches we passed, the way it often was here according to David. His uncle lived in the smallish town to which we were headed. He owned a hotel on the main square, where David would stay. Logan and I were booked into the allegedly lovely oil-dude lodgings of one Playa

Mamon, a guesthouse east of town on the ocean. First, we would drop off David in the center.

It was 5:30 p.m. when we finally reached the edge of Cumarebo. The outskirts of town steamed and shimmered with heat in shades of teal, rose, and orange. Homes and shops wrought of concrete and rebar stood beside those of sheet metal, plywood, and blue plastic tarp. Donkeys and chickens and toddlers crowded the road, machetes were sharpened on the cement of front porches and curbs, and all heads turned to watch us pass. Hips swayed and lips curled. The warm, greasy smell of the little cornmeal cakes called *arepas* and the white, melty cheese served atop them filled the air. Ears of corn roasted, fish dried, brown children hurtled behind all manner of kicked balls, and salsa and *cumbia* songs spilled out of houses and eateries and bars on to the increasingly narrow and increasingly paved streets of the relatively prosperous little town. It was, to my shocked dismay, eighty-eight degrees at this hour in the afternoon, this according to David's cheap little backpacker's thermometer. It was quite humid as well. I noticed that a creek bed beneath a bridge we crossed had more garbage in it than water. All eyes were upon us. Tongues would wag. There were new men in town, and they certainly weren't from anywhere around here.

2

Pucker up, Venezuela, because I've got a big wet one to plant on you. I looked at myself in the bathroom mirror. It was 6:45 a.m., day one of the Cumarebo saga. I did not think that it was too early to use that term. This job had all the earmarks of a whopper. We had a rookie along. We would doubtless encounter lots of thick, steep, and nasty terrain, critters you wouldn't want to tangle with, sometimes evil heat, stimulating bars, cute young women, a beach, and a complete absence of tourists. Cumarebo's arms were already stretched out to embrace us. Or was it to strangle us? We were the only gringos in town, and we were just young and good-looking enough to give pause to the gals. This much we had already noticed. We were in field-workers' paradise.

I thought of shaving and then blew it off. The night was ceding to daylight outside my room's glass windows. A lizard watched me brush my teeth from high on my bedroom wall, and a platoon of teeny black ants were hauling off the crumbs of the late-night coconut cookie I ate before hitting the rack. Our rooms were nice, the property of a strange German man named Gunther who owned and ran the place, a sprawling six-acre affair with grassy grounds running down to the ocean beyond its twenty adjoined guest rooms. It could also boast of a pool, a restaurant, and a bar. The food had been good the night before, but our new *Deutsche* friend seemed to be a bit south of eccentric. It was a very nice place, and probably worth the twenty-minute drive into town to pick up David every morning. Unless the bar at the inn was dead at night, and no local girls ever came out here. I mulled that possibility as I pulled my boots on and put my compass around my neck. I futzed about my dampish room as CNN in Spanish flickered on the screen of a small TV on a chest of drawers. I turned off the tube and the air conditioning, grabbed my pack, and stepped out of my room, locking the heavy wooden door behind me. I went to Logan's room and knocked on his door.

"Sup, dude?" Logan looked as eager as I felt. We walked to the dining area of the inn and to a very U.S. breakfast of scrambled eggs, white toast, and oranges. The coffee was chewy and black, the way I loved and expected it in South America. It was good to be back.

"Got your passport?"

"Got it," I replied, munching some toast with lovely mango jam and fresh, salty butter. We had already been asked for our passports at two gated highway checkpoints. Venezuela kept a close eye on highway traffic, and Logan had also explained that if a cop asked you to buy him a cup of coffee at a stop, you should probably hand him a small bill. It would only set Logan and I back by dimes, and we would be going through a couple of checkpoints regularly.

We drove into town to get David. I already liked the area. Everybody smiled and waved a lot. While Logan could pass for Latino, I stood out and drew attention. I actually enjoyed it. I was something new in a small town, and folks noticed. These were clearly people who liked to laugh and knew how to have a good time, even when they were broke. We'd be around for at least six weeks, we figured, and I already had the distinct impression that we had more than a few memorable days ahead.

⌁

The candy apple laughter of Luis and Diego's children filled the air. They were swarming. David was round and nervous. Roman was grumpy. Logan and I were primed and ready. Diego's pet monkey was berserk and understandably livid. The air smelled like rain.

Diego, Luis, and Roman were our *macheteros*, local guys who would help us cut through the forest and hopefully sidestep the worst these hills would throw at us. Diego and Luis lived within the survey area in a modest house of cinder blocks with their wives and children. Their goats and chickens were in orbit on the cactus-strewn hillsides surrounding their relatively enviable abode. They looked like good woodsmen. They were cousins, and both stood about my height, an inch or two shy of six feet, and looked to be made out of pretty tough stuff as well. They were happy to finally meet us. Their services had been arranged by Carl some weeks prior, and they welcomed us warmly on the dirt cul-de-sac below their house. Luis looked something like a Latino David Letterman, skinny and long-limbed, chipmunk cheeks and squinty eyes, but unlike Dave, Luis wore a wide, coarse, salt-and-pepper moustache, and he acted serious. Two fistfuls of thinning black hair sprouted above his ears and around the back of his head. A quick smile endeared Diego to me instantly. He wore round, wire-frame glasses and an old Chicago Bulls baseball cap, as well a moustache, and carried a bit of a gut. His hale, late-thirties face was creased with laugh lines, and his shoulders were broad and strong. Both of the cousins were brown-skinned and eyed, and had every appearance of hard-working country boys, right down to their flinty expressions.

Roman was a fat townie with a mullet that Logan and I would privately make fun of. I called it a Camaro crash helmet. Logan called it a soccer rocker. He was reticent and surly, an ill-mannered grouch who might not last long. His longish, horsy face fell into a scowl when we resolved to go ahead and work that day. We decided to go out despite massed and swollen rain clouds that flew low and slow above us like Imperial Star Destroyers or thick flocks of flying poison monkeys—I realized how much I hated the cage in which Diego's rancid little "pet" spider monkey was interned. The teeny prison was below their house and above us, fifty feet up the hillside. The poor primate was excited by these strangers, and flung itself wildly about inside a cube of chicken wire the size of a shower stall. Diego asked if I wanted to go see it. I declined.

We piled into the truck as the odd plop of rain landed like a grape on the tin drum that was the roof of the "Biwater." The Land Rover's nickname arose from a mysterious old sticker on its driver's side door. It was going to rain, but when? Smart would have been to take the day off, but Logan and I were looking forward to working in the cool weather, and we had all just packed our gear for the first day of install. But it was going to absolutely dump. The skies would open, but in one, two, or three hours? And just how much water was up there? We drove for a couple miles and left David and Luis at the start to the day's shortest and easiest loop hike.

Our entire geochemical program was south of the river, while Cumarebo and the only reliably above-water road, the highway, was just north. Diego had already explained that the river we would drive over every day on either of two sturdy, state-constructed concrete bridges could be impossible to get back across during a heavy rain event. He and Luis thought that today might be one of those days when no one could return to the highway or Puerto Cumarebo from the hills where we worked. The two bridges in question were typically completely *underwater* after an hour of the heaviest of rains. Big flash floods were an annual event here. The soil was baked and hard in the area, and would absorb little water. Our truck could apparently become stranded in the survey by floodwater in an hour or less, cut off from the highway and unable to return to town. We might end up spending the night at Diego's as a consequence. I looked over at Logan as he drove us to the starting point of the next loop.

"Just get back down to the highway fast if it starts raining hard, all right?" Logan reminded me in English. "Radios on!" Diego grinned at me goofily as we hopped out of the truck and stared into the woods. Logan and Roman sped away, familiar sounds returning as the drone of the four-cylinder diesel engine receded. A rooster crowed. Some cows groaned. Music from a transistor radio in the window of a nearby home floated faintly through the dark morning air like a rumor of another world. We put on our packs and slipped into the trees.

Thirty minutes later, cool water was running down my ass crack. My boots had filled with rain. The steep dirt of the hillside before me was crumbling like brown sugar, slipping through the grasp of the finger-like roots that held it together. Lightning struck itself above me in a dark gray miasma of cloud that had lowered to seeming treetop level, and the loud hissing of strong rain suddenly became the roar of a deluge.

"Diego!" I peered into the forest behind me. I could only see for about twenty-five feet. It was loud. I squinted at the screen of my GPS. We would have to go back. A hand on my shoulder startled me. Diego looked nervous, but smiled and shouted into my ear.

"Será un diluvio! Debemos regresar!"

"Vamos!" We turned in place, and I followed a quick Diego back downhill, slipping and tripping regularly. I called to him, grabbed his machete, and placed both his and mine inside the backpack he wore. It had filled with a couple inches of water in its main compartment, and our bologna sandwiches were floating open-faced within.

"Listo!" I shouted. Diego's agility was on display—I kept up with him only barely as we charged downhill. Thunder sounded like a bomb. Diego stopped quickly and put his hands above his eyes, peering downhill through a gap in the trees. I stopped beside him. We could barely see a creek below us, a hundred meters away, one we had crossed fifteen minutes earlier. It was leaping out of its banks, doing a great impression of a river. We looked at each other and shot quickly downhill. Our window was closing. We did not want to spend the afternoon or possibly the night out in this. I was already beginning to get a chill, something I never thought would happen in the hills outside of sweltering Cumarebo. Diego was starting to shiver.

We were waist deep in fast and pushy water a moment later, moving tensely across the creek, facing each other and holding hands. Four legs were much better than two, a trick I had learned in Colorado and that Diego knew as well. The water looked like boiling chocolate milk, roiling and frothing as the rain slammed into it. Green leafed limbs and logs floated by us regularly in a rush to the sea. Diego's round face was tight with fear, but his mouth formed into a rough smile. We were halfway across, and together we leaned into the strong current as cool floodwater water filled our pockets with dissolved hillside. We lunged for the far shore. We waddled to a relatively firm patch of mud and struggled back up a slippery bank to the dirt road where Logan had left us forty minutes prior.

The radio was useless. Despite our best efforts to keep it dry, water had found it, even inside the pack's best hiding place. I wondered about David. I hoped he and Luis could reach the highway. They could at least return on foot to Luis' house and spend the night there if they had to. So could we, but the plan was to head for the highway, where the truck could collect us all. We walked downhill on the now slick and muddy little dirt road, hoping to reach the westernmost of the two big concrete bridges before it was underwater. Our boots squished and burped in unison. I looked at Diego. He chuckled uneasily. Most of the homes along the unimproved road were made of concrete, often plain, unpainted cinder blocks with rusty sheet metal roofs; many of the owners of these homes were sitting on their front porches watching the storm from behind waterfalls pouring off their eaves. They all waved and some laughed—Diego knew most of them, and they all knew by now what we were doing. Word traveled fast in the countryside around Cumarebo.

The downpour continued unabated as we approached the bridge. We turned a final curve in the road and there it was, barely visible downhill below us. It was underwater. We trotted down the snotty mud of the road anxiously. People were gathered on both sides of the flume, under the eaves of a ramshackle auto shop on our side, and beneath a bus stop shelter on the far side. The forty-foot-long, twenty-foot-wide concrete bridge was a simple slab of concrete without guardrails. What was normally a calm and flat creek flowing ten feet below the span had transformed into a furious torrent crashing into and over it. I had never seen the like. Diego's eyes widened. The watercourse was a vicious cataract. A river-wide curtain of chocolate water shot six feet in the air where it hit the upstream side of the bridge. The waves and holes below were huge and violent, whole trees rushed past, and the water carved out the dirt of the banks like it was ice cream where the river changed direction. A drainage that usually held ten feet of water now barely held twenty-five. The power on display was impressive, and many had gathered to watch, albeit nervously. A couple more feet, and some serious flooding would happen in Cumarebo itself.

It seemed like a bad idea initially, but after taking it all in for a moment, I felt that we could safely walk across the bridge. Only a foot of water flowed across the top, and while it would be hair-raising to sploosh across to the highway side, only by some historic clumsiness would we fall over and be pushed off by a mere twelve inches of water. But the fury below the bridge would be hard to ignore. We wouldn't come out alive if we went in. Some kids would find us washed up on the beach somewhere near the mouth of the river with logs through our chests and bellies full of mud, I imagined. I looked at Diego and shrugged my shoulders. He knew what I meant. We walked across through a foot of opaque, coffee-colored water without incident, prompting a few others who were not on the side they wanted to be on to follow suit. Soon young boys were running back and forth across the bridge for sport. We hollered at them, but were ignored. They couldn't hear us in the still-heavy rain.

We walked to the bus stop and joined those gathered beneath a loud metal roof the size of a two-car garage. About a dozen people stood, sat, and crouched there, all watching as water began to find its way out of the big gulley and across the low ground beside it, toward the bus stop and the highway. I didn't even know the river's name. I asked a shivering Diego.

"El rio," he answered. I laughed. I smiled at a couple blokes smoking smokes and trying to stay warm beside us.

"Estan secos?" I asked, pointing at their surprisingly dry smokes. Both men were soaked.

"Si. De la tienda ahí," the man said, pointing across the street at a sundries shop. I told Diego I was going across the street to the store. I felt that we could be waiting there for some time, waiting all day maybe, as Logan and the truck might be trapped somewhere by floodwaters. I worried less about him than David. Diego was cold, and even I was getting there. I walked into the store knowing just what we needed. Rum, and plenty of it. I squished into the poorly-lit little *tienda* and asked for some smokes and a bottle. I produced my soaked wallet and a wet bill, wishing that we didn't have to carry our passports on us at all times, for mine was swollen with water. The woman handed me a big glass bottle of clear rum, giggling and staring out her front door expectantly. The rain was letting up slightly. I walked back over to the bus stop, screwed the top off of the bottle, and handed it to Diego. His face brightened as he took a deep pull, smiling and passing it back to me. I took a big gulp and handed the liquor to the guys with the smokes. They grinned widely and thanked me. After they each took a swig, they returned the bottle. I passed it to a plump woman in a soaked blue dress seated with her daughter on the concrete bench of the bus stop. She smiled and pulled on the rum, wiping her mouth with the back of her hand. Soon the bottle had made a complete round. Everyone drank but the girl.

After another hour, the rum was running low and the rain had almost stopped. The water ceased rising. Many people now walked across the bridge. The first car crossed, and then another. Diego and I were warm again thanks to the booze, and joked with a few guys who lingered, watching the river. We all quit the bus stop as the rain finished and went to stand near the bridge, marveling at the water's power. A group of people walked down the road from the hills of the survey area toward us. They crossed the bridge. Now, the still furious water flowed a few inches below the span. Most in the group of six adults were sobbing.

They spoke with pained faces to some gathered. One of the men explained to the assemblage that a woman had lost her life somewhere above us, in the hills, when she tried to pass through a low area filled with rushing floodwater in her car. Her body had not been found. Diego grimaced and shook his head.

"Que locura," he deadpanned. "What madness." Death was treated a bit differently in the Venezuelan countryside than in the United States. This was no tragedy to Diego—it was someone who had paid dearly for stupid behavior. I wondered how stupid we had been. We waited another hour before a soggy and bemused Logan drove with Roman across the bridge. He had been pinned down on a high point on the dirt road, unable to drive forward or back, and had waited with Roman as three feet of water crept up the Biwater's sides. I asked if he had heard the news.

"Yeah, dude. That sucks." He wrung out his soaked Yankees cap, producing a half-cup of water. Roman looked a little freaked out. "Where do you think David is?"

"At his uncle's, I hope. Or at Luis' house. If he turned around and bailed back to the highway at first rain like we told him to, he oughta be back in town by now."

"Let's run Roman into town and go by the hotel." Diego and I hopped in the Land Rover. Much to our relief, David had indeed walked down to the highway when the heavy rain started and hitched back into town.

Luis had simply walked home. We were relieved to find Davy seated comfortably at his uncle's hotel in dry clothes. We dropped off Roman, drove all the way back into the survey area to bring Diego home, and finally headed out to the Playa Mamon with water on the brain.

3

A puppy, a spaceship, and a penguin advanced on us. At least according to Andreas, the young son of the Playa Mamon's owner. We were watching thunderheads boil and rise over the hills of Cumarebo, picking out shapes in the gray and white billows as Logan checked us out of the lodge. We were moving to hotel rooms in Coro, having grown tired of the overly intimate and cloyingly cordial Playa Mamon. And it really had no beach either, as its name suggested—just a narrow strip of dirt between the brown sea and the neatly cut grass of the inn's grounds.

I looked at the sky. I saw a gnome having sex with a pickup truck and a boneless clown doing Pilates. I kept my impressions to myself. Logan walked back over to where I sat with our bags; he was grumbling about the final bill, and the fact that Gunther wanted to catch a ride into town with us. Gunther and Andreas rode in the back of the Biwater as we pulled out of the Mamon's paved, coconut-tree-lined driveway. All our considerable luggage was piled behind the bench seat upon which they bounced. Gunther had the demeanor of a jilted lover.

"Where will you stay now?" he asked.

"At the Intercontinental," Logan half growled as he gripped the Land Rover's big black steering wheel. I smiled, happy to have a morning off. My legs were a little stiff and sore.

"But it costs more, yes? I can make a better deal for you, you know this?" The German had only five other guests during our two-week stay. His former potential resort destination was not doing so well, and the new mood and president in Venezuela weren't helping matters.

"Gunther, we're not even paying, the client is. And we want to go out at night. It's dead out here at night. We like Coro. There's something to do after work there."

"And someone," I remarked.

"I can maybe get some girls to come out here, yes?"

"No. Discussion over, dude," Logan grunted. He looked over at me, grinned, and rolled his eyes. We were both quietly thrilled to be changing our location.

"OK, OK. You are free to do as you wish, of course."

"Oh, thanks. Thanks, Gunther," quipped Logan.

Gunther and little Andreas soon disappeared beneath the blue tarps of Cumarebo's main market. Logan and I continued into town and stopped to get coffees and nice croissants stuffed with eggs and cheese. My favorite barista was helping me, a stunning green-eyed and brown-skinned girl named Mai. After two weeks of breakfasts in the bustling and worn little store, I had started calling her "Sea Sugar."

"Mmmm. Sea Sugar's lookin' *good* today. I love her little skirt." Logan said in the code that was English. We both leaned into the high counter, smiling mischievously at Mai and her colleague Jennifer, which in Cumarebo was pronounced something like "jayngifer." I wished I was eighteen. We walked back and got in the truck.

"Where's all the twenty-something girls, man? It's time I got serious about catching one of these cuties," I complained.

"They're married! Makin' babies. But that's why we're going to Coro, bro! Bright lights, big city! You'll have no trouble there!" Logan was as usual enjoying the hell out of himself no matter what we were doing. I loved working with him. I held his coffee for him as he cranked the not-so-power steering wheel of the Biwater. We took a tight right and then another. Cumarebo's people walked and chatted and filled the narrow streets, a farmer harangued a street vendor, overalls stood beside miniskirts, and many still spoke of the flood. We stopped before the hotel on the square where David stayed every night. He emerged and hopped in the back, smiling and nodding to us as Roman rose grudgingly from his shady park bench and got in the other side. Now, as we had done so many times before, we would drive up into the hills, pick up Diego and Luis at their home, and drive further still to where our hikes would begin.

"I want one just like Sea Sugar, but not so, uh…"

"Fresh off her mom's tit?"

"Yeah. Less wholesome. Less trouble, anyway." And then there came the strangest noise. I thought at first, before even turning my head, that David was suddenly revealing a sense of humor heretofore unknown to us. As we rounded the plaza to head south out of town, a sound grew in the back seat, and it came from David's mouth. I turned my head around, thinking that David was unfurling some joke or prank upon his unsuspecting new friends. Nothing could have been further from the truth. David was having a full-blown and to all appearances epileptic seizure. I sprung into the back seat after a second of stunned disbelief and placed my hands on his head— he was in danger of swallowing his tongue. Every muscle in his body was taught to the point of snapping bones. His eyes were rolled back. He had involuntarily torn the inside handle from the truck's door. He half-moaned and half-choked out a loud, gurgling death rattle that was scaring the shit out of Roman. His tortured mouth foamed.

"Go to the clinic, dude. Go to the clinic!" I barked at Logan. "He's fucking epileptic. Oh my god, no way."

In ten minutes we had reached the clinic, all sick with concern for Davy. I called his uncle on our cell and he arrived there promptly, accompanied by his wife and their son. David was on his back in bed when they entered the room at the tidy little clinic. He was regaining consciousness.

David's aunt spoke to us in English. "He ran out of medicine. More arrived this morning, but last night there was none," she explained. "This would never happen when he takes his pills." Her face was filled with both concern and a touch of embarrassment. "We should have told you."

"Yes. He can't work anymore," Logan responded. "It's too dangerous. We really like David. We can't let anything happen to him." Logan's perpetually eager face was now somber.

"Let him work. Now, he has his medication. He will be fine. I give you my word. I take full responsibility. It would hurt him more if you send him home right now," his aunt beseeched. David looked up from his hospital bed.

"Logan, Tom—¿Que pasó?" He smiled weakly.

Coro was not beautiful, nor was it celebrated, and for it good fortune had made no exceptions, but Coro looked up to no one save God, and at times its honking and bumping and clanging seemed to me a joyous noise. With its car radios blasting the bubble gum pop music that was *cumbia*, its sardonic ranchers riding hot horses through dusty outskirts, its fishermen fishing, its office workers being official, Coro for the most part enjoyed being Coro. The seaside town could even boast of a bit of history. A Venezuelan revolutionary named Francisco de Miranda landed a force of men in Coro in 1806 and declared Venezuela's independence from Spain, however prematurely. That independence would not be enforced with any might until 1813, but the move proved prescient, as a scant few years later the same new patriots were led to eventual victory over the Spanish by the continent's most towering post-Colombian figure, that of Venezuela's Simón Bolívar. Francisco de Miranda would die in a Spanish dungeon. Most of Spanish America was freed just fourteen years after his ignominious death.

All but the wealthiest and drunkest in Coro were stirred to consciousness every morning by a steady and wicked heat present in all two seasons, these dry and rainy. A stiff wind often blew out to sea, pushing plastic bags and yesterday's newspapers into the weeds and willows of the town's waterfront, giving the impression that trash was not collected but distributed. But most of Coro was fairly tidy. Two hotels were the tallest buildings in town at around eight stories, and it was a rather average Latin American town of twenty thousand people. It had a couple restored colonial churches, an extensive, bustling, and stinky open-air market, and most of its homes and structures were concrete-walled and sheet-metal-roofed.

Logan and I were at our favorite bar in the middle of Coro. We were having nice cold beers after a rather casual day of work and an early return to town. To our left at the long wood bar sat our new gringo friend Benjamin, and Ben was on his soapbox. He drank lots of Scotch. He liked to talk, especially with two relative youngsters fresh from the United States. He had the pink face of a heavy drinker, buzz-cut blonde hair, wore new school and dark sunglasses, and might have been fifty. It was our third such session with the American ex-pat, a former oilman himself, a fifteen-year resident of our own Coro, of all places. His wife's family lived there.

"What a funny thing is happening in America! The Bush administration just filled a tall glass with mustard, put a dollop of refried beans in it, and called it a root beer float enough times that it's become the best root beer float ever! Perception is reality now! As Joe Goebbels said, 'there is no doubt that repetition makes people more likely to believe things for which there's no basis.' America keeps drifting slowly and surely away from its Constitution and that inconvenient little Christian 'Thou shalt not kill' thing. Now, they even admit they want to appear 'irrational and vindictive' to the rest of the world. And then they say that democracy is just what the nation with the world's third-largest oil reserves needs. And it just happens to have what the U.S. needs too," bellowed big Ben. He wasn't quite drunk yet.

"Oh, bro, tens of thousands Iraqi civilians have been killed by these 'smart' bombs as these 'imbedded' journalists make sure to avoid sending shocking photos and stories back to the States. What are they guilty of? Living in a Muslim country with lots of nice oil that the U.S. could invade without causing too much of a fuss. Hey, they *looked* like the people who brought us 9-11! Look at 'em! Bush said 'Sadaam' and '9-11' enough times in the same sentence that no one remembered that the hijackers were Saudis," offered Logan loudly.

Ben continued. "Right! But no Tonkin Gulf incident could be cooked up this time, so WMD's had to do, and Hussein's record. Sadaam *did* gas the Kurds, one of Turkey's favorite pastimes, and he used gas supplied by, well...us! But he was much less scary than the Iranians, and he hated them too, just like we did. He was *supposed* to gas them. Sadaam will survive the war and end up in a courtroom somewhere, but ten thousand John al-Does will feel the wrath of the strongest military in the world in their bathrooms or their gardens or putting their kids to bed in a high tech flash of death." Ben's face was beet red. He emphasized the flash of death part with a two-handed gesture. "Sadaam did have blood on his hands, and he was a bad dude. But he had a lid on Iraq. An invading force is gonna have to use the same tactics in order to maintain order among the sects and gangs throughout the country. Sadaam was more like Tony Soprano than Osama bin-Laden. Iraq had a secular government. They had some of the most educated people in the area. They had better infrastructure than everybody but Saudi. But *we* were better qualified to decide how their young, tense little nation should be run. Democratically. But that don't always work."

"Doesn't even work for us, apparently," I added.

"No, wait, now listen to this. I'm going somewhere with this. A slaughter of a whole different kind happened eight years ago in a country that was embracing this new form of government, this democracy, the way according to the U.S. that every country ought to be run. Rwanda. Suddenly Rwanda in the nineties had real democracy, not the fake kind, not the sort of oligarchy in sheep's clothing the U.S. likes, like here in Latin America. No, Rwanda had legitimate elections, good turnout, a free press, hell, Amnesty International itself encouraged it, and then, in 1994, a million Tutsis were murdered in an fucking blood orgy, slaughtered by hate-fueled, roving gangs who used machetes and clubs to murder their defenseless neighbors and their children, sparing no one. Think about that. A million. The U.S. couldn't have given a *damn*. What was in it for us? For generations, the whiter Tutsis had been a wealthy minority and the Hutus did all the work, were looked down on by the Tutsis, and were pissed. But wait! Democracy was coming, sweeping the globe! Suddenly, the Hutu had a voice! 'Hutu pride' was a slogan! They organized, voted, rallied to cries for an awakening by *Kangura*, the Hutu newspaper. The next step was mind numbing." Ben caught his breath.

"And then there's Venezuela," Logan chimed in. "Hugo's democratically elected. And now the U.S. has one of the most anti-capitalist leaders in the world as a neighbor. And he doesn't need an army or some terrorists to fuck with the U.S. He has his hands on the tap. He can take the bottle away and lock it in the cabinet."

"Yeah, that's right. He was elected all right. But he's the king of Venezuela. What's the king really want to do?" Ben smiled slyly, finished his Scotch, and ordered another. "You guys want one? I'm buying." We both nodded.

4

Like a fireman who runs back into a burning house to retrieve a child's doll and, upon returning it, is told that the doll "had a hat," Logan and I had just been informed by the grand pooh-bah at Pinkerton energy

202

that while they were fairly pleased with the job to-date, they would need to reconsider before doing further geochemical surveys. Though we all parted with smiles and congratulatory handshakes as we got in the truck, Pinkerton's regional exploration manager Hans seemed underwhelmed, not primarily with our speed, which had been mentioned, but with the method itself. While tales of frequent Africanized bee attacks and a major flash flood served to explain why we had not worked as fast as a crew of field droids might have, the method itself was hard to swallow for some exploration heads who had spent their whole lives applying armies of seismic workers and geophysicists to the problem of finding economic quantities of oil. Hans didn't like our sniffers, and had brought up all sorts of reasons why they might not work.

Hans likely arrived in Cumarebo with some prejudice toward soil-gas exploration. Someone else at his company probably bought the survey over drinks at some restaurant in Dallas or Sacramento or Tulsa, and that someone was probably not a geophysicist. Logan and I both felt a little miffed as we drove back toward Coro. We had only a week left with David, Diego, and the boys. David's family told us not to worry about him every day when we dropped him off at their hotel after work, as well not to speak of epilepsy, for his condition was something different, they explained. Maybe it was. He had begged us to let him stay, resumed taking his meds, and had worked eagerly and productively since his seizure. Our hats were off to him. I braked the Biwater to a slow roll at a police checkpoint between Cumarebo and Coro. A familiar, smiling cop waved us through.

"Do you want to go to Coco's? After we go shower?" The sun was nearing the horizon directly ahead of us in the effulgent orange haze of smog and dust above Coro. We had grown to like the town's great bakeries and fancy breakfast and coffee shops, its quality seafood restaurants, its nightlife—but we had yet to go to Coco's. It was Coro's hottest strip club.

"Yeah! We have to check it out before we leave. Diego seems to think it's some sort of paradise."

"I know. Let's go."

Logan and I drove across town with plastic-lidded Styrofoam cups filled with ice and Scotch whiskey between our thighs. We slurped our drinks through straws. I drove. Not illegal as long as we weren't crashing into anyone. It was twilight, and the heat was easing.

"Are we becoming alcoholics, Logan?"

"Becoming?" He smiled wryly from the passenger's seat, his white teeth bright against his deeply tan face and dark stubble.

"I mean, I don't know how much longer I should keep this up. We killed that bottle last night in three hours."

"I know, bro. We're bad. Bad influences on each other. We have too much fun."

"Actually, technically, we're not alcoholics," I mused, "we're power drinkers."

"Yeah, that sounds much better. But it's true, bro. The only stuff we're addicted to is adrenaline and endorphins." I merged the Biwater into light eastbound traffic on the highway out of town, the same one we took every morning to Cumarebo and the jobsite. Our new hotel's air-conditioning and restaurant were worth the half-hour commute, and while modest, Coro's nightlife hadn't been too bad. But most women within fifteen years of my age were indeed married, and those who weren't wanted pretty boys their own age, not Scotch-chugging, thorn-scratched weirdos from Gringolandia. Logan pointed out the little dirt road to Coco's in the fading light of early evening. I pulled into the highway's dusty median, stopped, and crossed the two westbound lanes of the highway through a gap in traffic. We followed the little road through a scrubby field to an island of trees and a low, orange-hued cinder block building with a rusty sheet metal roof. Four cars were parked there. A single naked light bulb glowed dimly above a gray wooden door with a big brass knob, one you would likely need an oven mitt to open during the heat of midday. But the sun was down now, and the sky had turned deep violet and dark blue above us. We parked, locked up the truck, and walked to the entrance.

We pushed our way inside. In an instant we knew that this was no high-class joint. I threw my empty Scotch cup into a metal trashcan that was once a paint bucket as the heavy metal door shut behind me. A surly bouncer sat on a stool near the door. He grinned at us lewdly, revealing an aversion to dental hygiene.

"Bienvenidos, gringos!" he hissed, appraising us. We walked to the bar. It was sticky and brown. I removed my elbows from it as soon as I placed them there. A woman emerged through swinging wooden half-doors to serve us. There were only five or six other people in the room, and they didn't seem to notice us. A small TV crackled in the corner. A low stage with two brass poles faced the bar across the room, and several square wooden tables stood around behind us. The place smelled like stale sweat.

"Algo para tomar?" The bartender looked like a weed in autumn. She wore what seemed to be a nightgown in a bad shade of teal.

"Whiskey para mi, con hielo y nada mas." Logan likewise ordered a whiskey on the rocks, which here meant bourbon. The bartender sat two drinks in plastic cups on the bar before us with a subtle smile. Logan asked her if there were any dancers on the itinerary. She said that there was no performance tonight. She disappeared through the swinging doors behind the bar. A moment later, two young women emerged from a hallway that led someplace other than simply to the restrooms. They sat beside us on stools at the bar and introduced themselves. Mine was named Olivia. Suddenly my libido was like a full-size household refrigerator tumbling end-over-end down the very steepest of hillsides with good speed, its doors flying open and off, pound cake, salmon, and ketchup flying out—Olivia was outrageously fetching. Logan said a quick hello to his new friend. I proceeded to introduce myself to mine.

"You dance here?" I asked in Spanish.

"Yes. But not tonight." Olivia's eyes smoldered.

"Where you from?"

"Maracaibo. Outside of Maracaibo," she said slowly in syrupy Spanish. Olivia's bee-stung lips were neatly coated with lipstick in a shade of dusty red rose. Her big green eyes looked bored, and her cherubic, porcelain face recorded some disappointment. Her straight black hair spilled halfway down her back. I bought her a drink, and her face brightened slightly. We talked. She was twenty-five. She had a kid who lived with her mom when she was working. She hated Coro, but made more cash here than in Maracaibo. Here she was the prettiest girl in town. She liked rum and Cokes. By the time the barkeep had brought her a third, she was leaning nearer to me. I could smell her hot breath and her perfume, both sweet like the sugary drink glistening on her lower lip. Her eyes lit up to an emerald incandescence. Her hand was on my thigh, her sticky mouth on my ear, whispering. Her grapefruits pressed into my arms. Her tongue found mine like a big wet nightcrawler. She was wise to the rise in my Levis. I ordered another bourbon. She asked if I wanted to go for a walk. Did I want to do this? Most of me did. Or was it the least of me? Was she a dancer or a working girl? Was there a difference? I turned to speak with Logan.

"Dude, I'm thinking of going on a walk with Olivia."

"Do it." He laughed. Logan's girl had given up on him. She seemed to have a cold. He had explained to her that he had only come to see the show and keep an eye on me. "I'll have another Bourbon or three." Olivia was getting silly and playful. She put her hand on my crotch.

"Are you ready?" she purred in Spanish.

"Yeah, I think so." And that was when the cops arrived, en masse, through the main entrance to Coco's. One of them approached us directly. He asked us for ID. I was quickly escorted out of the bar. I would sit in the back of a paddy wagon for thirty minutes before Logan could convince the Man to let me go. Whether Olivia was just a dancer or was in fact a prostitute was not an issue. Prostitution was legal in Venezuela. My only infraction had been my lack of a passport. My new friend was somewhere behind the locked doors of Coco's when I stepped down out of the van and got back in the Biwater. The evening was over. Logan and I drove home laughing.

"Bro, she was hot! You should have seen the look on your face when she sat next to you!"

"Oh, dude! I love her! I have always loved her!"

"I know, bro, I know. You and every other guy who's ever laid eyes on her!"

It was the final day of retrieval. The Biwater and the six of us had once again come under attack by bees as we exited the truck near a roadside sample due for plucking. We were just out of our seats when they hit us with typical fury. We ran up or down the road away from the Land Rover which, filled as it was with sweaty, salty packs and work shirts, was set upon by crazed *Africanas* mistaking these human-scented items for humans. We all stood a safe distance away, but soon realized that we would have to retake our ride, and the price could be pain and drama. Logan and David were above the truck with Luis. Diego, Roman, and I had bolted downhill. We stood around staring at the truck and each other for five minutes as the bees laid into our gear. Suddenly, David broke into a sprint for the Biwater.

Our jaws dropped. Davy had lost some weight on the job but was still chubby, and his belly bounced about before him as he picked up speed. His eyes were wide as saucers. His feet slapped the ground and his arms jerked back-and-forth with complete conviction. We all watched intently—David had vowed that no seizure could take him so long as he took his medication, but what might twenty bee stings do? My jaw tightened. Davy was nearly at the truck when he took the first two hits to his face. He slapped his cheeks as he reached the open driver's side door. He hopped in and quickly found the key, his face a mixture of horror and cringing purpose, the air around his sweaty, freckled dome thickening with bees.

"Go, Davy! Go!" I hollared.

The truck roared to life. David popped the clutch and the Biwater leapt forward, heading straight for us. David waved to us, motioning us off the road. The three of us crashed into the brush as the truck rattled by, picking up speed and the rush of air that would hopefully push most of the bees out of the truck. Davy was doing almost fifty as he wheeled out of sight on the narrow road. We listened anxiously. The sound of the Land Rover receded into the distance and stopped. We stepped back onto the road anxiously. Logan and the others came running down to join us.

"Bro! What got into him?" Logan cackled.

The sound of the Biwater returned. It was going slowly now. It approached. As it came around a corner and we all saw a smiling David, we let out a great cheer, hands in the air, faces alight with relief and pride. The city boy had created his own rite of passage and passed it with aplomb. David would later tell me and Logan that working with us had been the greatest adventure of his life. He told us that he would follow us anywhere, and that he wanted to work with us again more than anything. We were both genuinely moved by his courage and his fealty. If Falcon gave out medals, David would have one. As Logan and I left Venezuela, I guessed that we were unlikely to work in a significantly more perilous place anytime soon. I was terribly mistaken.

9 CHILDHOOD'S END

Africa is poor because its investors and its creditors are unspeakably rich.

— Naomi Klein

THE YEAR OF 1996 was an important one in Gabon. While crepes and sevruga were served in the restaurants of Libreville and foreign oil companies ferried hardware on flatbed trailers through the wide, hot streets of Port Gentil, the West African nation that had enjoyed three decades of prosperity finally arrived at that day that all nations blessed and cursed with oil reach—Gabon in 1996 reached peak oil. A nation that once led not Africa but the world in per-capita champagne consumption, Gabon had basked in the strong sunlight of easy money for almost all of Omar Bongo's remarkably long tenure as president, the longest in the contemporary world other than Fidel Castro's. Mr. Bongo occupied the post in 1967. The party had been cool if you could get in.

Gabon became an official nation in 1960, but was chaperoned closely by its French viceroys and foreign investors. Gabon never deteriorated into the chaos and violence that many of its neighbors did. It was special, many believed, and was even compared to nations like Kuwait when its first oil wells came in often and strong. The little nation had enough oil, in fact, that its relatively progressive leadership would develop the sort of modest public works and infrastructure that tended to make a rather broad group of lives better. There was even enough money left over to line the pockets of some big oil bosses and grease the wheels of the political machine when necessary. Gabon had enjoyed its prosperity, but seemed also to feel that it would never end.

But that was the sort of notion that drinking too much champagne might engender. By 2005, Gabon's nationwide oil production had fallen by a full third. This was no gradual decline. This was falling off a cliff. During the eighties and nineties, when the price of crude had often been low, Gabon borrowed money from the West. Now, about half of the nation's revenue was swallowed up by payments on those loans, and while the wild rise in the price of crude was helping to offset the drop in production, the writing was on the wall. The end of easy money was visible in the distance and closing fast.

Still, there were new discoveries to be made in Gabon, as the recent development of the nifty Atora oil field near Sette Cama on the southern coast demonstrated. Some geologists felt that more product lingered in an area to the north of the newly completed Atora facility and east of the great Loango national park, but how to explore it? Except for her two aforementioned port cities, the entire seaboard of Gabon ran wild. The establishment of Loango ensured that at least for the time being, one hundred kilometers of West Africa's most pristine coastline would remain untouched and uninterrupted, perhaps the only place in the world where wild elephants could be found walking upon the beach and even into the ocean's surf. They lived in a jungle and an ecosystem that could be accurately described as intact in 2005, home to an unrivalled array of megafauna that seldom if ever saw humans. Rich and expansive swaths of wet forest beginning just out of the ocean's reach on the beaches of Loango and stretching to the east in a vast green blanket were wholly unmarked by man, crossed only by the sort of avenues made by *Loxodonta africana cyclotis*, the same forest elephants that trod the beach, the undisputed kings and queens of Gabon's jungle. Here was a true no-man's-land, richly populated even in the twenty-first century with creatures that had never before gazed upon a human walking on foot.

Why did Gabon possess such wilderness? Gabon achieved her independence from French Equatorial Africa in 1957. While many of Gabon's fledgling neighbor states sold off their primary rainforests as timber, Gabon instead began selling its significant oil, the extraction of which was vastly less destructive to the forest. This jungle was not just a stunning place, but was one of the planet's largest lungs, second only to South America's Amazon. The productive Gamba and Rabi oil fields were like little metal islands in an ocean of green, and only by plane could the former be reached. The Rabi field could be gained via a very long truck ride from Fougamou to the north, and though a narrow dirt road continued further still to the new Atora field and lake Ndogo, the crude brown ribbon might be quickly rendered impassable by huge fallen timber and was the only road in a vast, uninterrupted carpet of flourishing wilderness. It could be argued that were it not for the oil, Gabon would have exploited its other natural resources to a much greater degree.

And now, the search for oil continued. The four of us sat on a turboprop plane winging its way south to Gamba from Port Gentil. We were reasonably tough and smart, as ready as we could have been, perhaps, but in the Congo, a creature so defenseless as man walking remotely beneath the double canopy and through darkly fertile bogs could ill afford to drop his guard, even briefly. Here, a team of four top Falcon guys and four equally well-suited locals might amount to nothing more than a box of toys. This was different than the jobs in the *junglas* of South America. The jungle's tenants were bigger here. Bigger and badder. While the Congo's animals could little resist the machines of man, they would suffer no fools on foot, no weak-looking and slow creatures sputtering about in groups of two balanced on their hind legs. Especially not in the backyard, where the kids played.

2

All eyes around the tarmac were upon us. A group of locals leaned into a tall chain-link fence enclosing the airstrip near a whitewashed concrete kiosk, the passenger exit. A hot sun ran smoothly across an empty blue sky upon its sidereal track. New white guys were here. Well, maybe. But who cared? They had big smiles. Yeah, but what were they doing? Working in the oil field? No. Too scruffy. They were met by one of the Vigons, the Frenchmen who operated the big fishing and guiding business outside of town. They must be going tarpon fishing. The old twin-prop plane continued spilling its passengers and cargo into the shimmering heat of mid-afternoon.

Wait—look, now—they're young. And not fat. They're carrying their own cases. And there's that handsome Jean Luc boy, Giselle's son, here to meet them. Off they all went toward Gamba in two nice Toyotas. Didn't he say he was going to work in the jungle soon? Those white boys were different, thought Sylvia. She shouldered a bag of fabric and sundries that had come on the plane and contained, she hoped, a vial of special perfume sent by her cousin in Libreville. She began walking toward the paved parking lot adjacent the airstrip. She scanned the vehicles there, searching for someone who could take her back to town. It was a long walk.

"Amelie!" Sylvia shouted. A pickup overloaded with white sacks of flour and sugar and a couple of open-air passengers was heading back to town. It stopped. Sylvia walked purposefully across the lot to where the truck waited. She slung her bag on her back and crawled atop the pile of goods to sit near her friend. The truck returned to motion as she found a good spot.

"Who were those white boys?" she asked mischievously.

"That's them. That's the ones I told you were coming." Amelie smiled.

I awoke upon a bed that I would learn to adore. Mosquitoes swam upstream against the current of cold air exhaled by an air-conditioner in the wall above my pillow, the fittest reaching my bare arms, chest, and face. I was awakened by their attentions, and sat up wondering if I ought to have started on a regimen of chloroquine. I swung my legs out of bed and stood. First light glowed in the east outside the horizontal glass slats of my closable window. I dialed it closed and walked to a chest of drawers upon which my clothes from the night before waited. I put them on. I opened the metal door to my room and stepped outside. Hot, wet air enveloped me and barged into my quarters. Before me were a gravel parking lot and a tennis court within a chain-link fence. I looked to my right. There was a light on in the room where Marcus slept. Behind and beyond our neatly whitewashed strip of adjoining cinder-block rooms, enormous and burgeoning trees fingered the sky, their limbs softly rolling in a light breeze, their leaves still black in the dimness of morning. A strange bird croaked from somewhere high above on a favored branch. Below the hill where our building stood, I could barely make out the waters of Lake Ndogo between some square little houses made of concrete. It was a very tidy fishing camp the Vigons ran.

We four were in our new theatre, but had not truly arrived yet. The fishing camp was like a slice of France in the jungle. I strolled to Marcus' door and peeked through his horizontally-slatted window. He was up. I tapped. The door swung wide and he smiled a greeting, looking behind me at the cornflower blue ripening in a massive sky, just barely large enough to stretch across the Congo Basin.

"Hey, are you the maid?" Marcus smiled.

"Yup. You want your something special now?" Marcus stepped outside grinning and squinting, his tall brow draped in half curls of sandy blond hair. His eyes were hazel-hued and bright, his skin taut and even, and Marcus never pretended to be anything but the fresh-faced and lanky part-time lobsterman that he was. He was good looking enough to turn a few heads, a slight cleft in his chin, pronounced cheekbones, a widow's peak where his tawny hair began—Marcus was twenty-four. And he was tough. He wouldn't have been invited to Africa had that not been true. He also lent our gang of four an illusory wholesome quality that might prove useful. "Nice rooms, huh? Good AC."

"Yeah, for real. I slept hard." Marcus rubbed sleep out of his eyes, his long fingers pushing the skin of his face around like a mask. "Hey, did you bring any body glitter?" Marcus tittered, convulsing, his eyes watering as we laughed and clucked in the pre-dawn.

"No. We used it all in Venezuela."

⌒

"How many Falcon workers does it take to screw in an ice screw?" asked Logan, grinning wryly. We all waited. "Two. One to push the screw into the ice, and the other to drink until the canyon starts spinning."

Marcus, Jack, and I laughed. I don't remember how the topic of ice climbing had come up, but if there was an entire continent where nonesuch ever happened, this was it. The boys from Gamba were talking among themselves in French or staring across the lake's glassy black surface from bench seats behind us. We pushed one of the camp's twenty-foot powerboats away from a concrete dock as two well-kept, twin Yamaha outboards came to life behind us. The skiff heaved forward. Our daily commute to work would begin with a fifty-minute ride across Lake Ndogo. We Americans had been cooked a breakfast of fried eggs and toast by a tall, slender, and deeply black-skinned young woman named Nicole in a little house near our rooms. "I think the cook likes you, Marcus," said a smiling Logan as the air began to flatten our hair and tug at our shirts. Our boat was fast to a landlubber like me. A great wake formed behind us.

"I've never dated a black girl," Marcus said loudly to all gathered. At least one of the guys from Gamba noted Marcus' comment with raised eyebrows, an apparent English speaker among our local hosts. English would not be our private code here as it had been in Venezuela.

"Sometimes as adults we look for things in our adult lives that we didn't get as children. For me that thing was Scotch whiskey. For you, Marcus, maybe it was holding hands with African girls," I offered loudly through the growing roar of the outboards. I got a laugh. We had to nearly shout to be heard as our boat was now flying across the dark water with zeal, unperturbed by a cargo of nine men and a pile of gear that included a huge chain saw, machetes for all, and packs full of water, radios, and food.

"Want a smoke?" Jack asked Logan.

"No, dude. I tried that start smoking gum. But it didn't work," Logan replied. Jack handed one to Marcus and one to me. We struggled to light them behind the cover of the little forward bulkhead.

"Psyched to be working again, Marcus?" I nearly yelled into Marcus' ear. He sat beside me on a plank of painted-green wood that ran from starboard to port across the boat's fiberglass hull. Two others just like it formed seating for twelve behind us.

"Totally. But I'm gonna miss the finals of America's Tallest Midget," he said, looking at me seriously. "Our culture is so vibrant in the States, you know?" Marcus could say a lot with a little. I laughed, happy to be working with these three lads again. Logan and Jack would only stay for install, and then it was up to me and Marcus to see this big job through.

Dawn came. The sun bobbed in the water to the east of us, obscured irregularly behind distant treed islands. Lake Ndogo was big, actually a lagoon, and the water portion of our daily commute wound around countless islands of all sizes. All of them were changing from black into lime and emerald where the sun struck their towering treetops. The boat reached full speed. I stared at the islands slipping by. Some were no bigger than a golf-course green, and others were much larger. Logan had already told us what to expect to encounter on the ground among those massive trees. He had been here before. But Logan tended to downplay objective hazards. I spun around on my bench seat, throwing my legs over it to face the rear of the boat. I looked at all the guys from Gamba with a smile, making my first attempt at French, a language I had studied in middle school, a fact that put me slightly and infinitely ahead of my countrymen. I imagined they would all pick it up quickly.

"Beaucoup éléphants?" I asked. A couple of them laughed. One furrowed his brow. And then another spoke.

"Oui. Beaucoup. Je m'appelle Jean Luc. Et vous?"

"Je m'appelle Thomas." We shook hands. "Je parle un peu, mais, je veux parler plus."

"Bon." Jean Luc smiled. He introduced me to the others, and soon all the white dudes had met all the locals, albeit in a stiff wind that carried some names away. Still, we were all happy to be acquainted. I wondered what they knew of our nation. We would begin learning about their jungle in fifteen minutes. I considered that just three days ago I was watching ESPN and eating at a brewpub. I grabbed my baseball cap just before it was blown off my head. It was specially issued for this job by Falcon and featured the official name of the oil concession we would be surveying. The guys from Gamba all got a hat too. I thought about what Marcus had said regarding the culture in the States. It seemed so far away as I stared across the water, but back across the pond, the hydrocarbon burn-fest raged on. America's mind was stuck in American idle. Real shows were fake, and fake ones real. Athletes who may have taken steroids faced indictment from a government that trampled the Constitution and lied through its teeth daily. A population whose news was disbursed by corporate toadies was still taking 9-11 at face value. Martha Stewart had just gotten out of prison. Oliver North had his own TV show. American kids were dying, blown apart in the streets of Tikrit and Karbala. Brad and Jen were on the rocks.

I wondered what Jean Luc thought of that. I would soon ask him. I wondered if we sounded like a nation at war. Livin' the dream, shop 'til you drop, live strong, no fear, don't worry, be happy, worry, shit happens, everything happens for a reason, no such thing as coincidences, love it or leave it, fear this, freedom isn't free—I guessed that the guys from Gamba had grown up in a society less in bloom with such extravagant banalities. In the United States, a fictitious teen wizard named Harry Potter commanded vastly more adult attention than did Mailer, Vonnegut, or Ford. Millions of grown-ups were in pleasant intellectual comas and at no risk of understanding their berserk government's goals and methods. Public concern about massive civilian bloodshed in Iraq could be summed up with another newly-born U.S. cliché: "Sucks to be them."

We were quickly off the boat and into a truck that had been specially adapted to wildlife viewing. In the bed of the Mitsubishi pickup were welded three lateral benches, much like the ones in the boat, but these had backrests. The Vigons were, after all, in the fishing and wildlife viewing business. The whole team fit comfortably in the back, and our skipper became our driver, the affable Vigon camp employee named Jacques. Jacques would require a good book or five for this job. His only role was to operate our primary vehicles, the truck and the boat, and he planned to sit in the cab of the Mitsubishi while we worked every day. He wanted nothing to do with walking around in the jungle, and he knew all about it. He seemed to regard us as partial fools in his affable French way.

3

The jungle awakened. A moist breeze ruffled my hair. The black flies called *mouche* bit hard into our necks and hands ahead of our swipes. A phalanx of muscular, contorted trees posed at the road's edge, flexing like bodybuilders, their veins bulging. I hopped out of the truck with Jean Luc behind me. Logan handed me my machete, handle first. I put my ball cap on.

"Have fun, bro. Be safe." Logan's face was the picture of gusto. The truck mumbled away. We were on a muddy little road that ended off to our west at one of Atora's new oil wells. Time for business. Seemed like just yesterday I was drinking Amstels on airplanes. Jean Luc and I were to place just six samples that day in a simple south-to-north line, and would in theory be picked back up on one of the little branches of the main road near our final sample. I had not balked at this job on paper, but on the ground, with my tin in my hand, the sheer size of the survey overwhelmed me. The samples were to be placed one kilometer apart on this job, and there were more than five hundred of them. The jungle beside us leapt to a height of about eighty feet within ten feet of the road's edge, and I could see into it for only half a stone's throw. I slapped the back of my neck with my machete, holding my GPS high in the air in my left hand. Jean Luc stared nonchalantly into the darkness gathered around the feet of the enormous trees. My GPS locked in.

"D'accord. C'est deux cents mètres à sud."

"Bon. Nous allons."

And then, with a few simple steps forward, we went back in time. We would now play by the same rules that our ancestors had played by for some hundred thousand years. We were, for all who would see us here, animals, just like them. But we were slow. And weak. We would smell very strange to all of them, and be terribly annoying to some. At least a dozen finely tuned and diversely talented beings who lived here were ranked solidly above humans in terms of their day-to-day survivability; these were creatures whose physical and social gifts far outweighed whatever advantage relative intelligence bestowed upon the human. Their odds of simply outlasting the week were demonstrably higher than were ours. For us, this would be no "fight club." This would be "flight club."

Jean Luc and I walked together as strangers for the last time. I watched him move, and he me. I held the GPS, so I led. I would soon show him how to use it, but first, I wanted simply to walk. To feel the ground. The topsoil was thick and spongy, soaked with water, slippery on slopes. The soil beneath this was sticky mud and sand. The trees shot skyward like columns, limbless, unclimbable, their arms spreading only when way above the ground. There were two distinct canopies above us, and what sun reached us was a grey half-light in many places. The jungle was loud. Many of the croaks and twitters came from the beaks of unseen birds far above, but other sounds surrounded us, sounds I did not yet understand. We walked. I placed my feet rather than dropping them. One sample was in, then two. Jean Luc watched me install the samples, mild shock registering in his thoughtful eyes. That was it? That was how we—looked for oil? Jean Luc was handsome, though he didn't act it, a face well proportioned and full of poise, a slender nose, a smooth brow, an athletic body. Though his expression was normally one of dispassion, he would let slip a smile now and then as he struggled to understand my poor French, a subtle lift of his mouth's right corner. He looked a fair bit like Michael Jordan, so much so that Logan would nickname him "vignt-trois," or "twenty-three," MJ's number with the Chicago Bulls. The ladies loved him, I imagined.

Though we could usually see about fifty feet straight up, visibility through the brush at human eye-level was limited, sometimes as little as thirty feet. Tall bushes, ferns, and springy shoots leapt out of the mud everywhere except where animals large and relatively small had walked trails through the undergrowth. We followed these if they went our way, but they rarely went straight. Only humans would want to go straight. Small, sluggish creeks and stagnant oxbow ponds variously gurgled and festered across our path in the low areas between the hillsides. A few of the little creeks held clear water, and they might all have juvenile crocodiles, I was told by my guide. The word happened to be the same in each of our native tongues. No big deal, just don't step on one. Lethargic mosquitoes were everywhere, but they were easy to kill and still easier to ignore. It was like twilight in many of the thicker areas despite it being midmorning. There was almost a sense of being inside a covered arena or beneath a huge, green circus tent in certain parts of the forest. We were under the big top.

A sudden noise off to our right gave Jean Luc pause, a swift, diffuse motion behind some thick growth, a couple of heavy footfalls, and then nothing. My heart pounded with surprise and without fear. I was delighted. I could not believe it. I had been within a hundred feet of...I turned to look at Jean Luc.

"Éléphant!?"

"Non, Thomas, buffle."

A wild cow? We approached our third sample location. Jean Luc certainly moved better here than did I. There was thick, gooey mud in every flat-bottomed draw we crossed, mud that oozed greasy and putrid-looking water and was replete with dinner-plate-sized impressions made by some very large, round feet. The rotting mat beneath our boots smelled to me vaguely and strangely like Roquefort cheese in spots, but upon the well-drained, steeper hillsides, the smell of decaying leaves like that in any deciduous autumn forest rose from the ground, familiar but odd in so tropical and ferny a place. While thick and tight in spots, the drippy low growth was largely free of thorns, and was for the most part as easily hacked through as the type of plant my mom introduced to our living room when I was younger.

I looked closely at the bark of the huge trees. I held leaves inches from my face. I breathed in deeply and held the air in my lungs. I was in the jungle. *The* jungle. It was somehow less alien than it should have been, but already, I felt different than I had ever felt on a Falcon job. Jean Luc was patient with my poor French. It had been a dry rainy season so far, he explained. Still we ran into the direst of bogs with some frequency on the way to the next sample site. Jean Luc had proven remarkably adept at quickly felling a type of small tree with a very straight trunk and relatively few limbs. These were leaned and dropped in pairs with great splashes of sour brown water across the deeper sections of swamp to form barely adequate, comically unpredictable bridges. Jean Luc's balance had been breathtaking. He always crossed first, his tired, black leather city shoes disappearing underwater as the tree trunks shifted and bowed beneath his weight, his shoulders and hands jerking like a mime's, his brow furrowing and relaxing, his fleeting smile dissolving into serious concentration. I crossed less elegantly using chopped, younger versions of the same tree as three-meter-long walking sticks, two meters of which went underwater. I had as yet not swam, but had jerked and contorted enough to make Jean Luc laugh out loud. Was there quicksand here, the kind I saw on TV as a kid? I crossed yet another fen on a couple of felled little trees. Jean Luc and I stopped on a soggy hillside once across. Our pant legs dripped slime. Some bird cawed louder than the others from far above.

I pointed at my boots and tried some French. "I brought two more. You have them tomorrow," was what I tried to say.

"Ah, oui?" Jean Luc's smile flashed. I looked back at my GPS. It had lost signal while we crossed the bog just behind us. The tight double canopy would be a problem for our hand-held GPS's.

"We must go up. We lost...communication," I mumbled, pointing at the little black box that told us where to go. Jean Luc nodded and continued uphill. I followed. My eighth-grade French was bubbling up to the surface of my mind like trace hydrocarbons. I asked in French if he had a big family.

"Yes. Two sisters, one brother. One house." He replied slowly but eagerly in English. Jean Luc walked effortlessly and quickly. He wore a bright orange Smithsonian jumpsuit made of cotton. He was among those who had worked as a guide and assistant when that group conducted its wide-ranging bio-survey of the area. This was Jean Luc's jungle as much as it was any man's, and he seemed to know it well.

Between us and some rumored sky stood the towering trees, sighing and swaying in time, muttering, reaching down like parents to dress us in shadows. My feet seemed poorly designed for this root-bound and deceptive ground. I was getting tired after seven clicks of steep hills. We paused in a brilliant opening in the forest where the sun came blaring through a gap in the canopy, a trumpet blast of light that turned olives into emeralds all around us. Birds cawed and cooed and rattled in perplexing vocabularies above, the loudmouths of the jungle. The jungle. We breathed inside her like embryos. Her bright green face looked up at the sun as rivers flowed down the creases around her eyes, ageless and helplessly *alive*, alive beyond control. Chromosomes floated through the outstretched fingers of the trees above like confetti above a grand parade of creatures, ourselves conspicuous among them. I gazed stupidly at my plastic compass. We walked, returning to the gloam.

Another noise. Loud too, but this time Jean Luc's head jerked around to look behind us as quickly as mine, both toward four-o-clock. A great form, a silhouette, sat barley hidden from us by a veil of trembling oval leaves just forty feet away. Jean Luc watched with some interest, telling me to be still and quiet with a gesture of his right hand. It sensed us only slightly after we sensed it. Startled, it rose to move away from us, its massive daub and lead flanks shuddering up from repose to become walls, its huge ears tucked to its sides—it pushed through a springy stand of saplings and trotted nimbly away to some other jungle neighborhood. In five seconds, all sound of it was gone.

I looked at Jean Luc wide-eyed. My mouth changed from the roundness of surprise to a smile of discovery. "Éléphant!" I stated with the glee.

"Oui. Éléphant," Jean Luc uttered casually, grinning at me. "Un éléphant. Une jeune fille."

⌣

"I want to grow coca in Bolivia." Logan guffawed with enough volume to be heard over the roar of the engines. The lake slipped by us as the laboring twin Yamahas whisked the water into froth and sent it into the air behind our hurtling skiff. A great wake followed us, a giant white dovetail in the brown water.

"I want to be an assman. Or maybe start a school for the dead," Marcus stated loudly. We all looked at him curiously for a few seconds. The wind pulled his sandy hair straight out from his head. He giggled.

Jack spoke in turn. "Rodeo clown. I'm gonna fake my own death here in Africa, and then I'm going back to the rodeo to find some good clown work," he yelled.

"I guess I want to preach. Yeah. I'm gonna get me religion. Give me chastity and give me constancy, but do not give it yet!" I hollered. All of our next career choices were out in the open. When Falcon went under, we'd be just fine, thank you. I noticed that Jean Luc and another of the Gamba boys listened to us without seeming to, nonplussed looks on their mugs.

"How big was your elephant?" Jack asked.

"Fucking big, but Jean Luc said it was just a teen. A girl."

"Was she hot?" asked Marcus.

"Yes," I shouted, "I would've done her." Soon we were walking up a paved path from the dock to out rooms. The boys from Gamba walked before and behind us, all of us chuckling, jawing, carrying machetes and appetites for supper, as well as various other delights that a man might desire and reasonably expect to find in the evening in western coastal Africa. We were quickly showered and assembled in the fishing camp's restaurant beside truly cold beers.

"They have pizza," I mumbled. I pulled on my Heineken. "Is that her?" I asked toward Logan as I glanced above the water-stained, cream-colored paper of my menu.

"Yeah. That's Amelie. Oh, shit, look what she's *wearing*, bro!" Logan's voice cracked into hilarity. Marcus placed his menu down on the brown wooden tabletop. We all stared. Amelie was patently ravishing, more apparition than reality, and all with a "why, I don't know what all you boys make such a *fuss* about" naiveté that many women of her beauty could never pull off. Her skin was perfect dark chocolate, her chestnut eyes laughed, and her hips, her butt, her Mesopotamia—she was coming to take our orders.

"Does she speak English, Logan, or is this code?" Marcus muttered, unable to take his eyes from her as she approached our table and commenced flirting with Logan, all the while beaming, turning, glancing at each of us, her skin damp from the kitchen's heat. Amelie's body screamed woman, but her face said girl. Her cheeks plumped when she smiled, which was often, and her almond eyes were angled slightly down from the temple to the slight bridge of her elegant and slightly ski-jump-shaped nose. Her hair was set in precise cornrows and finished with little red and yellow beads that gathered about her strong shoulders. She was precisely adorable, twenty-three years old, a force of nature placed on the planet to help ensure the future of the species. We would survive, I imagined.

Moreover, Amelie spoke some English and smelled like a mango. I was developing an erection. "Was that a ring I saw?" I asked Logan.

"Yeah, bro. She's married."

I ordered some fish from about ten choices on the surprising menu. We would eat well, it seemed. We all talked. Gradually, I fell into a somnolent silence as the beer slowed the machinations of my mind. While my cohorts talked quietly, I stared at the flame of an orange candle burning coolly between two other guests at a smaller table across the dimly-lit, wood paneled dining room. I watched the couple. They were older and white.

They sat there speaking quietly, so really happy to be together, her hair like silver wool, his face like raw ground beef pushed into shape by the deft hand of a sculptor, while outside, the sky melted in salmon and peach and topaz, and most everywhere elephants said good evening to one another in ways that humans could not.

4

I did not find Danielle particularly anything when I first saw her. She shuffled sassy though the blue evening light, orange handbag around her slender black arm, her odd little bob of straightened hair holding her head like a pair of black mittens. She was shorter than me only barely, voluptuous, athletic, and maybe about thirty—a tough call. She wore bright white lipstick, but only on her lower lip. Her big dark eyes were bored when she drew close enough for me to see them, her lips thick but not wide, her nose straight down like a shark's fin.

"You oil?" she said with no affection.

"Yup," I replied. I smiled and held the door to the restaurant for her. I followed her inside, noting a certain gait and dearth of pretense on her part. She liked men, and wanted their eyes on her, that much was clear. But she was still a *lady,* I guessed. Her tush swung lazily back and forth like a bell as she walked two steps ahead of me. She took a right and went to a stool at the bar. Her scent was of rosewater and a little sweat from the walk to the Vigon camp from Gamba. I took a left and went straight to a chair at a round wooden table and sat opposite Marcus.

"I'm having a super day," said Marcus. "I didn't get lost!" We were the first Americans to arrive for supper. It was evening on the second day of install.

"Me too. But I'm kinda beat. I couldn't decide whether to go straight to bed after showering or stay up all night and drink way too much whiskey. I'm like an old married couple," I deadpanned.

"Is that the plan?"

"Our third night in country, job's going good, and no Scotch shortage, either. I predict foolishness and excess."

"I bet you're right. And I didn't do a pre-drink stretch or a warm-up or anything." Marcus and I were being watched from the bar, discussed, perhaps even rated. I wondered how I was faring. "Those two seem to be way curious about us," he said quietly. He smiled at them.

"Indeed," I stated. I smiled over at them too. No reaction.

"Hi ya, boys! How's the jungle?" Catherine emerged from the kitchen, her husky voice the bullhorn of all womanhood, one that blared in at least three languages. We had all met her the night before at our first dinner in the Vigon camp. She was the barkeep, hostess, and muse, and was also the wife of a Vigon. Danielle and Sylvia watched closely as Catherine brought two Heinekens to our table and clunked them down, green beer-sweat dripping down their aluminum sides. Catherine was also sweaty from a hot kitchen.

"Any elephants, gentlemen? Any lady gorillas make you love them?" Catherine cackled, Marlboro red in one hand and the other on her big hip. Her mahogany face was pretty like a lion's. Her accent was African French, but her English was damn good. She studied in Port Gentil.

"No jungle love," I muttered tiredly and smiled. "Just lotsa walkin' through water."

"Uh-huh. You boys look tired. You need whiskey. Calories. I'll bring you two on the house." Marcus and I looked at each other as she walked away. Had we already been killed and through some mistake gone to heaven? She was quickly back, a bottle of Dewar's in one hand and two tumblers in the other. "You two help yourself." Catherine marked the level of booze with a grease pencil and stuck the crayon behind her left ear. "I have to go help in the kitchen. And talk these two stupid girls at the bar out of getting mixed up with you two," she pointed at each of us with a well-manicured index finger, its nail painted in blue metal-flake. "We're out of ice," she said as she walked slowly away.

"Wow. Way cool." Marcus poured one for me and another for him. "Does it seem like we might get laid to you?" Marcus said, eyebrows raised and tumbler to his nose.

"Yes."

This time, the elephant wasn't running away. It just stood there. The wood handle of my machete was soaked with brine from my hand. My arms from my elbows down were throbbing with the itchy needle pain of ant bites. The elephant was less than sixty feet straight ahead of us in the middle of a broad trail made for and by his kind. He faced me, and seemed a bit conflicted. He really did seem to be weighing his options. With a lazy swing of a right front leg the size of a high-school tight end, the giant started toward us. I almost threw up. My head turned in slow motion before my body could like a planet, my left eye waiting in the darkness of fear for the dawn of Jean Luc's face—yes, he knew what to do, he could trick it with some spell, finally, finally there he was, Jean Luc, and...

Flight. I spun and hurled my feet before me, whipping my machete and GPS into the air and sprinting madly back on the trail. No! Not on the trail! Jean Luc grabbed me by the shirt and yanked me off the path and into the tangled brush without slowing down, his face tight as a drum. Boughs lashed our cheeks and arms as brown water leapt from the puddles where our boots fell. We finally stopped and turned around, crouching low, myself shaking with adrenaline. Jean Luc put two fingers across his lips. Quiet. My heart exploded over and over again in my chest, my mind coiled like a snake, my ears listened, and then...nothing. Jean Luc stood up casually and said "it's fine!" at full conversational volume as though he had just checked the air pressure on a tire. He then walked over to a handy and enormous tree and commenced whacking on it with the back of his machete. He produced an impressively loud series of thumps by striking one of the elegant pre-roots that extended like the folds of a gown from the tree's great base.

"What?" I struggled to catch my breath. "Why is it OK?" I was on one knee in four inches of slime, grabbing a little tree with white knuckles. I was nauseous with adrenaline. I realized then and there that there was absolutely nothing we could do against an elephant. Realized? Even schoolchildren in Kansas knew this.

"He is old. He could not tell what we are. Not aggressive," Jean Luc said plainly in French.

"Oh." My throat was the only dry place on my body. "When are they aggressive?" I stammered back in his tongue.

"When babies are around."

"Oh. Babies. I see." I walked behind the tree to check my shorts. It occurred to me that if the Congo Basin was a book, it would be seen as depending too much upon hyperbole.

Logan and Jack were leaving. Install was complete, the job's final sample plunged into the muck that very afternoon. Though constantly exciting, install had passed without injury or serious incident. Another potential African job was surfacing and required attention in the form of reconnaissance. My two best friends were driving to the Gamba airstrip and hopping a plane to the Democratic Republic of Congo. Things were a lot trickier there than in peaceful little Gabon. I wondered whether Marcus and I or Jack and Logan would face more danger in the next three weeks. Two more locals would join our team of eight to replace them for the relatively easier process of retrieval.

I looked at Danielle. She was giddy without being cheerful. I paid for our third round of cocktails. Danielle's chocolate thighs were poorly concealed beneath her short, bright orange skirt as she wiggled around on her barstool like a teen. She sucked the last of her whiskey sour through its ice with a red straw and a coarse hiss, licked her teeth, and tried to understand my French, squinting at me. I spoke more of that tongue than she did English.

"Voulez-vous coucher avec moi, ce soir?" I stated quietly but with a curious confidence, recalling having learned this little bit of French sometime in junior high, as we called it then. Why did I know how to say that? Was it was in a pop song? I looked at Danielle's face, her eyes gazing into some unknown distance behind the bar. Catherine looked at Danielle and giggled from the kitchen as she spoke with the short, bald cook.

"Oui," she purred, turning her eyes but not her face toward me. Very well. That was settled. Marcus appeared also to be in the company of a new and special friend. He grinned at me, incredulous. Marcus' gal Sylvia was a doll. They were propped up on each other at a table in the room behind us. Catherine sauntered back over to the bar and leaned into it from her side, smiling at the two of us.

"So, what do you think about this war the U.S. is fighting?" she asked.

"It's criminal," I uttered. "It's shameful."

"You're an American. And you seem to be a reasonable man," she said with a giggle. "How is it that after 9-11 the U.S. stood there and acted like they had never hurt a flea? Like they had never, ever killed civilians in, oh, let's see—Vietnam? Or how about Central America?"

"I know. I know. And not three thousand. Millions. But a lot of people in the U.S. don't even know that. And they wouldn't care."

"They oughta care! Those people ought to educate themselves. Don't they know their shit stinks too?"

"No. I mean yeah, they should." Danielle and I rose from our stools together as Catherine smiled warmly and took my money. She placed her hand on my arm as I turned to leave and drew her head toward mine.

"You got a nice girl with you, boy." Catherine was almost lit, and she was a very happy drunk. Her breath smelled like wine. "You have fun tonight."

"Thanks, Catherine. You have a good night too," I said and smiled.

Soon Danielle's clothes had melted off into puddles of faint color on the floor in the cool darkness of my room. The air-conditioner whirred away noisily as I put a hand on her breast, another on the wetness between her thighs, pressing against her so whitely, practically glowing in the dark. My blood rushed south. She scratched her breast and yawned. She didn't want to kiss. We went to the neatly made bed. We plopped down on the thin, black flannel blanket with a bounce, our hands moving across one another's goods. We paused. She looked at me eye to eye closely, and then leapt back into herself, her arms falling to her sides. Was she famously demure, or was I simply a bore? Was she shy or practiced? Might she be both?

She pushed me onto my back and knelt above me, her knees outside my hips. Danielle grinned, the whiteness of her teeth flashing, and impaled herself upon me with conviction. I remembered how good it was possible to feel. White and black collided and colluded. We were hot and getting hotter, becoming truly acquainted. Our timing. Our angles. Now we had an understanding. Now we were communicating. Skin slid hotly against skin, a wet noise, a sigh, a coo. I was plunging like a silver spade into the moist, dark earth between her pulsing thighs. I grabbed her ass and crushed her into me. Her face was open and breathing like a flower's, a flower growing out of me, her little black bob of straightened ebony locks bouncing to our rhythm, her boobies jiggling, her eyes half-shut and regarding me wickedly, full of sly sweetness.

5

We were well into the first week of retrieval. As Jean Luc and I walked down the shoulder of another hillside on a faint trail made by wild pig traffic, a piercing cry erupted from the brush, a shattering, bloodcurdling cackle. We both spun in place to behold an angry and large chimpanzee in the trail behind us. We froze. His gray face was full of grave intent, and a handful of others cowered behind him, at once curious and unsure. A youngster advanced to cringe behind the big male and peek at us. He was an uncomfortable thirty feet away.

Our challenger was in a half crouch almost like a man, ready to spring quickly in any direction. His eyes were full of anger. It might have been the strangest moment of his life. It was among mine. Jean Luc muttered "grand singe," holding perfectly still, both of us gazing at a primate that looked to weigh about one hundred pounds, and those full of muscle. His face changed subtly as we regarded him. His brow released unsurely for a split second as through fear or the briefest thought of conciliation, but returned to a furrowed resolve. He looked at the machetes we both gripped, then back at our faces. He was tight-lipped and made no sound, his mind working hard. My knuckles whitened around the wood handle of my Tramontina blade. His chest rose and fell, his nostrils flared, and his arms were tense with potential. He was covered with coarse dark hair everywhere but his face, and looked directly at us without releasing his gaze. He looked every bit steeled for a fight, a large and unpredictable thug defending his turf in a rough neighborhood. But we were entirely bizarre. Now that he had a good look at us, uncertainty mixed with hostility on his face.

"Agressive?" I hissed, feeling a now familiar nausea, and like Jean Luc, not moving a muscle. The tone and volume of his affirmative reply indicated that I had asked a very stupid question. He whispered back to me that I should move away first, but that I should not turn my back on the taut monkey. I walked carefully backwards, cognizant of a concern in Jean Luc that he had not yet displayed. In twenty awkward back steps, I could no longer see the bad-ass male. Jean Luc did the same until we turned and walked forward down the hill, careful to do so slowly lest we show fear or weakness, two things I had plenty of.

I wondered if, in a parallel life, I was sitting in a mobile home in Buena Vista, Colorado, clad in a dress and painting my nails. And maybe Chomsky wrote books about NASCAR. My laptop was open on the big wooden table we had hauled into my room to serve as the job's data entry hub. Marcus had used Photoshop to place my head on the body of a hot bikini-clad woman. I was working on his. It was afternoon on the tenth day of sample recovery. Just ten more days of work remained. We sipped cold cans of Heineken.

"Logan would never do this," I mumbled.

"No. He's not this silly."

"A lot of guys would never do this."

"And that makes us?" Marcus asked, amused.

"More complete men. We have imagined ourselves as hot chicks. He shall be the greatest who is the most manifold, Nietzsche said."

"Nietzsche? Dude, there is nothing Nietzschean about this." I laughed. It had been an easy morning, as each of our four pairs of men had to retrieve only those samples placed on a day of install that was foreshortened by the mechanical failure of our truck three weeks prior. After our usual hour-long return trip across the lake, we were back by lunchtime. Tomorrow would be different. Tomorrow we would attempt to recover those samples that languished farthest from the places of man, the most distal samples we had placed in the body of the survey. The northernmost lines of the job were too remote to be accessed in a day, and we would be compelled to sleep on the mud in light tents, sufficient perhaps to keep us from the rain and the flies and mosquitos, but no shelter from more dire encounters. I tried not to think of it. My trepidation arose from the fact that we were having increasingly frequent encounters with the most purposefully menacing of the jungle's children. "You gonna see Danielle tonight?"

"Probably. I wish she'd stop coming by every day. I need to sleep one of these nights." After another early wake up and yet another boat ride, Marcus and I and our two local companions, Jean Luc and Louis, would split into pairs and retrace the tracks we pressed into the mud during install in the most decidedly fearsome portion of our massive survey. During install we had enjoyed a honeymoon of sorts with the Congo. Beginner's luck. A grace period for the new geeks in the jungle. We had been practically rowdy, enjoying a certain saccharine courage then, intrepid before an unknown peril. Now both Marcus and I were nervous, and I was privately managing some growing dread. We knew who was out there now, and we knew that they knew all about us. They were not the cobras, leopards, wild pigs, buffalo, nor even the elephants, although that latter group might possibly be gossiping abstractly about us in their own way—they were the chimps, and in the huge but small neighborhood of the Congo through which we trod, we were the latest news upon their lips.

The gorillas surely spoke of us as well, likely remembering us as simple aliens, less threats than curiosities. They were patently polite when we happened near them, and in the event of our unexpected presence reacted only with mild interest, slipping elegantly away to disappear into deeper sanctuary. Pound-for-pound the most powerful creature in the woods, the gorilla was shy, and we only glimpsed them a couple times. The kindly gorilla's smaller cousin, however, preferred and even savored confrontation. Chimpanzees were more than simply territorial. They could be almost warlike, organizing from time to time into hunting parties, pursuing, capturing, and eating the smaller red-capped mangabey monkey, a species that we saw almost daily and had reacted to us with nothing but quiet curiousity. Not so the families of chimpanzees and their doyens.

Though our first and closest encounter with them had ended uneventfully, it had not been our last. We were followed by a livid male for over half a click a few days prior, and he put on quite a show. Even Jean Luc thought it was creepy. Now I was haunted by dark possibility. My attitude had changed irrevocably. I walked uneasily, a stranger in a strange land. I was expecting chimps everywhere, and we encountered them more often. My resolve was melting, my sense of purpose gone, but more than simply this, I was beginning to wonder how appropriate any harm intended me by the local fauna might be. I felt like a marionette during the long days now, walking no longer with joyful purpose but marching, stung by my conscience as much by wasps and ants, a shell at night as I groped Danielle in the darkness back in Gamba.

I was a mere tool. I was making a day-wage to help a large multi-national decide where it might best drill, where it might hack a path into the homes of these many happy creatures and deliver the roar and diesel breath of the drill rig. The tenants here had every right to assail the first foot soldiers of man's impending presence, even if it amounted to just one oil well. This place was among the last intact wilderness on the planet. Was I as deplorable as a colonial profiteer of the nineteenth century? Were we simple hydrocarbon copies of them? I missed the confidence that Logan's and Jack's blithe attitudes allowed them—for my two best friends, our activities remained as natural and inevitable as the morning rain. I was not helped by being conflicted. I was slipping into the darkness of doubt and the danger according uncertainty.

I was having trouble placing one foot before the other in the slippery mat of leaves below us, feeling myself walking toward a jury that would surely convict me. Jean Luc's cotton jumpsuit was uniformly dark with his sweat and that of the jungle. I was soaked as well. We had two more samples to retrieve before we reached the same campsite we had spent the night in during install. I was feeling less like Indiana Jones than *persona non grata*. Now I was paranoid, straining to hear the sound of our next adversary before it heard us, marching without a vestige of conviction. Camping seemed like madness.

The massive trees swayed in a stiff breeze above us, holding hands, nodding to one another, dripping, obscuring the sky, piling shadows upon us. We moved deliberately, our loads heavier than usual due to the camping gear we carried. The day was waning. Our four-wheeler waited eight clicks to our east on the faintest of drivable trails within the survey. I stepped bleakly, ten paces behind the ever-deft Jean Luc, looking more at the darkening ceiling of leaves above us reflected in the glass screen of my GPS than at the directional arrow beneath that told us where to go. I watched Jean Luc, his machete swinging smartly through the twiggy saplings crowding our course. I imagined what thoughts filled his head. I wondered if he considered this whole affair to be a worthwhile opportunity for both him and his colleagues from Gamba, or just another chance to die in the jungle.

They needed education and opportunity, not no-future, one-off oil jobs like the one he was currently doing at his own peril. We had discussed just this topic as much as my broken French would allow during our jungle lunch breaks. While Jean Luc had expressed no contempt for the oil patch and was making a decent wage, he seemed to be lukewarm and even melancholy about all of this. He was smart. His co-workers were to a man more cheery about having any work at all. But none of them had a chance of getting the training necessary to land one of the coveted jobs at the oil company's production facilities. These were reserved for a few nationals who had studied in Port Gentil and Libreville and beyond that, mostly foreigners. Furthermore, even those shining, rumbling production facilities could be gone in less than a decade.

I really liked Jean Luc. I admired his skill in the thick stuff and his courage. He may have resented what I represented, but his generosity had made a kind of friendship possible between us, and he would likely have conceded that I was not the average visitor. He knew that I respected him. I had learned more from him than he had from me. He liked the boots I gave him, and liked that we took turns carrying the pack and taking the point. As we approached a dense wall of thicker low growth, he slowed his pace ahead of me and tipped his head up slightly, smelling the air.

A great whoosh exploded from the tight copse of brush directly before us. The slimy ground shook with thuds. Before we could react, a tight wall of green just twenty paces ahead of Jean Luc emitted a withering trumpet blast and the hulking, lurching gray mass of a startled and furious cow, her trunk high, her dirty tusks pointed at Jean Luc like lances, her ears furled wide. I wheeled and began my latest sprint as if in a dream, as if underwater, much too slowly, my mind collapsing. My knees lifted and dropped, my arms swung, my eyes shot from bough to bog with manic instinct, and somehow, with anvil thuds dropping behind me, I remembered that I must make a move, left or right.

I broke left. I was an animal now, wet and slick with the sweat of penultimate volition. My body careened with a surreal agility. A trumpet exploded behind me, but not just. I leapt and blocked a branch, fought a fall, shifted a shoulder, plunged, splashed, my legs springs. I ducked left again behind a huge tree and into a fragile ball of meat and bones between the long, radiating fins of its base. The breath of the angry mother leviathan came in perturbed wooshes behind me in the gloom of twilight. She had stopped running and was paused, listening, her senses reaching out around her. My whole body was tight as a mousetrap's spring. I breathed in and out quickly in quiet little gasps. The giant cow huffed and puffed on the other side of my tree. She was unsatisfied. She was twenty feet away. I prayed to some distant powerless god, I begged, beseeched, tasting my helplessness, a thin gruel of spit in my mouth, my pointless little arms tight about my left knee, my other pressed in the cool mud of the jungle, the Congo, mother of all of this. I was a tick, a barely noticed pest, an itch that through neither malevolence nor intent but through a simple reflexive motion was about to be scratched. The cow wheeled slowly, tasting the air carefully with great sweeps of her colubrine trunk. She began to move away. I thought of Jean Luc. I thought of the calves. Where were they?

I heard no sounds of young elephants in the foliage nearby. She was heading back now, placing her feet softly in the pasty mud and dung and leaves. Soon she was gone. I withered in dread. Jean Luc and I still had two clicks to camp. The light was failing. We could surely not go back to the Yamaha. We had to carry on to the agreed-upon coordinates. We had to meet Marcus and Louis at the campsite. We had to get there soon and somehow try to build a fire in the dripping darkness. Only a fire would offer us some hope of a safe night on the ground.

⌣⌐

Jean Luc and I reached the camp coordinates in total darkness. We soon heard Marcus and Louis. They were late arriving there, and also barely. My headlamp cast a frail, ghostly beam ahead of me as I stumbled into the little opening in the trees we would call a bed. Our little fire pit was still recognizable as a pulpy stain of ash on the ground, a mocking reminder of our previous jovial confidence. Marcus was physically ill and barely greeted me. He tumbled to the ground and on to his back. Jean Luc was already looking for wood that might be dry on the inside. He was uneasy. I gave him the light off my head. I was almost paralyzed with dread and bone tired. I sat like a toddler on the wet ground beside Marcus, head between my knees. My mind was deeply bruised.

Only the oily blackness. Only the teetering of the ego, the free fall. But then, for some reason, I remembered that it was so much less than what others faced. No man was shooting us. No war threatened us, flashing in vulgar whites and oranges in the night. No power sought to disappear and torture us. No perverse ardor for some false cause. Only the jungle surrounded us. Ours was a mere misadventure in the trees. I thought grimly about the Darfur and slumped into my knees. I thought of the dead innocents in Iraq. I thought of the very expendable U.S. soldiers there. I got up to help Jean Luc look for wood.

After fifteen minutes of bumbling numbly about, I sat on the ground beside Jean Luc in the puddle of light that my headlamp provided. He and I peeled soggy bark from twigs and smallish logs as Marcus groaned his way through a can of sardines beside us, drinking water in small gulps from a plastic bottle, mumbling strangely, beside him a gorilla skull that Jack had discovered during install and left in camp. They had been harried by elephants too, or vice versa, one kilometer to our north on their parallel line of samples. Jean Luc's ears were wide open. He listened to the jungle closely, as a mechanic might listen to the sound of an engine in need of repair. There was plain concern in his face below the headlamp he wore. The elephants were down for the night, he told me, but chimps moved about in the gloom, and we needed flame. We needed something that said "don't mess with us." Jean Luc heard them in the not-so-distance as we gathered wood—he tapped my shoulder and pointed after hushing me with a finger across his lips. They were close. We worked quickly stripping bark. I did my best. My fear filled me like strong alcohol buzz, slowing my fingers, but Jean Luc was here. I kept repeating this fact in my head. Jean Luc would not let something horrible pass. The jungle would not hurt Jean Luc, and neither those near him, I pretended.

He began arranging our modest pile of dry twigs. He worked quickly, a magician before a restless crowd, preparing a display that would justify the high price of the admission. He arranged the hopefully willing tinder as only a human could, making a place for the best trick of the Homo sapiens to be loosed and take hold, the nifty discovery that countless dark thousands of years before had lent a slim advantage to the slow and defenseless creature that would eventually dominate the world beyond the Congo. A neatly shredded and fairly dry copy of my field map waited beneath a fine little teepee of twigs. I handed Jean Luc my lighter. He turned the little wheel atop the Bic and a flame emerged with modern convenience to dutifully lick the rough edges of our shredded map. A new flame took hold in the little pile of shredded fiber. I wondered where the paper came from. Alberta? Louisiana? I would have paid handsomely to be in either of those places. A faint chirping was audible from the unsure darkness to the west of camp. It was repeated thirty seconds later. Our tentative flame survived in its nest of paper below a tight tent formed by Jean Luc's dark brown hands. He was utterly focused. His full lips were pursed inches from our fragile orange hope. Smoke issued barely, carrying the weak scent of a magic that even chimp nation would not contest.

Jean Luc cajoled the flame with a firm patience. Our tinder was at best damp, but after fifteen minutes of careful attention, our flame spread to the slenderest of twigs just as it finished with our map. There were different noises to our west, the odd quip or brush of leaves, the softest whispers—we were not alone. Marcus was unconscious or the like, stirring from time to time to groan and peer at us before drifting off again. Louis was asleep in a tent. Jean Luc nodded at me to add one stick and then another above his promising shrine of fire as it grew slowly. Smoke floated up between our faces. He blew on the flame carefully, and it grew to the size of the palm of a man's hand. A swish here and a rustle there told of large bodies nearby, close enough to remind me where my machete was. I did my best to say "they are coming closer" in French.

"Oui," Jean Luc responded plainly.

"Agressive?" I asked, matching Jean Luc's affected cool.

"Je ne sais pas. Possible," he whispered. "Peut être non, mais..." He trailed off, intent on our precious flame. It fluttered poorly, losing strength. The sickness of fear wrenched my guts again. We needed more dry fuel. I turned and moved to Marcus' side. I put my hands on his chest. I felt up and down his torso until I found the crinkle of his map in his breast pocket. I shoved my fingers in and grabbed it, waking him up. I removed the map from its ziplock bag and offered it to Jean Luc. He placed the paper quickly below our small flame. Yellow light grew between our wet faces as Marcus sat up.

"What'r you tryin' to do?" he muttered.

"There's chimps like right over there, bro. We need fire."

Marcus stared at me blankly and again reclined. Jean Luc grinned at me subtly. The fire was growing on its own now. I realized that I had still never seen fear on his regal face nor dread in his sharp auburn eyes. In ten long minutes we had a modest campfire. I looked at Jean Luc. His face relaxed as he glanced more casually into the darkness around us. Marcus would never know what a boon his lack of consciousness had been for him. I knew that I owed this man from Gamba my sanity and maybe my life. I retired into one of our flimsy little nylon-mesh tents at some time well after midnight. I lay on my side, my knees drawn up to my face. Louis had slept through all of this in the other tent. Marcus snored beside me. Morning would come late, and I would not sleep. Jean Luc would not lie down, instead tending the reluctant flames of the fire throughout the night until a dull blue light filtered through the high treetops to remind us all of another day's beginning.

6

I walked empty and etiolated behind Jean Luc. The sun washed the jungle's highest leaves with light in another world above us, a faraway place where joyous flocks of unknown birds celebrated a new day. We had our first sample of the day in hand, and seven more awaited my nervous attention along our course back to the Yamaha. Jean Luc had doubtless come to regard me as a spineless freak over the past few hours, I imagined, and I agreed with him. I had met more than my match, and was looking inside myself as I walked, searching my inner landscape for some landmark that might help me navigate back to myself. Jean Luc seemed to understand that I had lost my way and treated me with deference, respecting the drama consuming me, whether real or simply self-indulgent.

My mind sketched in the air before me. Lack of sleep had me tripping. We ran into a large group of boars foraging on a broad hilltop. Jean Luc stopped and turned, cautioning me with a glance. As some of the hogs trotted quickly away from us downhill, a few large males lingered to formally face us, a defensive gesture that was not empty—wild boars were quite capable of mounting a damaging attack. All the local boys had said as much. I reacted with dispassion. I was exhausted, at least psychologically. Jean Luc and I each moved to the base of a climbable tree, of which there were a serendipitous and obvious few. I commenced whacking my sapling's trunk with the back of my machete as Jean Luc hurled some hard-shelled, apple-sized seed pods at the hogs in succession, an effective tactic. The big males sprinted away, puzzling and grunting. We continued.

We reached our Yamaha around three in the afternoon. As soon as we stepped into the sunlight and saw the sky blue sky above the trail, we were set upon by *mouche*. We walked back into the shadows of the jungle to lose them—in the relative darkness, the relentless biting flies mounted no attack. The irony of returning to the jungle's murk and peril to find relief from anything was not lost on me, but the false safety of a nearby vehicle and a drivable path were enough to make me smile. I hugged Jean Luc, quite surprising him, but winning a grin. I had been spared in a pardon that rang like great bells around me, their unheard peals filling no one's ears but mine. Jean Luc looked at me strangely, kindly, offering me the final sip of our remaining water. I insisted that he drink it. But he was not thirsty.

Once shabby and expected, Gamba now shone like heaven. Danielle's face was bright as she walked beside me through town and back to the Vigon camp from the anemic grocery we had just left. I had bought canned fish and little bottles of rum and chocolate bars for four men. They rested in their rooms, preparing for their night among the wild things. Tomorrow four of our friends from Gamba would have their slumber party on the mud, camping just as Marcus and I had on their remotest lines while we four slept in beds in the safety of the Vigon camp. I was at very least concerned for them, but I downplayed the close encounters of our camping trip. I realized that most of these guys just weren't as scared of the jungle as I was. Being back in Gamba was enough to fill any sag in my sails.

"Bring a little white gas for a fire. Just don't get it near the samples," I suggested to Henri, the effective leader of our next camping party. "We wished we had."

In a couple mornings, I felt like myself again. Only a few days remained. I sat on my bed facing Danielle, looking at her face, the scent of her fancy new perfume rising between us. It was 6:15 a.m. We would have only a few more days together. I rose, straightened my knees, and shuffled to the shower. First light glowed feebly through the cluster of trianglular holes in my shower's concrete wall, placed there, apparently, so the mosquitoes could come in. Suddenly, there was a hand on my waist, and Danielle was standing beside me in the trickle of cool water. Frothy soap, giggling, a kiss of slick wet lips, a look for me from her that said I was a fool to be anything but whole. I had learned much about Danielle. She owned a little bar in Gamba, and was regarded by her peers as a success story. She had bettered herself and her life, as well those of her sister and brother and parents. I asked her why she kept spending time with me and sleeping in my bed.

"Because I like you," she said in English, beaming.

Where had I gone? What was I doing? We hurtled across Lake Ndogo with Jacque at the helm, delivered once again to our day's work under the big top. My hands waited at the end of my arms for orders. My legs were strong servants. My mind was sharp at the tip and along the blade, but at the base it was unsure, lacking the sort of inexorable conviction that made great men do great, um…things. One question burned brightest within me.

"Do you want cheese or tuna?"

"What?"

"What sandwich you want?"

"Cheese." I looked at the treetops as though at a diorama. We piled back onto land at Atora and all eight of us gathered our machetes, GPS's, and water bottles yet again. The bulk of the samples were already in hand, already in coolers back in Gamba. These last days would be easy, in theory.

I hadn't said a word on the morning boat ride, and I scarcely remembered it. I kept thinking to myself that it was time for me to stop looking for oil in foreign countries.

⌣

"To working with the finest men in the world." Marcus was standing at the head of the largest table in the fishing camp restaurant, delivering his toast in turn. He had a way of holding his words up in the air and letting them sparkle. We were in the restaurant drinking, our friends from Gamba beside us, our trial at an end. To a person we were all giddy—even Jean Luc was jolly, having a rare beer and the odd gulp of rum from a bottle passed around the group of a dozen men. I stood. It was my turn.

"To walk your boots to the end of their lives, to lean into the same rain that mats the hair of the ape and the boar, to taste the soil, the air, the unflinching march of the seasons, to be theirs, to look upon the works of man from the forest's cover as a spy and to see only sound and fury, signifying nothing. To be wild, far from couth, to borrow abandon from a flask of wine and wander through a starry night where mysteries are better questioned than solved. To give new and better names to birds and snakes and trees, to sing loud to nothing and not care how you look or act. To let one's mind wander far away, hoping it to return, as a dog you have taken on a long walk in a place without people. To have a hunch that the gods think you're all right. This is the field!" Three Johnny Reds had truly loosened the screws at the back of my tongue. Cheers followed my grandiloquence. Marcus tittered, rum-lipped. Jean Luc looked at me, bemused and smirking. He stood as I sat.

"To see…" Jean Luc's English was nascent, but had improved after six weeks with me at his side. He looked not around the table, but straight at me, smiling widely. "To see a man who fear elephants…look in his pants to see if they clean!" The table exploded with laughter.

10 SHARKS AND SARDINES

It's amazing I won. I was running against peace, prosperity, and incumbency.

— George W. Bush

O UR WHITE JET plane vaulted skyward with force. The state of Texas and the whole nation spun slowly beneath us as the 737 banked lazily to the south. Cars pumped along freeways below like blood cells in the veins of a giant and petulant teenager with nacho cheese and human blood under his fingernails. Way off to the east, beyond the earth's curve, the Washington shelter for the ethically challenged was packed to brimming. People everywhere compared themselves to other people, some real, and many imagined. Rice and bombs were prepared for export to other nations. Dogs had microchips placed in their shoulders. Bible-thumpers were pouring over careful plans to become indignant about something other than the horribly bloody and distinctly anti-First Commandment invasion of Iraq—perhaps it would be Potter, that popular, pagan teen-wizard. Maybe it would be some comment by the "anti-war progressives," a group I was having a hard time locating on the television. I thought that said group could have helped those followers of Christ who owed their opinions on U.S. foreign policy to Fox news to be more, well—cerebral would have been too much to ask—maybe they could just have reminded Christians what their boy said about vengeance.

I recalled a sign I had seen some time ago down below in Texas. It read: "Abortion stops a beating heart." So did war, but offing adults was just *so* different. You got to see the looks on their faces.

I reflected, my forehead against the plastic of the window's inside. The United States in 2005 was still among the wealthiest nations in the history of the world. It still had a very large middle class. One thing such widespread wealth tended to do to upper- and middle-class people, especially in the States, was to make them feel like they had done something to deserve their uniquely privileged lifestyles, something good, and that they were special people, more than simple winners of the "born in the USA" lottery. Because that's how the world worked. Good things came to good people, and we had good things, so...that old American notion that "you get what you deserve" still played quite well at home. It was a hard way to look at things if you lived in rural Honduras and a hurricane just killed your parents and obliterated your hometown, but it usually worked just fine if you lived in a loft in Petaluma.

Certain Americans who for better or worse were in the public eye were even suggesting that there was no such thing as coincidence, that "everything happened for a reason." Strange news indeed for that Honduran girl. This sort of breathtaking egocentrism had actually caught on in 2005, was even dispensed as some species of wisdom by Americans wearing knowing looks all across the nation. I glanced to my right at Ms. Middle and Mr. Aisle, or 26B and C. Mr. Aisle was all business, salt-and-pepper beard, copy of the *Prensa Libre* opened wide, but Ms. Middle was a *gringa*, an American, and she was eagerly on her way somewhere new and exciting if the shiny new Guatemala guidebook between her denim thighs was any indication. Clean, newish jeans, a yellow tank top, Burt's Bees lip stuff—Ms. Middle was going to Tikal, I guessed slyly, looking at her knees. Very sharp. She would likely go through Antigua too, where I was headed. Most tourists did. I wondered if Ms. Middle believed in coincidences. I wondered if I should talk to her. I imagined the Iraqi woman whose son and husband were killed in different parts of Mosul on the same day. What a coincidence! Oh, wait—there's no such thing! They were meant to be murdered on the same day! This sort of repugnant anti-thought could only have flourished in a country where half the people lived in a corporate-sponsored fantasy world bearing only a vague resemblance to reality on planet Earth, a world where bad things never happened to good people and good people never did bad things. And no gray areas. America hated gray areas. Black and white. With us or against us. No thought involved.

Ergo, if middle- and upper-class people were good, then poor people must have done something wrong to arrive at their plight. Something other than misfortune must have resulted in their very sad and very small lives. You got what you deserved, right? But most of the world's people were poor. And most of them did not fight, thieve, or even connive. They survived, comforted in the knowledge that the rich people of their own world famous human race had visited the moon and could blow up the whole planet if it became necessary, which it nearly did back in the early sixties. I looked into the blue sky above Texas through my little window. I imagined some powerful and benevolent alien race arriving on Earth and deciding to hold a planetwide popular election, an absolute orgy of that cherished practice we call democracy. The poor wouldn't just be the biggest voting block. They'd be the only one that mattered. What if this imagined worldwide popular election was instead a referendum with a single question. What if it asked "keep things the same, or change them?" What if the question was "suffer in silence, or struggle for justice?" What if it was "who would Jesus bomb?"

"Hablas muy bien Español."

"Gracias, tu también." I smiled at the sultry barkeep as she giggled. I extended my hand to shake hers above the dark wood of the bar at Reilly's. "Tomás. Mucho gusto."

"Marta. Igualmente." Marta was a local, born and raised in Antigua, a *panza verde*, or "green belly"—a couple of hundred years back, the huge volcano towering just south of town, aptly named Agua, belched out enough water to completely flood the town and turn many of its less fortunate residents into bloated green corpses. But Antigua survived that and many other natural disasters, and few locals or travelers would argue that in 2005, it was one of the most beautiful towns in Central America.

"I predict that Congress will amend the Constitution to allow animated characters to run for public office." Conner drank a gin and tonic, for it was still morning, and sat on a stool at the bar beside me with yesterday's *NY Times* unfurled. Conner was an instinctively sardonic thirty-something, a hyper-educated, handsome, and world-weary part-time drunk. He had perfectly imperfect hair and a quick smile for anything truly new or clever. Conner was from Long Island. His manner recalled James Dean.

"Ah, yes. The Shrek administration," I imagined aloud. It was starting to rain. The crowd moving by in the street cooed and twittered behind us. Passersby pressed into canary yellow and ochre walls along the shiny black cobblestone streets to escape the rain beneath wooden and tin eaves. Most of them were foreigners, and many spoke English, but locals could be found scattered among them, a farmer here and there, a street vendor selling dazzling handmade textiles, a uniformed child heading home from school for lunch. Antigua's stores and bars and residences were all entered through doorways in long, gapless walls that defined each city block, creating a feeling of both unity and exclusivity. Antigua was the Aspen, Colorado, of Central America, also in the mountains, also a very popular place to play. Now I would live here, at least for a while. Conner had done so for a year or more. The rain outside filled the street with a benevolent roar, eclipsing all human noise but the odd shriek or burst of loud laughter. The heavy wooden doors of the bar were always flung wide during business hours, and a gaggle of *turistas* pressed into the smallish area between the bar and the deluge on the street behind us.

"Twain said thunder is good. Thunder is impressive. But it's lightning that gets the job done," spoke Conner, his eyes not leaving his paper.

"Relámpago. Sí. Dude, I think I'm in love. With the bartender."

"I know some people who can cure that. Right here in town. They can cure most diseases here. Even love. And I can't believe you use that word. You seem rather smart until you say that." Conner caught the eye of the object of my desire and raised his glass, shaking the ice within and grinning like the Cheshire cat.

"What, dude? I'm from Colorado, bro. No, really, I think I love her." I finished my Moza, a local dark beer, and lit a smoke. I offered Conner one. He took it. Keane came on the stereo out of the shoebox-sized speakers on the stone wall high above us. "So did you meet that guy last night at the party who said he made cheese out of human breast milk? I think he was from Croatia."

"No," said Conner, wincing.

"Did you hear about that gringo who killed his wife and kids in Costa Rica?" I asked louder over the roar of the rain, feeling a strange pair of damp breasts press into my back as the space behind us filled with shelter-seekers.

"I'm sure he had his reasons." Conner laughed, a fresh cocktail supplied him by Marta. "I don't remember much from last night. Bad Conner slipped out of his cage. I almost had sex with a fifty-year-old tory." Night was what Conner and I waited for. At night in Antigua, all the shoppers and tick-list tourists found their way back to their hostels and hotels and the drinking set emerged, full of lust and guile, travel dingy, elegantly moist, consciously unselfconscious, chaste harlots and innocent criminals, self-made wackos selling nosebleed seats to the revolution, sexual omnivores, and legions of single women dressed for the tropics. The callow sat with the sophisticates. The sybarite walked beside the Mennonite. I already loved it.

"Hey oil boy, tell me what happened with Enron," said Conner, his eyes still on his paper.

"The best analogy I've heard is that just as in poker, you can win without good cards. For a while. You can win in the energy biz without really having any. For a while."

2

The United States used its unaccountability to great effect in Guatemala in the early fifties. The little country just the other side of Mexico had two good presidents in a row starting in 1945, good, that was, for the average José in Guatemala. The U.S.-owned United Fruit Company begged to differ. United Fruit paid very little tax to Guatemala, relied on practical slave labor, and furthermore owned large tracts of fertile land that were left fallow for years, land that might have produced affordable food for people inside Guatemala. The term "banana republic" was invented to describe nations like Guatemala, countries that had the fruit that U.S. consumers wanted and suffered for it at the hands of their self-appointed, U.S.-backed, and deeply corrupt governments. But in 1945, the little nation elected a populist to the presidency.

Guatemala's first fairly-elected president was Juan José Arévalo, an unabashed reformist. After achieving its independence from Spain, Guatemala suffered through a long series of corrupt autocrats, the style of leadership the U.S. preferred in Latin America. Arévalo presided from '45 to '51 over a Guatemala that enjoyed unprecedented freedom in political life and suddenly had social security and a new constitution, one influenced greatly by that of the United States. Labor unions were born and labor laws codified. Sweeping agrarian land reform was seen as the way to improve both civil rights and conditions for the rural poor, a remedy for the deeply entrenched system of *latifundia,* slavery made tenable, the old-school, patrician way of keeping agricultural profits high by keeping wages low. Really low. This is where United Fruit came in. One Allen Dulles, brother of U.S. Secretary of State John Foster Dulles, happened to be a primary stakeholder in United Fruit, a company that became iconic for what it represented—that the U.S. government's allegiance to big business always trumped the rights of individuals and the sovereignty of governments in Latin America.

The firm known as the "octopus" by its employees was served notice by the Arévalo administration that it would have to bend a little. Change was coming, and while it certainly wouldn't have to leave, the huge company would have to begin to respect the people and the rules of the country where it harvested its products. Arévalo and his immediate successor Árbenz were not just anyone. They were the first two fairly-elected presidents in their country's history, both populists, like-minded men who were not corrupt and would not become so. Árbenz's victory in 1951 represented not simply approval but enthusiasm on the part of the electorate. Guatemala might stand up and walk on its own with a bit more time. It was flirting with true representative government, U.S. Constitution style. But Árbenz would not get that time. Already, Kermit Roosevelt's new CIA was orchestrating a bold new experiment in subterfuge in Mohammed Mossadegh's Iran, this called Operation Ajax. Mossadegh was a democratically elected nationalist prime minister who took on the Anglo-Iranian Oil Company, now British Petroleum, with his nationalization of Iran's rather extensive oil fields. He was about to be toppled. Guatemala was next. Operation PB Success was about to begin.

It didn't take long. Árbenz was quickly out, and the reactionary Castillo Armas was in. Of note is the fact that the overthrow of Árbenz served to galvanize the emerging radical ideology of a young Argentine who happened to be in the neighborhood at the time, one Ernesto Guevara. Armas immediately disenfranchised half of Guatemala's electorate by removing the voting rights of the illiterate. He also seized what little land had been returned to peasant families for subsistence farming. Armas saved the day for big business. Corporations could again do whatever they pleased, and were once again well above the law. Thirty-five years of some of the most brutal and atrocious kind of smoldering civil war ensued between those who sought to restore their good government and the changes it brought with it, and the jackals for hire that killed and terrorized the people that Arévalo and Árbenz tried to enfranchise. Arévalo would later write the famous and widely circulated fable *The Shark and the Sardines*, denouncing U.S. actions in Guatemala and Latin America at large. Today it's agribusiness as usual in Guatemala. The Central American Free Trade Agreement was even ratified, another harsh blow to the small farmer. The poor were quiet for now. Tourism was getting bigger. So was crime. Most countries that suffered long civil wars had lots of guns floating around out there. In case you felt like robbing a gringo.

⁓

I met Sydney at an after party just off the main plaza at some locally owned restaurant that became a speakeasy after midnight, when the bars were supposed to close. Antigua was cool that way, and after a few weeks there, you learned where to go get a drink and hang out after twelve. The town was still free of those Carlos and Charlie's-style affairs found in parts north, Mexico's party towns primarily, but I imagined that soon a "Cortez and Monty's" or a "Tupac and Pizarro's" would pop up. It seemed inevitable. But in 2005, Antigua still had vestigial class.

Sydney was buzzed. My gringo friend Davis was well over six feet tall and black, as some gringos were. He was staying at my place, and had met me at the covert watering hole. We had better luck meeting girls as a team.

He and I sat down with Sydney and her local admirer at a four-top because there was nowhere else to sit. Suddenly I was talking with a California girl. Her pretty face was earnest and bright as she listened to my story. She was in full bloom, lit up by beer and travel, her tan shoulders bare above a tangerine halter top and a pair of ripe oranges. A deft hand indeed had drawn her mouth and eyes, elegant cursive to the block lettering on my own face. Her long brown hair was pulled back into a ponytail, and her magnetic, mahogany eyes did not so much advertise as betray a precocious mind. I watched her as I might watch a magician as she spoke slowly, explaining where she had been traveling, the usual stuff, but I beheld her with a vague sense of expectation. She had a different *onda*, a singular vibe, her scent, her shadow, the freckles on her tan cheeks—she leaned closer to me, now indifferent to her Latino suitor, closer still—her wet lips nearly touched my ear.

"You're kinda cute," she mouthed.

And then it was on.

Sydney would be the hazard I was unprepared for, the elephant behind the tree. She was not beautiful. She was beauty itself, at least to me, and a light burned so brightly within her that it nearly shot hot white rays out of her mouth when she spoke. She talked slowly. She walked slowly. She kissed me slowly, with a sticky heroin euphoria filling her iridescent chocolate eyes. She was little, if only physically, and her clothes covered her strong and lovely young body only just. She liked to drink, and she liked the boys. Pure naphtha was she, as well just signed on as a barkeep at Reilly's, the best bar close to my apartment. Where she now lived. With me.

I was still in a haze of disbelief. I watched her in the morning as she brushed her teeth, bare white butt jiggling, long dark hair spilling down her back, a tattoo, a simple, five-pointed star above her beltline on the right. Who was she? I hadn't looked twice at her that night in the bar before we met, but now a strange new fire burned within me. She was *it*. I was already smitten, and I concealed it quite poorly. She spoke good Spanish. She liked to drink. She read a little Chomsky. She even knew about United Fruit. And she and I did the goat dance very well. What more could I want? But it wasn't about want. It just was. I was about to realize that I had never really been in love before.

"Have you seen my iPod?" she asked from the back porch, collecting her dry clothes from the line. I sat at my laptop writing.

"Yeah. It's in here on the chair." I sucked on a bottle of Gallo, Guatemala's favorite beer. The clock on the wall read 3:30 p.m. The door to the little concrete patio of my apartment had a metal latch that had to be tweaked just right before it would open. The strong afternoon sun had turned the cement near the door hot, and Sydney's feet were bare.

"Ow, ow, ow, Tom!" I jumped up and shot through the little kitchen to the back door. I let her in. She hopped in onto the cool tile of the kitchen and threw her arms around me. "You saved me. Thank you," she said. She kissed my mouth and launched past into the apartment. "Are you gonna walk me to work?"

"Yup. Gotta go get some meat too. I'm gonna make *carnitas* tonight. You get off at one, right?"

"Yeah."

We walked down the highway from the apartment until it became a street, and in ten minutes, we were officially in town. The *túk-túks* were everywhere. They would be around only a bit longer, about to be banned by a city ever so concerned with its image and stature as the loveliest town ever. They went by other names in other parts of the world, but the *túk-túk* was, in Antigua, a small-wheeled open car for hire. Most were red. Their little gas engines burped and gurgled beside us on the black cobblestone as we walked down the sidewalk. Bougainvilleas hollered in manic scarlet voices from the tops of walls. Sydney drew a whistle from a passing car. She wore a little white skirt that said "pink" on the back. It troubled me only a little. We talked. Sydney found occasion to inform me that she was a serial flirt and make-out queen. But it meant nothing, she explained. She assured me that she was with me now in a way that made me feel weak and somehow unevolved. We reached Reilly's. Time for Sydney to tend bar. Time for me to have another beer.

All the people who lived around my apartment and along our way to town were folding laundry, eyeing fruit, swatting flies, and wondering why Sydney was living with me. Did I look fifteen years older than her?

I was pretty sure I didn't, but a few "what a lovely daughter you have" comments would be ahead as Sydney could pass for seventeen if she needed to, and the best I could do was about thirty-three. No matter. She was twenty-three, old enough to like coffee but too young to like Scotch, young enough to rail against her country's foreign policy with zeal, but old enough to acknowledge her own privilege and immense good fortune. She handed me a Moza and refused my cash. Her smile was intoxicating. I sat at the bar and drank it in. I bid her farewell after my beer with a pecky kiss and ambled down the cobblestone to the main market.

In ten minutes I was there. It was always pungent. The scent of pineapples, freshly-hewn meat, flowers, spilled Pepsi, and urine mingled in the warm air. Huge blocks of white cheese sat uncovered in the sun. Teens mixed together on the gravel behind the blue tarp stands where their parents sat and sold all manner of quality foodstuffs. Pigeons saw to the scraps. In the sky, a rainstorm was being prepared for later in the day. A dark cloud grew above town like a drop of ink in a glass of water. Not far from the market's steamy bustle, tall, swaying eucalyptus trees stood side-by-side on the steep hillsides just above and outside of Antigua. These hills were the thighs and knees of three massive volcanoes that crouched on two sides of town, Agua, Fuego, and Acatenango. Some nights, from my and Sydney's second-floor apartment, we could see Fuego's magma flying skyward and quickly back to earth to drip down the big peak's highest slopes. The tallest buildings in town were only three stories, but most were one. Good views abounded in Antigua.

Smiles were plentiful in the market. Courtesy was in style. The warmth of human kindness was not lost in the pursuit of the quetzal, the monetary unit of Guatemala, as well its most celebrated bird. I stepped up to my favorite meat stand and was greeted by a smiling brown man with a deeply wrinkled face and a white apron stained red and umber. He called me *joven,* "youngster" in Spanish, and his eyes sparkled with some mischief. Most Mexicans would have told you that *carnitas* was to be made with pork, but I bought beef shoulder roasts and cooked them forever atop the stove in good stock and hot peppers until the meat fell apart. I then baked the meat until it became a bit dried out and even crispy at the edges. It had become a twice monthly ritual for me. The meat kept for weeks in the fridge, and could later be featured in a Thai dish or even a *biryani,* the sort of richly spiced meat dish I had eaten in Yemen. I loved to cook, especially, I would soon discover, for Sydney.

3

The price of crude was soaring. While I was not working and would not do so for a while, my ear was to the ground for sounds from the patch. There were many. Hugo Chávez was trading oil for cattle with Argentina, literally bartering with his southernmost neighbor—no currency involved. His vision of a South American trade organization was being realized in a strikingly old-school manner. Hugo was becoming an icon and a lightning rod. Chile had a female presidential candidate named Michelle Bachelet, a moderate socialist who concerned herself with the gap between rich and poor in her relatively prosperous nation. Ecuador had a populist candidate named Rafael Correa who sought his country's presidency. Correa spoke Quechua, held a Ph.D. from the University of Illinois, and was no adherent of the sort of free trade agreements that the United States was trying to foist on Ecuador. In Bolivia, Evo Morales was about to renationalize his country's significant gas industry. Lamentably, Colombia's popular reformist candidate, Ingrid Betancourt, was still held by the FARC. But South America was slowly and surely slipping away from U.S. influence and U.S. exploitation.

Che might have been encouraged. The poor and indigenous, for the first time ever, arguably, had reason to believe that something better might be coming, at least for their children. The United States was well distracted in the wake of its bloody and criminal oil grab in Iraq and Afghanistan. Between one hundred thousand and a half-million non-combatant Iraqis were dead, killed by a nation that pretended to follow the teachings of Christ, the "prince of peace." Nothing more peaceful than a dead person. There was less indignation in the United States about this horrifying and utterly shameful massacre, a crime that would come back to haunt it again and again, than there was about France's failure to join the party. "Freedom fries" and not french fries were served in a nation with a half-wit starring as commander-in-chief and the compassion of a viper.

People in Guatemala knew all about war. They watched their families and neighbors die as Armas was succeeded by a series of despots culminating in Rios Montt in the early eighties, a figure who made Sadaam Hussein seem rather easygoing. Just as Hussein had been, Montt was well-liked and supported by Washington and the Reagan administration. He was trained in Fort Benning, Georgia, at the infamous School of the Americas, widely considered the best campus for those seeking master's degrees in torture and terror. As Americans listened to the Gipper prattle on in his uniquely puerile way about communism in Central America, Montt's death squads raped, tortured, and massacred Guatemala's indigenous men, women, and children. Their crime was to demand rights for themselves and a representative government in Guatemala City. Their graves were scattered across the steep hills around Xela and Huehuetenango and most everywhere in the highlands, their stories ignored and discounted by the devils who watched as they were killed and terrorized by hired jackals, men in name only, demons who never raised children, farmed, or fished in the Guatemalan highlands a single day in their lives. There could be no punishment to match their crimes.

"You're not driving home," Sydney said darkly to Terry. Terry was an Irish friend of ours who also tended bar at Reilly's. He drove a little old Dodge pickup named the Millennium Chicken.

"It's a good thing the road is curvy, 'cause I'll be swervin'!" Terry shambled out the door to Reilly's. It was just after midnight. The bar's owner Zack looked over at me and Sydney and produced Terry's car keys, jingling them about. We laughed.

"Good job Zack! That was quite a performance he put on tonight," Sydney said, smiling at me. I sat at the bar as Zack kicked everyone out.

"Yeah, not a dry seat in the house," I quipped. Sydney giggled, wiping the bar clean and dumping out the tip jar. It had been a great night for tips.

"You can keep drinking, but you can't do it here," Zach bellowed into the street as he pulled the bar's heavy wooden doors shut. "Time exists so that everything doesn't happen," Zack belched, "all at once!" He was a big lad with curiously large arms. He was full of Gallo and bourbon.

We were all nearly drunk. Conner and I were allowed to stay. He was the bar's best customer, and I had to walk Sydney home. Soon we had swept the whole floor and counted all the loot. Zack and Conner would go to an after party. Sydney and I decided to go straight home. We walked up the cobblestone street toward the ornate, mustard church called La Merced and its small park, now empty but for a few midnight revelers. We continued for two more blocks after a jog left, holding hands and pitching woo. We stopped to neck against a building for a moment in the darkness. We carried on until we had left Antigua proper and were walking along the highway toward the little neighborhood called Manchen, where our apartment waited.

"What're you gonna do tomorrow? I work the day shift. Sucks." Sydney looked over and up at me sideways, walking beside me like a child in her mild drunkenness, her freckles wet and flashy beneath the sodium streetlights, her smile smoldering—I loved her so much. I was mentally ill in a way that was quite new to me, and now I knew what all the fuss was about. I had really only been in the saccharine kind of love before in my life, and my question now was why? Why here and now?

"Probably drink wine, try to write, and clean the house."

"You're neat, but you're not clean. It's true."

Suddenly the street began to shrink in around us. I became aware of a change in the night air. A figure approached in the darkness beneath some trees across the highway to our left, walking with purpose in a path that would intersect our own in ten or fifteen seconds. Sydney did not yet know. A tall stone wall bordered the sidewalk to our right, boxing us in. The figure left the shadows and emerged onto the asphalt highway, into the faint light from the streetlamps.

"Sydney, turn around and walk the other direction."

"What?" Too late. He closed quickly. With a jerky motion like he was pulling something hot from his pocket, the silhouetted stranger ripped a handgun out of his jacket and pointed the muzzle at Sydney's face from eight feet away. A streetlight buzzed dimly above him, lighting his face enough to see it. He was very young. I shouted.

"Oye!" He pointed the gun instead at me. Relief filled me. I spoke like a taut snare drum cracked by a lone stick. Sydney cowered behind the metal pole of the streetlight, now behind the kid with the gun. Her posture betrayed her fear. "Que quieres? Plata?" I looked at his face and at the pistol. Sixteen, maybe seventeen. Nickel-plated .40 caliber. I was agitated, but I was not afraid. He saw this. He was the scared one. I produced my wallet from my right front pocket and tossed all the bills inside it on the dark ground. I replaced it in my pocket. I took two strides toward Sydney, grabbed her by the hand, and pulled her up the street into the darkness. We walked and did not run.

⌒

Cars hissed by in the dim light of early morning on the highway below, where he had been. I bit a nail, an indoor gargoyle; my laptop told me to go to the window and throw it outside into the muttering rain. There was a fog caught breathless between the towering eucalyptus trees on the hillside behind our building in the first light of dawn. They stood around dripping, acting like they couldn't see us inside. Sydney was asleep in a ball beneath blankets on the couch in the darkness, white TV light crackling and spitting before her. I sat before my computer in a cone of orange lamplight at a table beside the couch, trying to write something to someone. I got up and went to sit beside her. She stirred and put her arms around me. I held her and kissed her, loved her with all my might. It had been disturbing, perhaps even at some depth, but it had been brief, and we had been strong. I felt fortunate for having been with her. This was no chivalry on my part. I knew now that I most certainly loved her in that way that mankind so exalts, that peculiar selflessness that endures after the supernova of ardor becomes a steadier and less violent fire, the insanity that everyone seems to yearn for, everyone yet to taste it, at least.

⌒

Would Che have robbed us? Robin Hood? I drank some pricey local coffee, hard to find in a nation that exported nearly every last bean, and ate a slice of really fine quiche Lorraine at Café Condensa, on Antigua's main plaza. Sydney's voice rose and fell across from me at a heavy wooden table. She ate a triangular slice of robust whole wheat toast with strawberry jam and butter. I watched her jaw muscles as she chewed, munch, munch, munch, swallow. God, she was a beautiful creature. We were excited to be going to Monterrico. We had a rented motorcycle and were headed to the budget-list destination and its black sand beach on the Pacific side after breakfast.

"Wouldn't you steal from wealthy tourists if you were poor and lived here?" I asked through a mouthful of eggs.

"Well, steal, maybe, but not rob with a gun. We're not wealthy. Well, maybe you are, oil boy," she said with a smile.

"Yeah. That's what I mean."

"In like a clever and harmless way. Yeah. I guess. If I really had no opportunities. But I think I might have some."

"Yeah, you might. Lots of good people here don't. Most don't."

"But good people don't steal, right?"

"I suppose they don't. They certainly don't point guns at people. Unless they're named Butch or Sundance..."

"Or Che? Right, revolution boy?"

We were soon flying down the road on our rented 150cc bike. Sydney wore a little backpack with all our things inside and held her arms around me tightly. I felt at times as though she was giving me the Heimlich maneuver. We stopped so that she could take photos of the *paisaje,* the landscape, its people, their dwellings, and their animals. Horses kissed the ground here and there in modest pastures where the jungle had been hacked and burned back in favor of the type of grass that livestock needed.

"Look!" Sydney spotted a flock of parrots, an emerald amoeba floating about among the treetops. Soon we were on a flat-bottomed barge motoring through a mangrove swamp, Sydney and I and some boatmen who sucked down a nice cold beer with us. We three and the bike were the only cargo. I licked a bead of sweat off Sydney's nose. "Gross," she complained. I marveled silently about the things she considered gross and those she did not.

In a little while, we stood on the charcoal sand of the beach and looked out to sea, out toward the rest of our lives, or perhaps we beheld an imagined scene inside the mind of a character from a book that was never written.

⸺

Sydney and I lasted about five months as a couple. We would leave Guatemala for Honduras and then Nicaragua before her disturbingly universal appeal to young men and a mutual, seasonal allergy to sobriety would drive us apart. I missed her deeply as soon as we parted ways, but I was beginning to realize that booze had been my real girlfriend the whole time. For the last couple of years. I had been quite faithful to her, though Sydney had never really threatened to come between us—Sydney loved her too. It had been one hot threesome. But now I had to leave her after leaving Sydney just months before, leave each of her incarnations, a cold beer or nine on a hot day, a fiery glass of Scotch in winter—if this weren't enough, she would go out that very night and party with all my friends, make them more brilliant with her presence, pass out with them. Tonight I was alone, back in the United States. Tonight, I would read about gout on the Internet and smoke yellow Spirits on the drippy porch of a little cabin in the chilly and wet ponderosa pine forest. Tomorrow, I had plans to go climbing with Logan and Jack. My Falcon colleagues were still my best friends.

It was snowing at nine thousand feet in Boulder County, and not the faintest wind blew. My tobacco smoke rose slowly up through a yellow cone of light cast by a lone bulb above me. Great round snowflakes spun quietly earthbound, falling carefully atop each other in piles. It was a fine place to come home to, the United States of America. I owed it a big thank you and a part of my income. I paid. I stared into the darkness from the porch of my rental and thought about how capable the United States was of kicking its own bad habits, the biggest being petroleum and violence. Increasing paranoia about climate change had people in the U.S. thinking about their "carbon footprint," but no one suggested to them that they should also consider their human blood "footprint." I thought about all the people I had met in my travels. How good they had been to me. How I was treated like a prince in Yemen, an infidel made to feel a brother. How a middle-class white boy had been all right with the moneyless *campesinos* of Bolivia's meanest Chaco. How jungle man helped wolf boy. There's bad types out there too, and a shocking number of them are in power, but for the most part, the world is home to some fine, upstanding people. People who wouldn't do you wrong, and who knew what that meant better than did Washington. People who hadn't thrown their hands up and said that it was too hard to change things. People who never said that those in charge knew better than we did as they killed those we didn't.

How to find oil and gas without really trying. That was the title I might have borrowed for the last decade of my life. I loved imagining the musical. What I had actually found, and what was vastly more important, was that the only allegiance I need have was to the human race. The world had become my neighborhood, and while I was helping find the addictive and problematic fuel it ran on, I wasn't quite sure that I was doing much to make it a better place. I had found that many of the otherwise smart and caring people of my native country were still easily distracted and made fools by their government, their media, and the material prosperity they carelessly enjoyed. Just as Homer Simpson said of beer, I had found that oil was the cause of and solution to all of the world's problems. Thankfully and frighteningly, we would soon be running out. The biggest crux modern humans would face was just around the bend. Soon we would all have no choice but to stop being so very thirsty.

AFTERWORD

MARK TWAIN WROTE, "Travel is fatal to prejudice, bigotry, and narrow-mindedness." It is also dangerous to ignorance, and undermines propagandist buildups to criminal wars of conquest and plunder. Travel helps us understand that the vast majority of people in Iraq and the rest of the world are normal citizens who have nothing to do with the jihadist groups whose images flash gratuitously across our screens and minds, nourishing the fears that propel the wrong people into power in this, the world's richest and most bellicose nation. It is the sad truth that one of the things American leadership has been exceptionally good at is convincing its citizens that its elective wars are actually fights for democracy, liberty, security—that its murderous meddling in Latin America and poor nations around the world is for the good of the people living there and not for control of their myriad resources.

The intellectual ghetto that is the mainstream American TV media makes this all too easy. The latest innovation in American reportage, "imbedded" journalism, is as inherently self-defeating as it is embarrassingly obsequious. It is also, very likely, quite portentous. Add to this an onslaught of films and video games fueled by a morbid ardor for all things war, and you have a hothouse for raising children who think that invading other countries is all well and good. It is no stretch to imagine that nations like Venezuela and Bolivia are decent odds to host some sort of armed conflict on their soil in the next ten years, some self-serving U.S. operation on live television that results in lots of dead civilians and plays just fine in the States. Maybe it could even be a pay-per-view event. The Iraq war also happens in a TV for most of us. And TV shows are produced and controlled by people behind the scenes, as we all know and love to forget. Someone makes sure that we only see when the other side kills, and that we see that again and again. When we kill, it's like a score update on ESPN.

The U.S. government is highly skilled at turning perception into reality. It knows how to make dissent look like treason. It denies the mere possibility of its own wrongdoing and attacks the character of its detractors, especially well-informed ones. In short, it abuses the misplaced trust of the American people. People who know nothing about Sabra and Shatila, the Plain of Jars, the Maya and Fort Benning, about Turkey and the Kurds, Nicaragua—there is a very long list of U.S. sponsored terrorism. The damage has been done in these places, and nothing can undo it. People in the United States scratched their heads and asked "why do they hate us?" after 9-11. One of the many answers to that question is that they hate us because we don't even know what our government is up to. Whether it was the populists we took out, like Torrijos in Panama, Árbenz in Guatemala, Ortega in Nicaragua, even al-Beidh in Yemen, or the bad guys we propped up after them, here, they're all just a bunch of no-names, speed bumps on the way to the sort of obedient oligarchies we can do business with on our own terms. Terms that were and are very unfair to the people trying to live in those countries.

Our government favors only those nations that truckle well, and now outright invasion is a very real possibility for those that don't. The most recent Iraq invasion killed at least one hundred thousand civilians, people who would have been delighted to show you their home towns and have you over for dinner if you were visiting, maybe even kick the ball around. They're dead now. If that doesn't bother you, even just a little, then I wouldn't want to go fishing with you. Or listen to any opinions you may have about U.S. foreign policy. You should not even have the luxury of not letting it bother you. But you do. If you saw it up close, you better believe it would. What the U.S. bought with these lives and those of its own soldiers was access to Iraqi oil on its terms, more control over the region, and more ways for billions of tax dollars to end up in corporate pockets. Though many try to tell us otherwise, the transaction is, quite simply, their blood for our petroleum. A tired anti-war cliché that happens to be true.

The U.S. has orphaned tens of thousands of children in Iraq. Children who will want to know exactly what happened to their parents and their country as they become adults. We may argue all we want about the justification we were given for the invasion, even attempt to make a flimsy case that what the U.S. did was prudent. All that is moot. What we see now is that there's nothing like an invasion to foment some real high-octane hatred where there was not enough for the zealots and killers to harness before. This metaphor is made more interesting when you consider that the octane rating of gasoline is not an indication of power or strength, but a measure of a fuel's resistance to premature combustion during compression inside an engine's cylinders. The higher the octane, the less prone it is to exploding before the right time, when the spark is loosed.

A wildly disproportionate reaction to 9-11 against an uninvolved party is how many see the Iraq invasion. Informed people know that the much-anticipated second U.S. invasion of Iraq was in fact made possible by 9-11, and was not a reaction to it. But that's what the U.S. neo-cons want. They want us as a nation to be perceived by the rest of the world as vindictive and irrational, casually ruthless at times, scary to be sure. At the same time, they want our citizens and allies to believe that we are the very beacon of goodness. Saved the world back in 1945, we did. Maybe we did, and how great is that. We do owe much to the brave servicemen and women of the greatest generation, and we ought to remember Dwight Eisenhower's famous warning about the military-industrial complex. Since Eisenhower's prescient farewell address, the very same MIC that he spoke of has waged and supported some of the most brutal campaigns of the horrific twentieth century in Southeast Asia, Central America, and the Middle East, using young men and women who little understood the true nature of those conflicts. Yes, using them. The U.S. MIC is healthier than ever before. It is capable of anything, both marvels of killing technology and despicable depths of depravity. Millions of civilians have had this made terminally clear to them in the past five decades.

Our recent actions in Iraq have brought nothing but shame upon our nation and its people, and have made the world a much more dangerous place for all of us. It's easy to be an armchair fan of wars of conquest and empire from within the castle walls. But it is only invulnerability and isolation, both physical and moral, that make such a thing possible. U.S.

citizens who casually dismiss civilian casualties in Iraq will most assuredly not be saying things like "collateral damage" and "that's the price you pay" if the next chapter of the story includes another 9-11. They'll be asking their government why it didn't protect them. But the sword cuts both ways. All violence is the same. Bullies love to dish it out, but they can't take it, and they call it something else when it happens to them. It's not "terrorism" when they do it, and a "police action" or a "liberation" when we do it. Accept your government's use of preemptive violence and the resulting civilian casualties, and you invite the same thing upon yourself. Live by the sword, die by the sword.

Truly intelligent nations reject invasion and occupation as transparently sinister and decidedly untenable foreign policy. Truly strong countries demand that their government do unto other civilians as they would have other governments do unto theirs. The U.S. government says it is fighting terrorism. It says it needs more and more money and soldiers to do so. But terrorism is a tactic. You cannot declare war on a tactic. More importantly, the United States has used and is still using this tactic itself. Terrorism, simply put, is war waged on and among civilians. There is a school for it in Georgia. Another lesson is taught in Iraq. Was 9-11 avenged? Need it have been? When will Iraq be? Wars are fought by the poor, who are hired, pressed, or brainwashed into service, for the rich and the zealous. If the cowards in Washington had to do the fighting, diplomacy would enter a new golden age. Misinformation and schlock patriotism are the shot and the chaser they give you. Don't drink too much.

Made in the USA
Lexington, KY
29 March 2013